IMAGES
of America

DYERSBURG

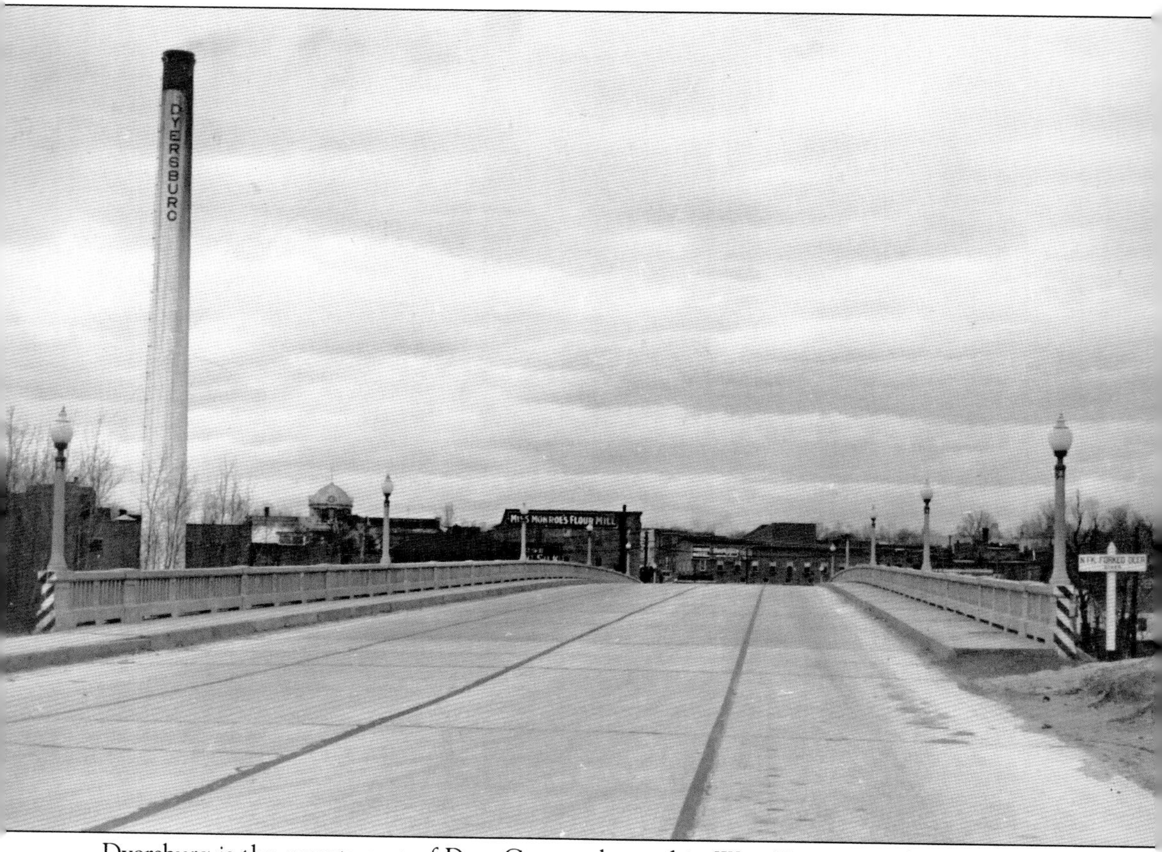

Dyersburg is the county seat of Dyer County, located in West Tennessee about 70 miles north of Memphis. The town of Dyersburg was first laid out in 1825 on what was then called McIver's Bluff. A long bridge over the Forked Deer River connects the town with the well-traveled route that became Tennessee Highway 51. (Courtesy Dyer County Historical Society.)

ON THE COVER: In this c. 1900 photograph, cotton wagons fill the town square during the busy season, when handpicked cotton, or "white gold," was being delivered by wagon to the cotton gin (the white building with the smokestack). By 1935, there were more than 5,000 farms in Dyer County, most producing cotton. The rich soil of the area could produce as much as twice the state's average yield. At the gin, the cotton was purchased, processed, and compressed into 500- to 600-pound bales. Because the main street in Dyersburg was congested with cotton-loaded wagons when the gin was in operation, the horse-drawn water pumpers from the town's fire department traveled through alleys at the rear of buildings to get to fire scenes. Forked Deer Hardware, with its sign visible at left, is believed to be the oldest continually operating hardware store in the United States. (Courtesy Tennessee State Library and Archives.)

IMAGES
of America

DYERSBURG

Bonnie Daws Kourvelas

ARCADIA
PUBLISHING

ISBN 978-0-7385-8729-5

Published by Arcadia Publishing
Charleston, South Carolina

Printed in the United States of America

Library of Congress Control Number: 2010936162

For all general information, please contact Arcadia Publishing:
Telephone 843-853-2070
Fax 843-853-0044
E-mail sales@arcadiapublishing.com
For customer service and orders:
Toll-Free 1-888-313-2665

Visit us on the Internet at www.arcadiapublishing.com

For my mother

Contents

Acknowledgments		6
Introduction		7
1.	Court Square	9
2.	Buildings	23
3.	Businesses	47
4.	Street Scenes	57
5.	School Days	67
6.	Floods and Other Disasters	83
7.	The Mill	93
8.	People	115
About the Organization		127

ACKNOWLEDGMENTS

My deepest appreciation goes to Danny Walden of the Dyer County Historical Society, because without his help, this book would not exist. Danny's passion for preserving the history of Dyer County is inspiring, and it is my hope that this book will lead others to lend their help and support to this group. I also thank Earl Willoughby for his unfailing knowledge of the minutiae of Dyer County history and his wonderful talent for preserving and telling its most entertaining stories. Danny and Earl share my belief that history belongs to the public and should be freely shared in order that all may benefit.

Special thanks go also to Gaylon Reasons, who founded the original Facebook group, "Grew Up in Milltown in Dyersburg," that sparked the idea for this book. Gaylon spends many hours locating, scanning, and posting the images of his hometown, keeping the memories alive for future generations. Contributors to his group, including Paula Ledford, Linda Ward Sellers, Roberta Summar, Sandra Gibson Phillips, and others, generously shared their personal photographs and cherished memories of growing up in Dyersburg.

An enormous debt of gratitude belongs to Billy Parmenter, longtime employee of Dyersburg Cotton Products. In the waning days of the company's existence, he had the foresight to gather up and preserve the mill's photograph archives when no one else wanted them. Had he not done so, they surely would have been lost in the fire that later destroyed the mill. He generously allowed us our pick for this book.

Thanks so much to my editor at Arcadia Publishing, Maggie Bullwinkel, who patiently rode out the ups and downs of this project and didn't give up on me!

Most of all, my love and appreciation go to my sweet husband, Nick, who rode along to keep me company on the many trips up and down Highway 51, and to my children, Jeremy, Julia, and Annie, who kindly ignored the growing piles of papers, photographs, and notes taking over the kitchen table. And I thank my mother, Edna Stephens Daws, and the memory of my grandmother, Callie McGraw Stephens, for one of my most cherished childhood memories—summer evenings spent in the porch swing on Harrell Avenue in Dyersburg, listening to the cicadas.

Unless otherwise noted, all images appear courtesy of the Dyer County Historical Society.

INTRODUCTION

In 1818, a treaty was struck between Gen. Andrew Jackson and the Chickasaw Indians who occupied the rich wooded lands in West Tennessee. Under the treaty, the Native American tribes ceded the land, and settlers quickly poured in from Middle Tennessee, East Tennessee, North Carolina, and Virginia. Knoxville newspapers of the time commented on the constant stream of covered wagons passing through town, headed west.

In 1823, the Tennessee General Assembly established Dyer County, named in honor of Col. Robert H. Dyer, who had served under General Jackson in the War of 1812.

Rich, fertile soil left behind by ancient glaciers created some of the most promising farmland in the world. Dense forests provided timber; poplar, oak, gum, hickory, walnut, chestnut, beech, cypress, and other trees grew thickly. Legend holds that in those days, a squirrel could travel from the Mississippi River to the Atlantic Ocean without ever touching the ground.

In those first years, John McIver and Joel H. Dyer donated 60 acres for the new county seat at a central location within the county known as McIver's Bluff. In 1825, Joel Dyer surveyed the town into 86 lots, and the first courthouse was built on the town square in 1827.

The earliest crops of corn and tobacco were eventually replaced by cotton. From its location on the Forked Deer River, Dyersburg grew quickly, especially once the *Grey Eagle* made the first successful steamboat trip in 1836.

Although the battles of the Civil War reached nearby Fort Pillow and Shiloh, Dyer County was spared the worst of the fighting, as no major battles took place within its borders.

The county's first real industrial boom began in 1879 when the steamboat *Alf Stevens* shipped timber from A.M. Stevens Lumber Company to markets in St. Louis. The Stevens company established a large sawmill in 1880, the Bank of Dyersburg opened that year with total capital of $10,000, and another timber industry, Nichols & Company Wooden Bowl Factory, began operations in 1881. Just a few years later, the Newport News and Mississippi Valley Railroad arrived, and a branch line called the Dyersburg Northern linked Dyersburg to Tiptonville. The railroad links encouraged new industries and businesses. For example, in 1884, investors established a cottonseed oil factory. This company remained locally important through the 20th century. By 1914, Dyersburg had become the junction point for three different railroad lines, led by the Illinois Central. A new combination depot was built at the nearby town of Newbern.

By the 1920s, most of the timber of Dyer County had been felled and replaced by cotton fields.

The American textile industry, based on the factories of England, had already been well established in the northeast when it began to move south in the 1880s. Mill owners were looking for nonunion labor, as well as proximity to where cotton was being grown. Mills existed in Trenton, Tennessee, and in Mississippi when a group from New England came downriver in 1928 looking for a good spot for a cotton mill. Dyersburg gave them a warm reception, and Dyersburg Cotton Products was born. It would survive the Great Depression to become the centerpiece of the town. The "mill town" concept came with the mill, and as many as four generations of Dyersburg residents worked there.

Cotton and cloth could be easily shipped in and out because of Dyersburg's location on the Forked Deer River. This proximity to rivers also led to danger, however; western Dyer County was plagued with floods on a regular basis, especially in 1927, 1937–1938, and the mid-1950s.

During World War II, the Dyersburg Army Air Base, located at the border of Dyer and Lauderdale Counties, became the largest inland B-17 training base in the eastern United States. Because of the efforts of Congressman Jere Cooper, it retained the Dyersburg name even though it was actually closer to the town of Halls. Thousands of young airmen arrived for their training, and bombers filled the skies over Dyersburg.

After the war, other crops—soybeans, milo, wheat, and corn—eventually began to take their place alongside cotton, although the growth, harvesting, and ginning of cotton remained deeply important to Dyersburg well into modern times. In 1969, the establishing of Dyersburg State Community College helped boost opportunities in the area, and in 1976, a new bridge was completed, becoming the only highway bridge over the Mississippi River between Cairo, Illinois, and Memphis.

Today, Dyersburg is the regional hub of a 10-county area, and its farming community has been joined by new manufacturing and retail efforts. Its classic Southern town square with its lovely domed courthouse brings the past to mind, but the town continues to look to the future and strive to reinvent itself for a new century.

One

Court Square

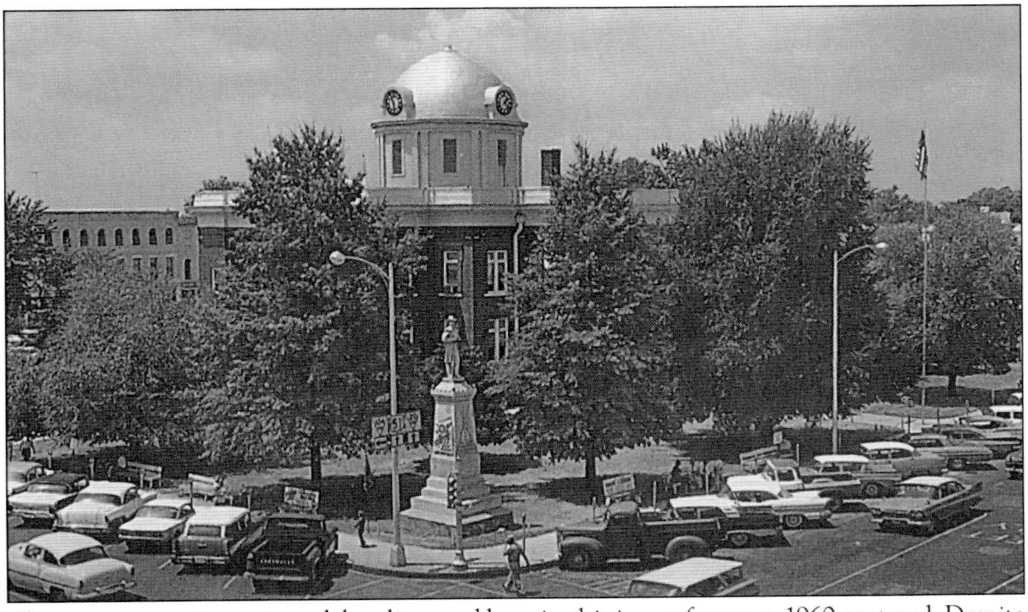

The town square is manicured, bustling, and busy in this image from a c. 1960 postcard. Despite suburban growth in the post–World War II years, the square has remained the hub of activity for Dyersburg for many decades. (Courtesy Gaylon Reasons.)

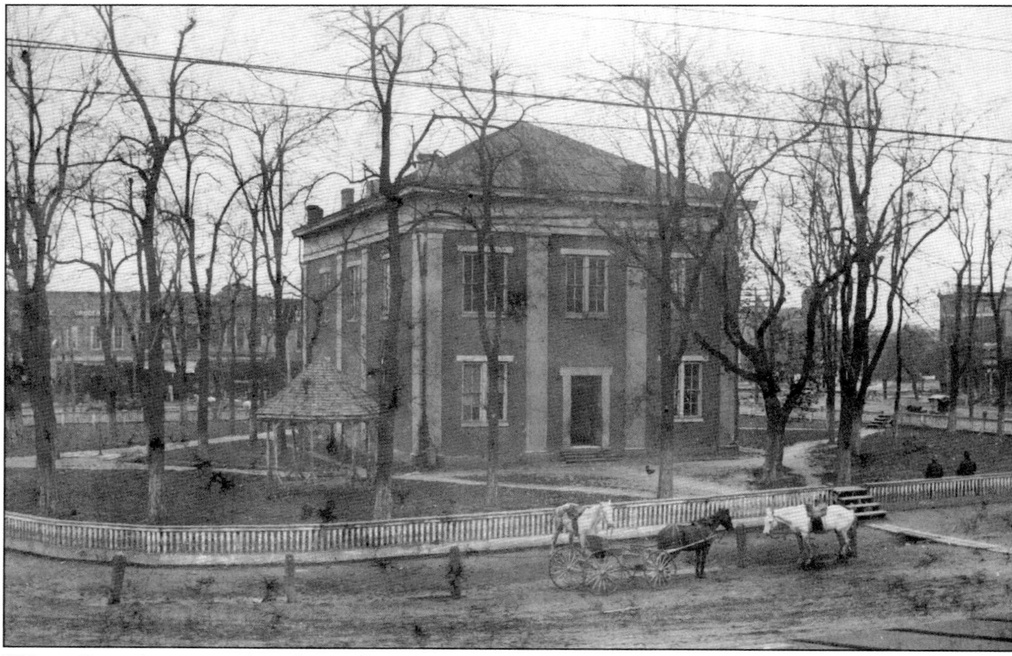

When Dyersburg was first formed, court activities were held at a private citizen's home until a small log courthouse could be built. Two later versions were constructed, but in 1864, an outlaw Confederate soldier, Tom Mays, set fire to the courthouse, destroying it and most of its records. The walls remaining largely intact, the brick structure was rebuilt. It is seen here around 1905. (Courtesy Tennessee State Library and Archives.)

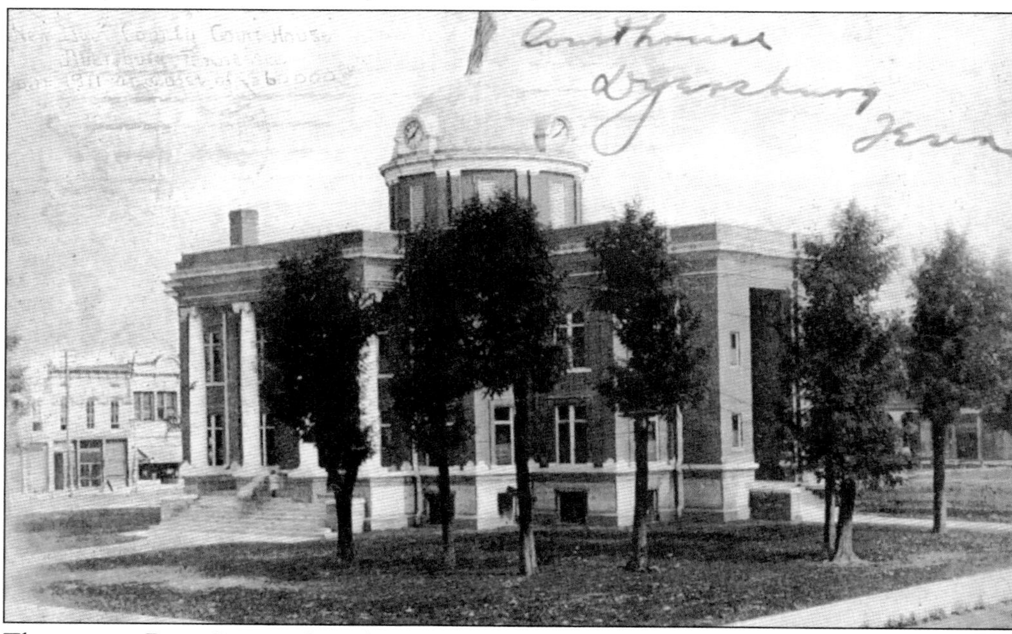

The present Dyer County Courthouse is a graceful and imposing three-story brick building designed by local architect Asa Biggs and constructed in 1911. It is the centerpiece of a downtown historic district listed in the National Register of Historic Places.

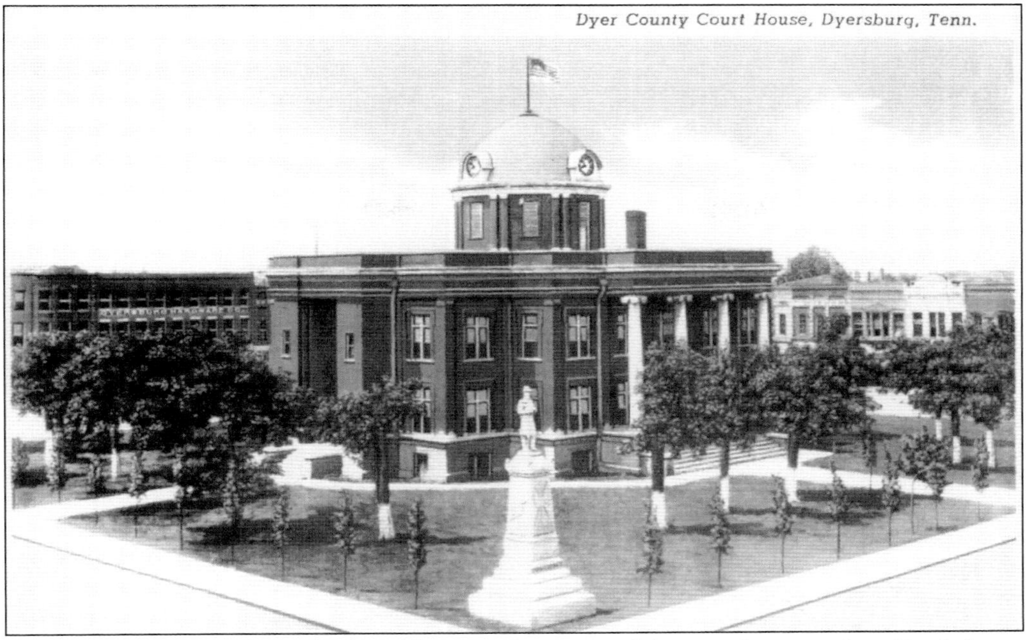

Many vintage postcards can be found bearing the image of the courthouse and its Confederate Civil War statue, nicknamed "Johnny Reb." The statue was unveiled on April 6, 1905, which was the 43rd anniversary of the Battle of Shiloh. A time capsule was buried beneath it.

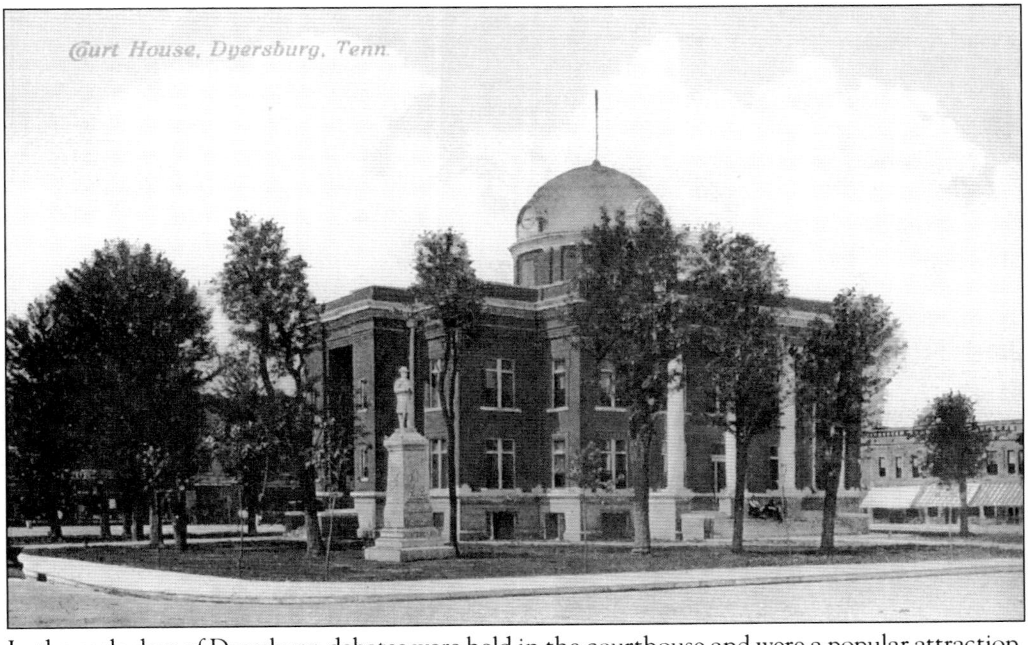

In the early days of Dyersburg, debates were held in the courthouse and were a popular attraction, featuring topics such as "Who was the greater man: George Washington or Lafayette?" Debates often turned into daylong events, including horse racing, cockfighting, and dancing. Various church groups also met in the courthouse until they could raise money for their own buildings.

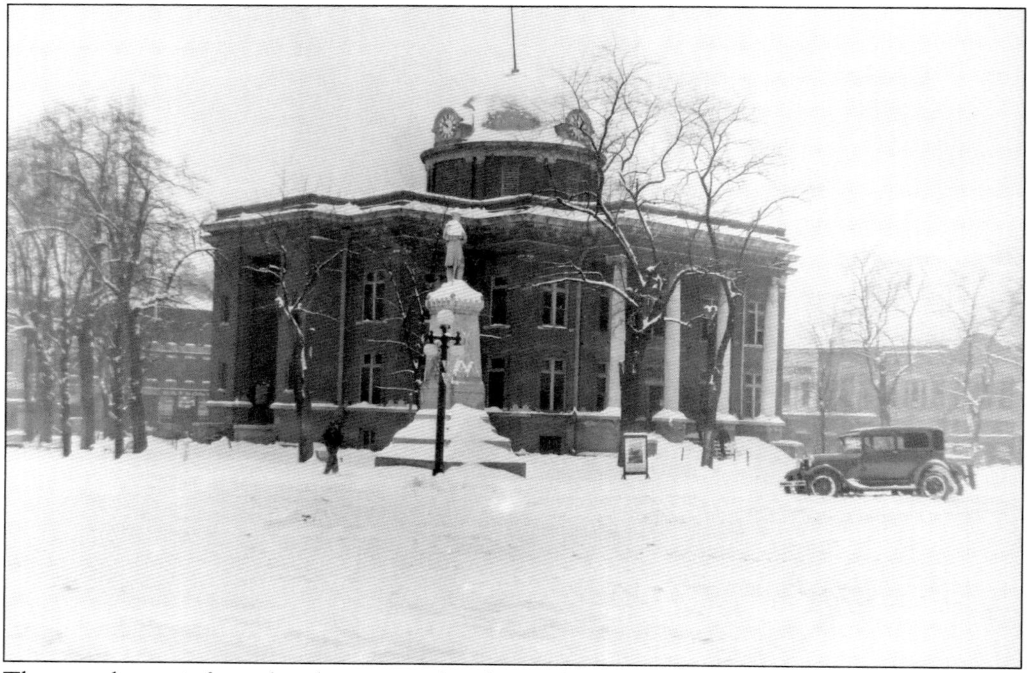

The courthouse is frosted with snow on this day in the 1920s, the decade when the town square was first fully paved for automobile traffic. The process was slow, however, and at times merchants would pool their own funds to get alleys paved.

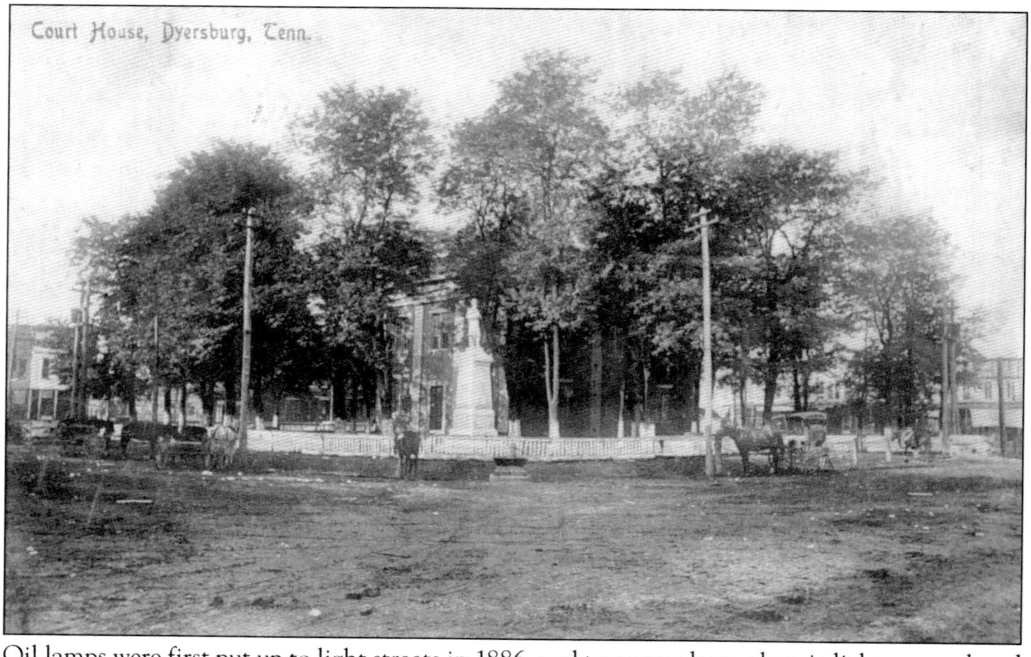

Oil lamps were first put up to light streets in 1886, and two years later, electric lights were placed throughout the town. That same year, a water company was built downtown, and the first telephone arrived in 1891. The town has had a newspaper since 1865, when *Neal's State Gazette*—now the Dyersburg *State Gazette*—was established.

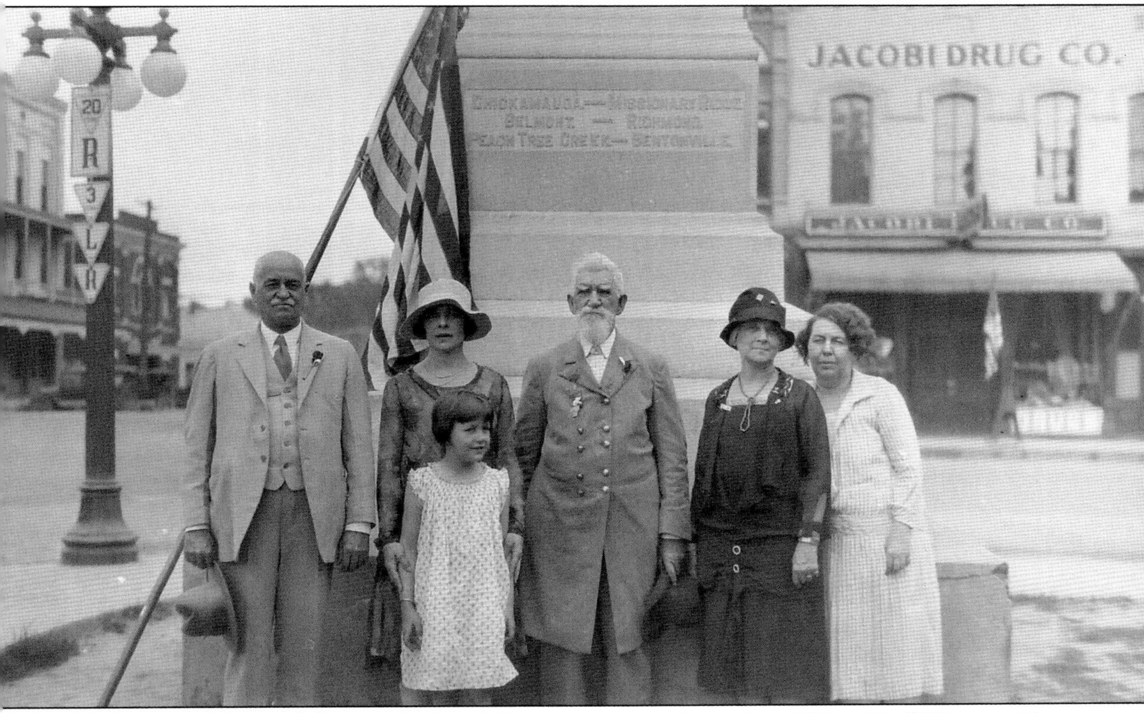

A group poses in front of the town's Confederate statue. At far right is Ellen "Nell" Reed, wife of longtime town pharmacist Dr. John Reed; she was active in many war memorial groups. The identities of the other group members, including the old Confederate veteran, are unknown. This photograph is believed to date from 1924, when the statewide Confederate Convention was held in Dyersburg and the Reed family hosted a large reception in the veterans' honor. (Courtesy John Reed.)

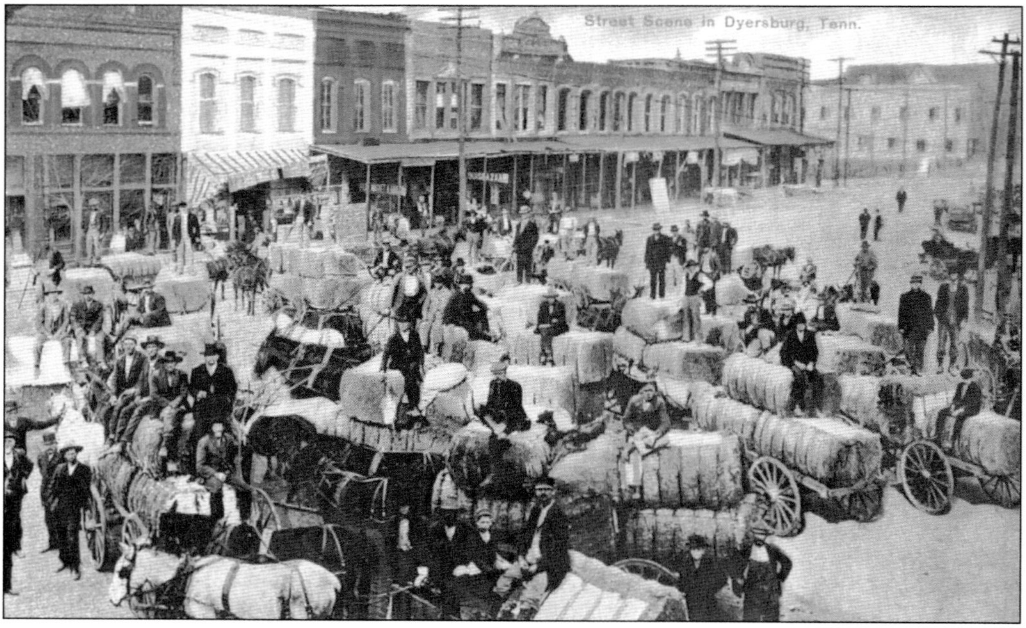

These vintage postcards depict cotton time in Dyersburg: above from about 1900 and below from 1909. Every autumn at cotton picking time, wagons jammed the square, bearing their loads. Until soybeans, corn, and other crops became competitive, cotton was the main crop and lifeblood of Dyer County.

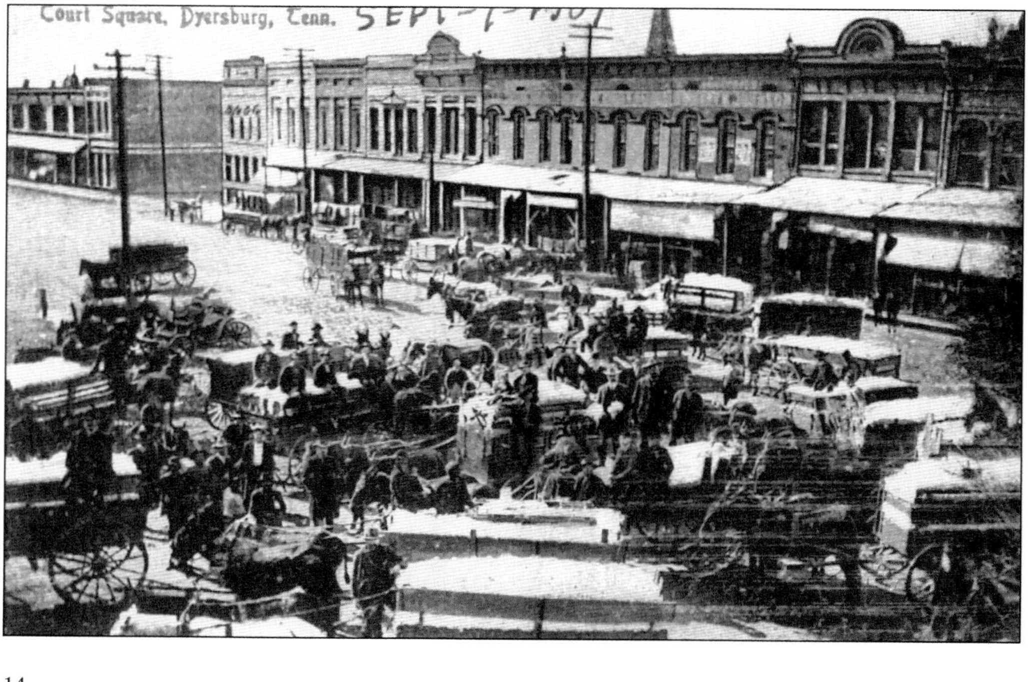

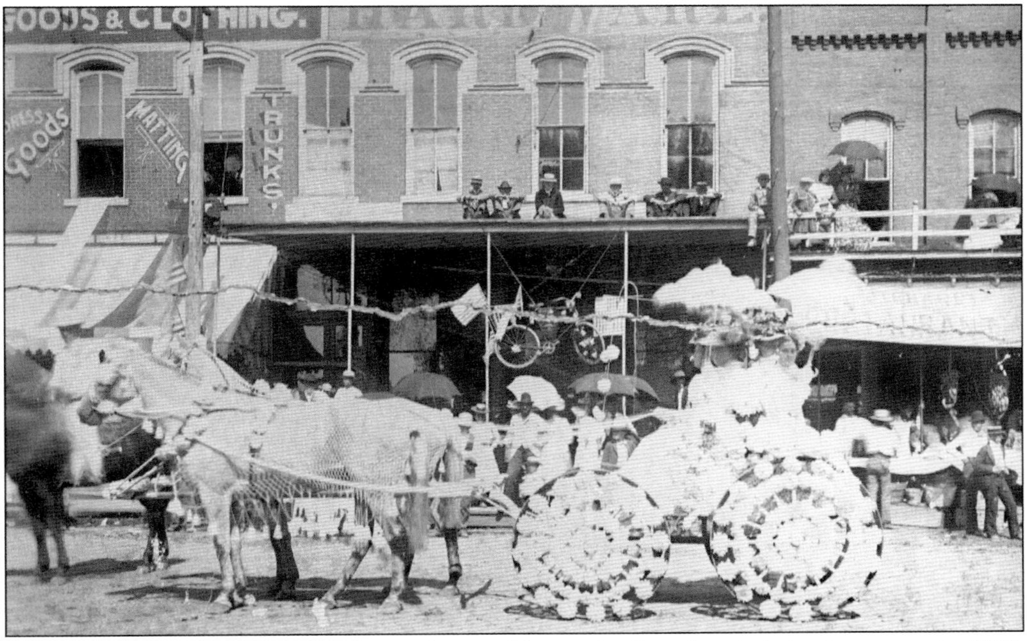

The Nichols family of Dyersburg is ready to celebrate the Fourth of July in the square in 1899, having decorated their wagon and come to town. Independence Day celebrations were large in the town's early days, drawing farmers and their families from miles around. (Courtesy Tennessee State Library and Archives.)

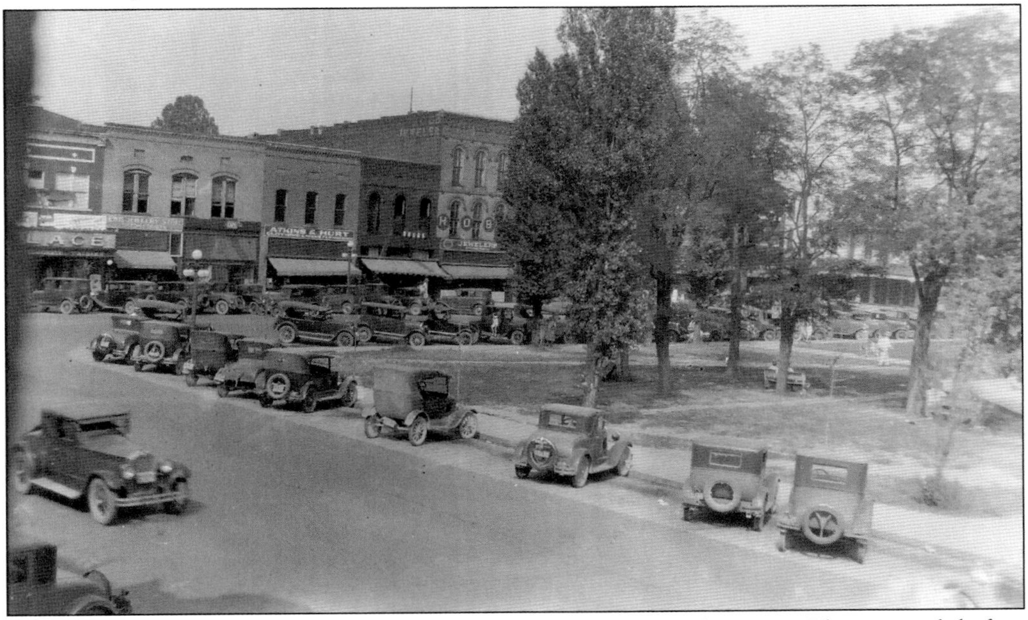

Automobiles line the curbs on a busy day in the town square in the 1920s. The automobile first came to Dyersburg in 1902 when Frank H. Shepherd bought a car in Memphis and spent three days driving it home. By the decade of the 1920s, cars were everywhere. Annoyed by having their horses frightened, farmers at that time demanded the speed limit be set at 20 miles per hour in the city limits. (Courtesy John Reed.)

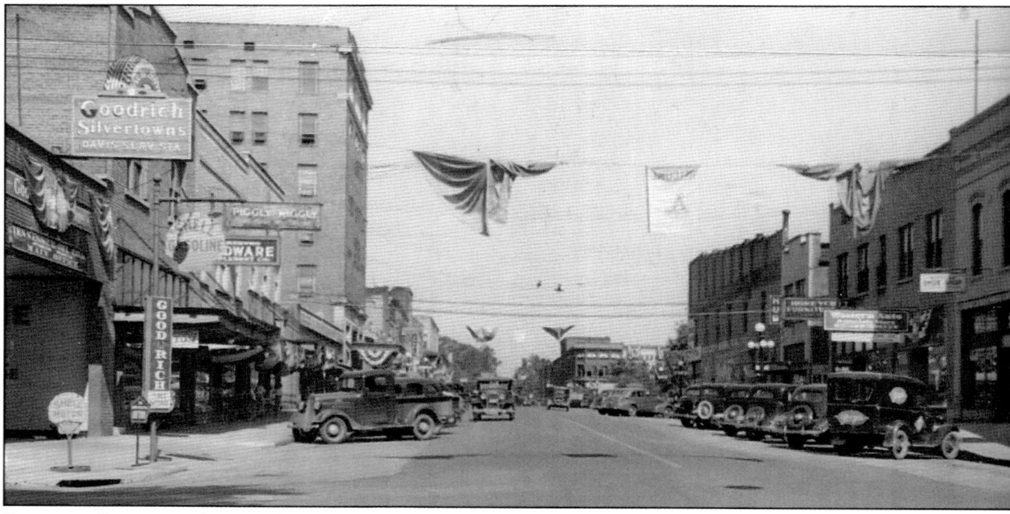

Patriotic bunting drapes the square in the late 1930s in this view looking east. The bunting was probably in honor of Independence Day or another patriotic holiday. Older residents recall that no one ever locked their vehicles when they left them parked at the square. In the earliest days of the automobile, residents would sometimes sit in whatever car was nearby as they chatted with friends and had to be reminded that cars were not park benches. (Courtesy University of Memphis Special Collections.)

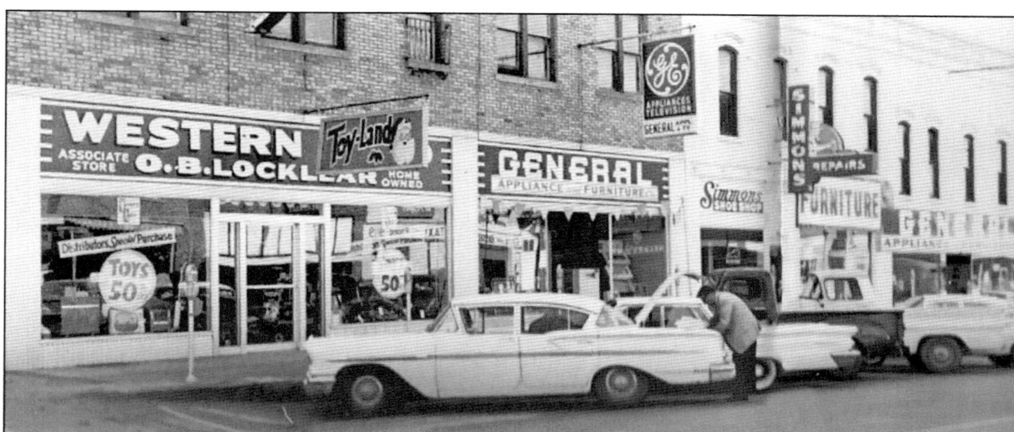

The Western Auto store with its Toy-Land dominates the western side of Court Street in this c. 1960 photograph. The General Appliance store survived and thrived, eventually buying out the businesses on both sides of it.

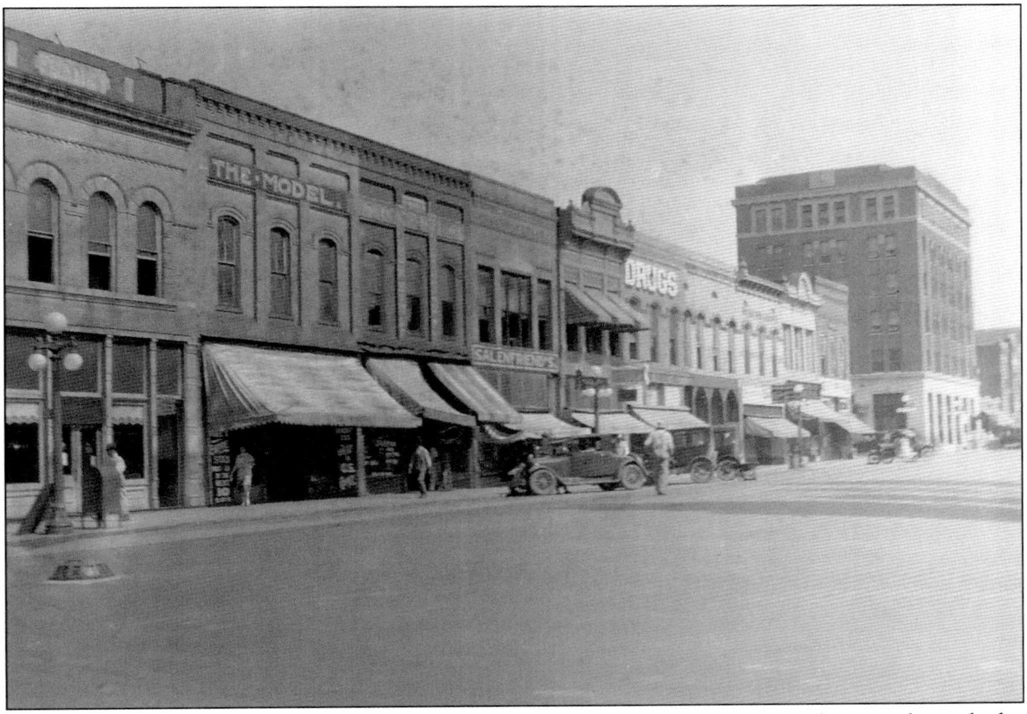

Two views of the west side of the square, from the 1930s and the 1960s, show changes through the years. As time went by, awnings disappeared and protruding brick pediments were removed for safety reasons, but the historical buildings retained their unique arched windows. The building at left was still a bank in the earlier photograph, but by the 1960s, it had become city hall and had a new facade.

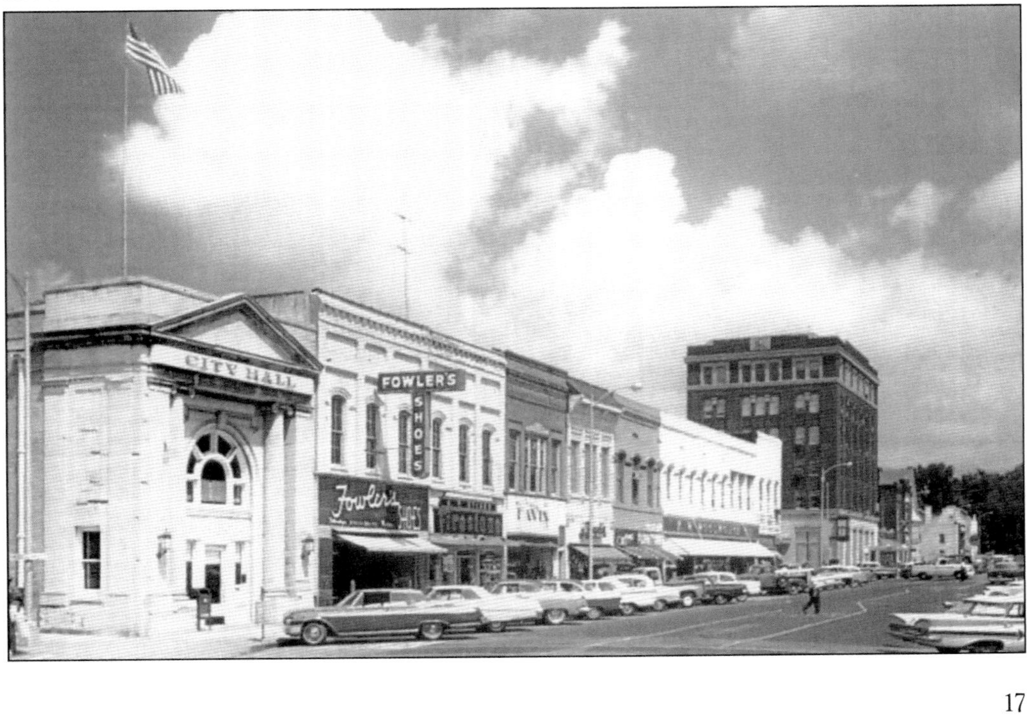

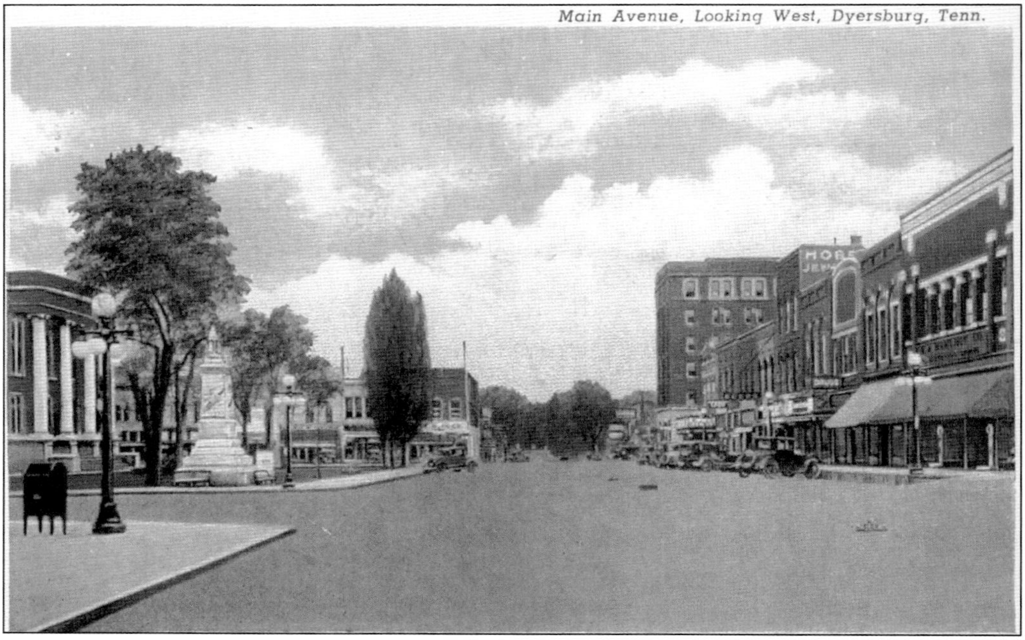

A vintage postcard shows a view of Main Street, looking west, in the early 20th century. The white globe lights at left decorated the square from its earliest years. They were later replaced, but in 2010, the State of Tennessee granted funds to have identical lights installed on the square once again.

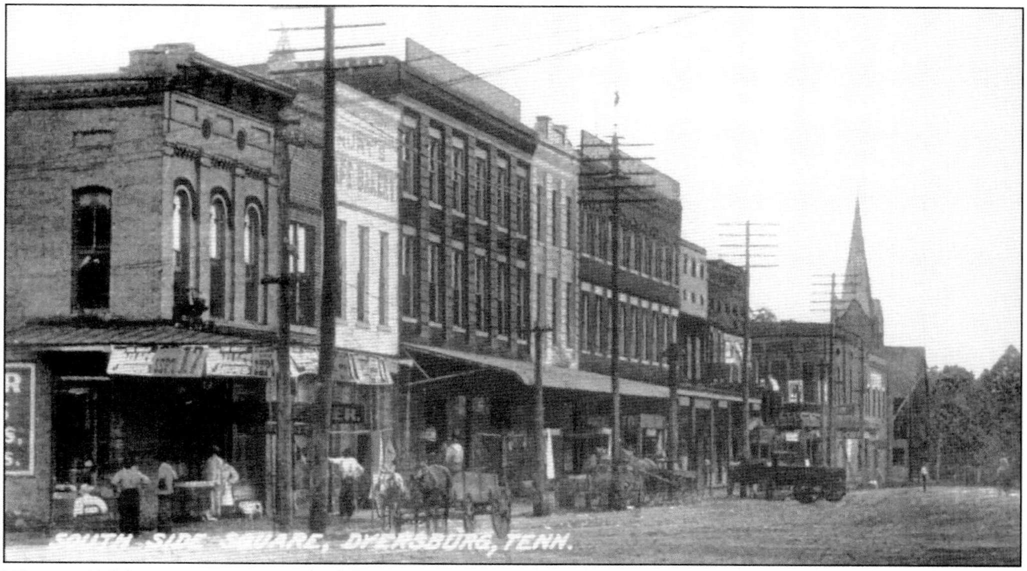

This c. 1900 vintage postcard of the south side of the square includes the original First Methodist Church building with its tall steeple. It was demolished in the 1920s when the new church—a large Mediterranean-style building—was constructed on the site of the Neal estate at the north end of downtown.

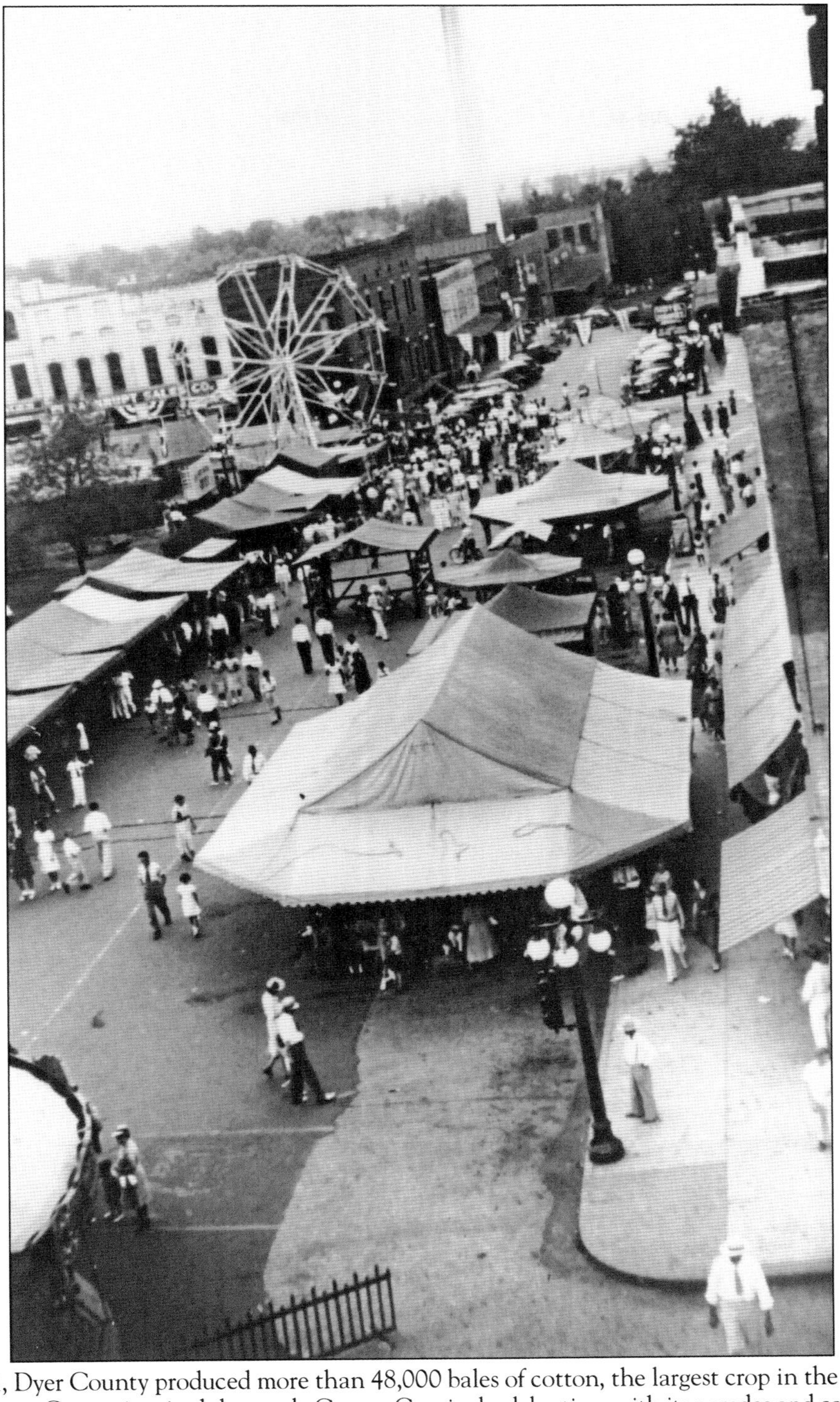

In 1931, Dyer County produced more than 48,000 bales of cotton, the largest crop in the state of Tennessee. Cotton inspired the yearly Cotton Carnival celebration, with its parades and carnivals, including this one in the mid-1930s. Citizens traveled from surrounding counties to ride the rides and play the midway games.

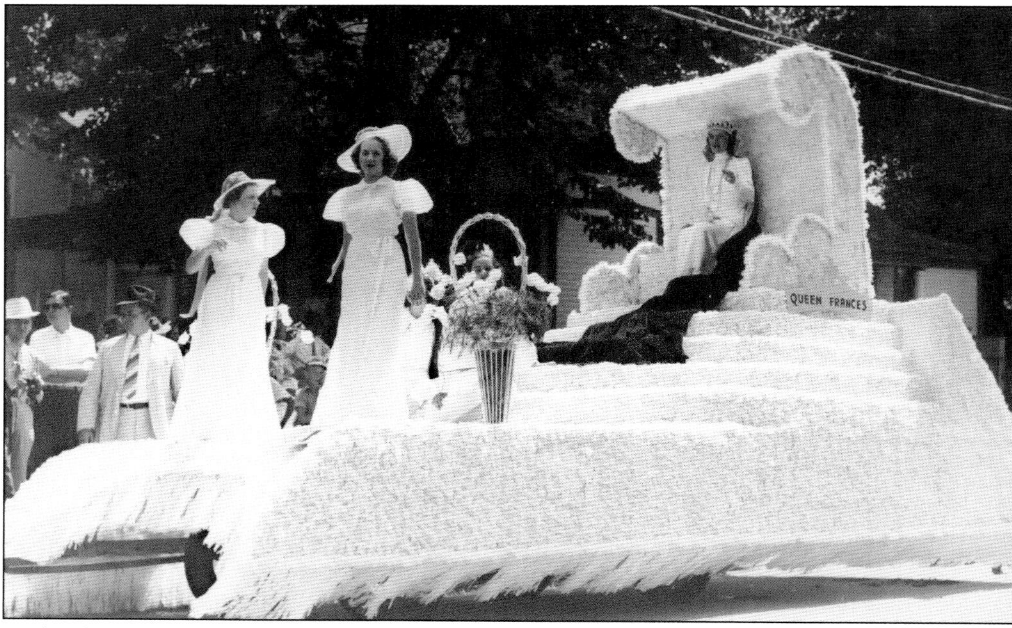

In the depths of the Depression, Dyersburg and other southern cities began to celebrate Cotton Carnival to promote the sale of cotton and to provide entertainment for the citizens. Parades were held in the town square, along with pageants, trade exhibits, social extravaganzas, band concerts, and street carnivals. By World War II, there were 28 cotton gins in operation in the county. Today, there are no active cotton gins in Dyer County, although a cotton boll remains on the city's seal. (Courtesy Chris Gibbons collection.)

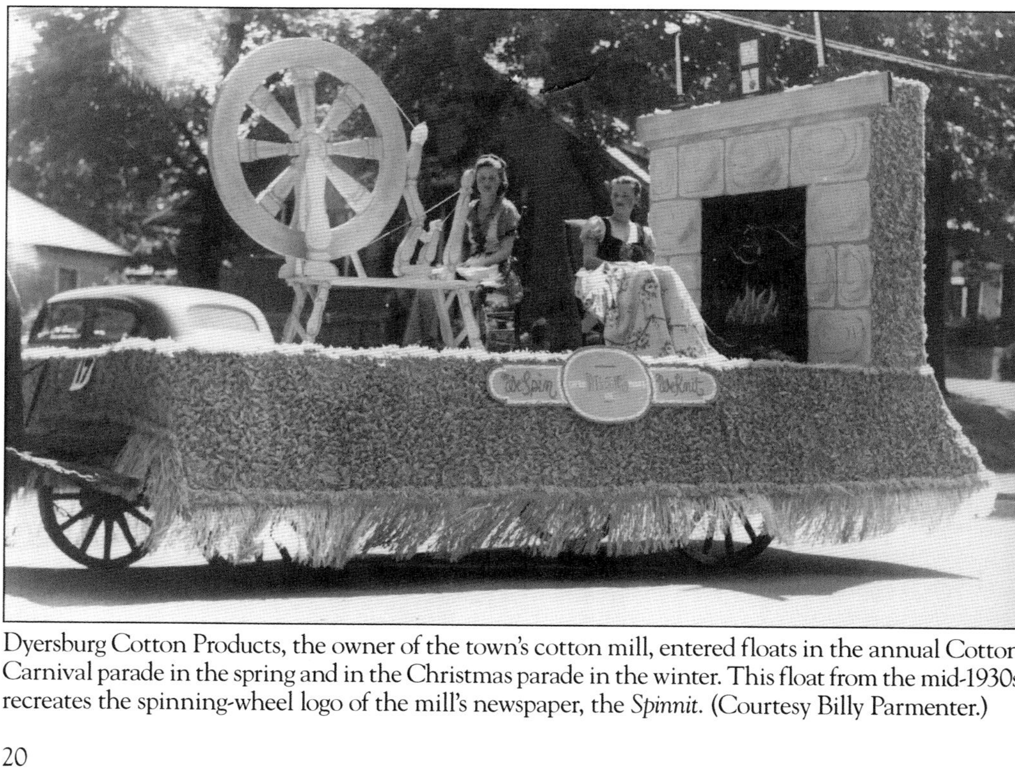

Dyersburg Cotton Products, the owner of the town's cotton mill, entered floats in the annual Cotton Carnival parade in the spring and in the Christmas parade in the winter. This float from the mid-1930s recreates the spinning-wheel logo of the mill's newspaper, the *Spinnit*. (Courtesy Billy Parmenter.)

Before and during World War II, the area around South Main Street and Cedar Street was nicknamed "Whiskey Shoot" and "Sharecropper Street." Airmen training at the nearby Dyersburg Army Air Base were frequent visitors. The building advertising whiskey for sale and a café later housed Dyersburg's Juvenile Court, which is perhaps rather appropriate.

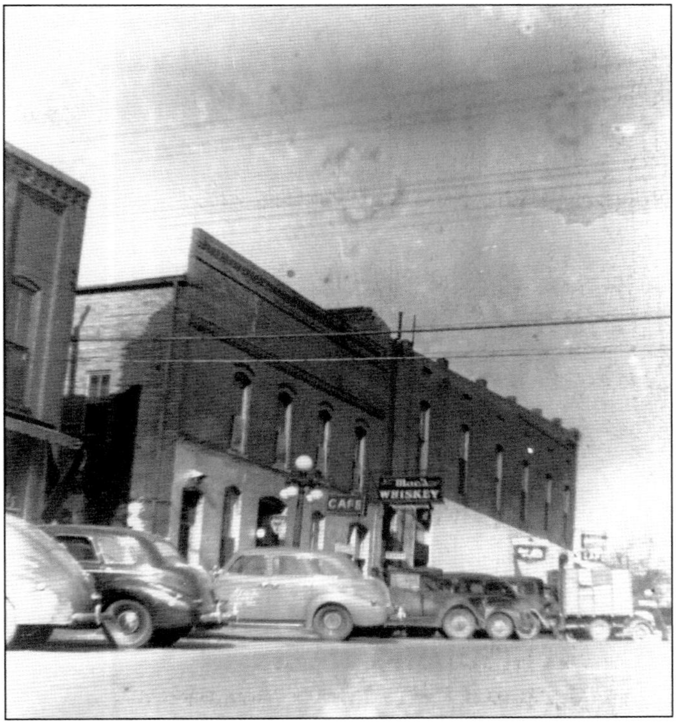

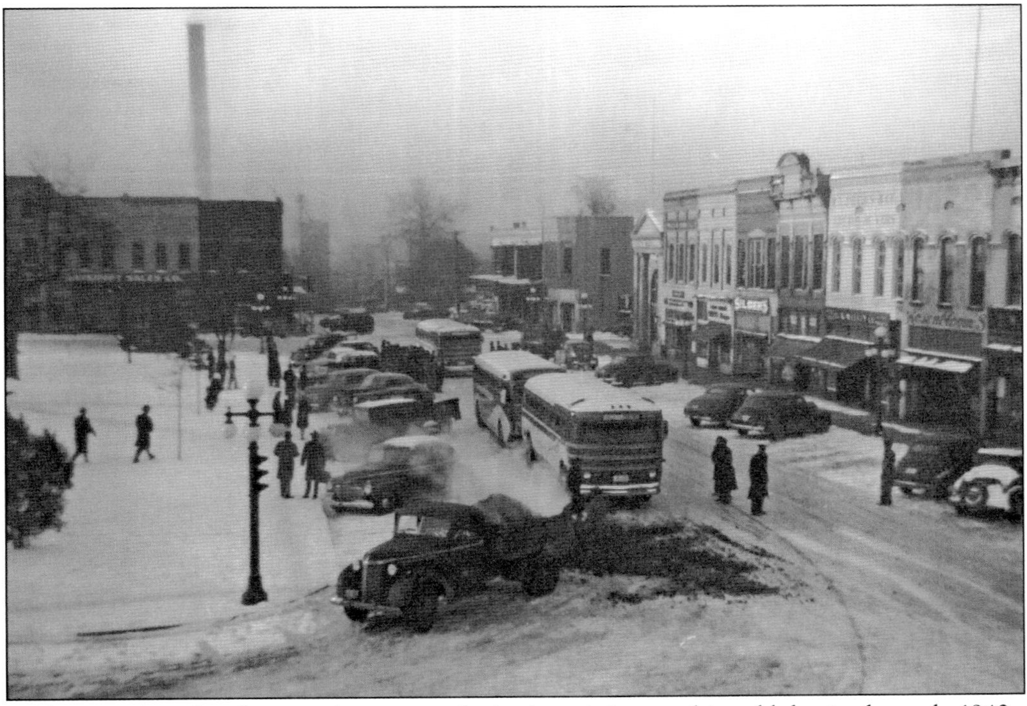

Soldiers are boarding buses to leave town for basic training on this cold day in the early 1940s. In the snowy street can be seen dark coal cinders from the nearby plant with the smokestack; the cinders were spread over the ice for traction.

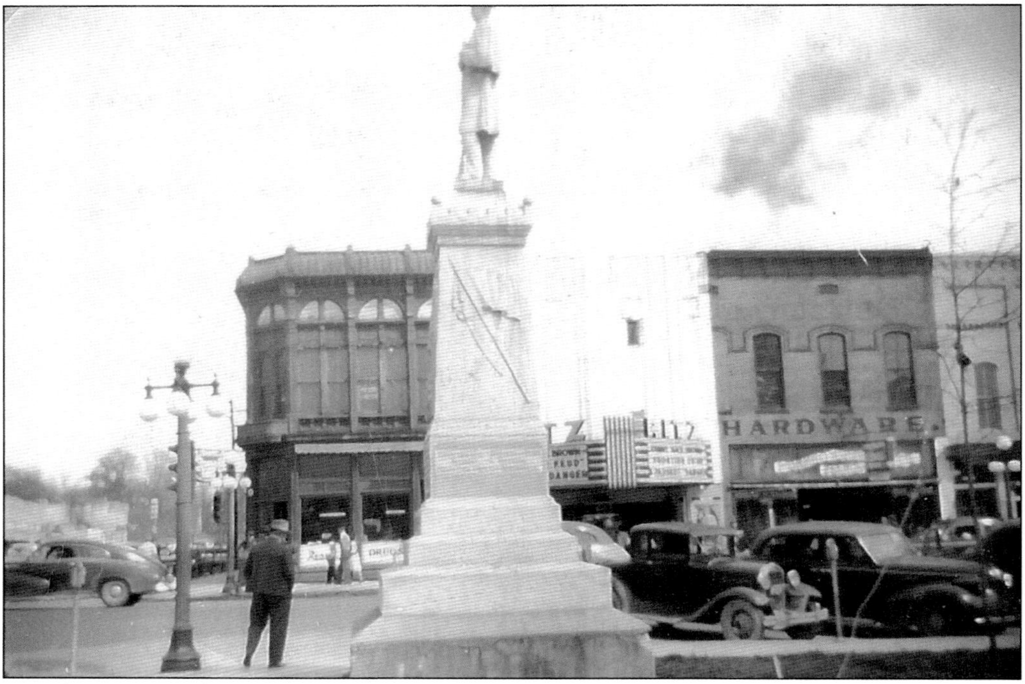

Dyersburg's Confederate monument was unveiled in 1905 amid much celebration. The newspaper reported that "eight acres of people" attended that day. However, the event had been delayed and rescheduled because the statue first arrived with a US belt buckle rather than a CSA buckle, and it had to be sent back to the sculptor.

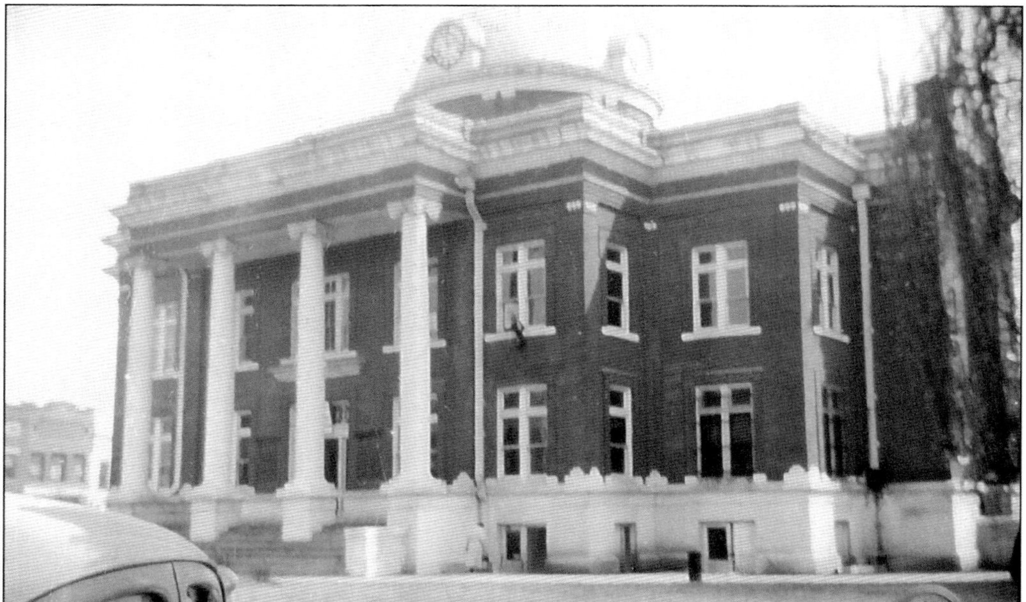

The courthouse has always been a popular spot for picture-taking. The clock tower has faces on all four sides. It stopped working in the 1960s. Various fundraising campaigns through the years have aimed at restoring or replacing it. (Both, courtesy Sandy Deel.)

Two

BUILDINGS

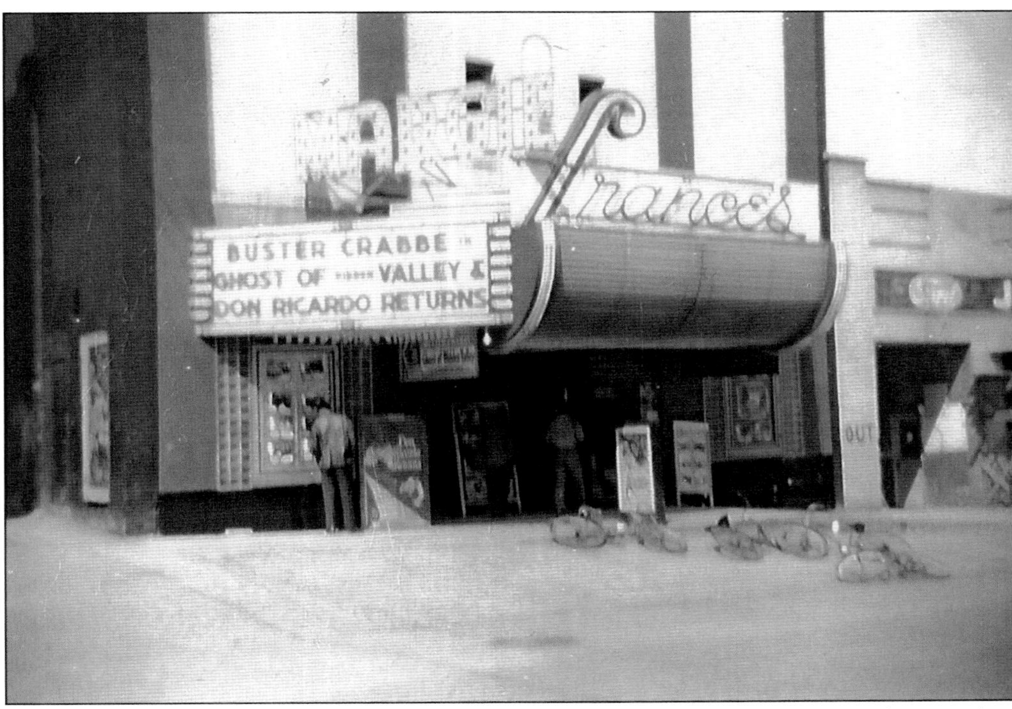

The Frances Theater with its lovely, stylized marquee was a cool and inviting spot for Dyersburg youngsters to abandon their bicycles in 1946 and dash inside to watch the thrilling adventures of Buster Crabbe. The theater was named for Frances Fowlkes, granddaughter of the man who opened it. (Courtesy Sandy Deel.)

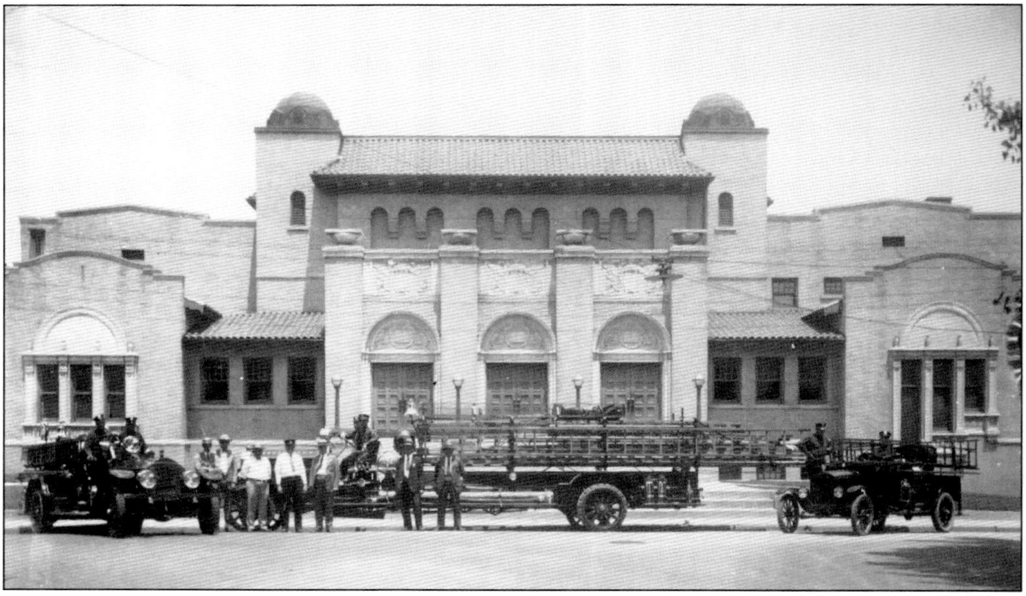

Dyersburg's fire company poses in 1928 in front of what was then the newly constructed First Methodist Church on McGaughey Street. The fire company's building was nearby, housing two trucks. One was called Boy Scout, and the other was called Girl Scout. (Courtesy Tennessee State Library and Archives.)

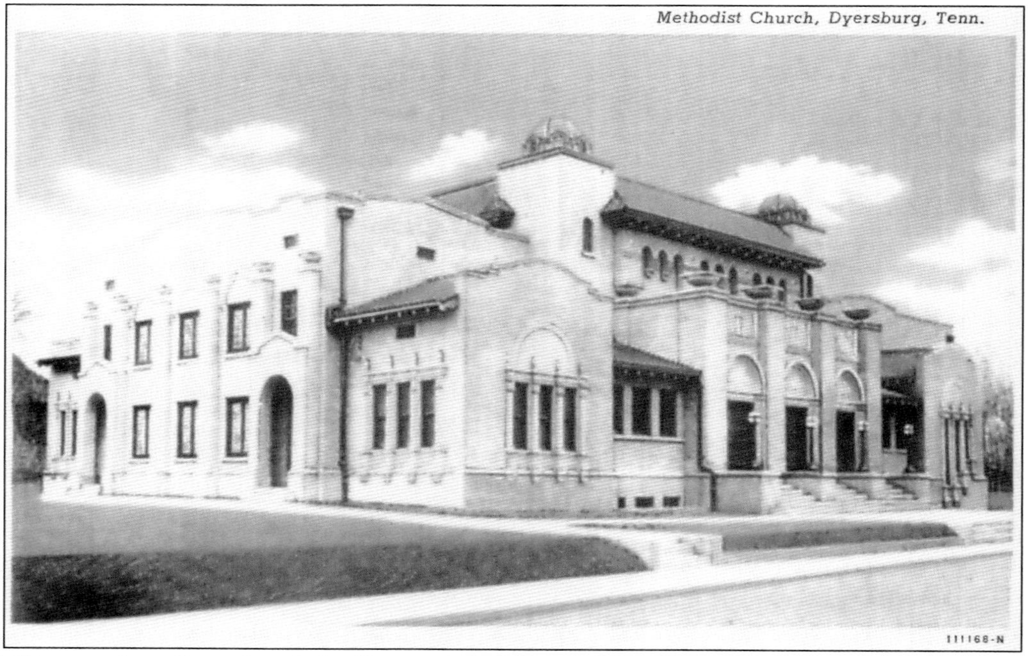

This sprawling, Spanish-style building replaced the smaller and more traditional First Methodist Church with its steeple, which once stood on the town square. First Methodist was the first church in Dyer County. This imposing structure, with its green accents, was built in 1923 on the former property of Col. Tom Neal, who in 1865 founded what became the Dyersburg *State Gazette* newspaper.

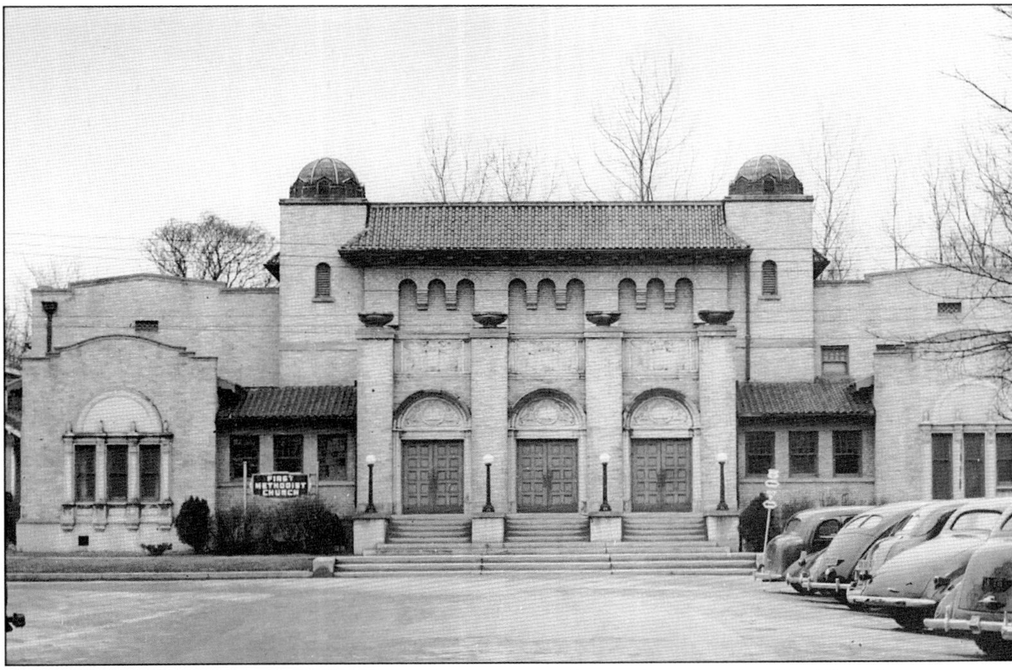

In 1840, Robert M. Tarrant held a courthouse revival, and First Methodist Church grew out of this meeting. Two previous church buildings existed before this one, which was constructed in 1923. It is pictured in the 1940s (above). The photograph below, from 2010, includes the historical marker that now stands on the lawn. The church prides itself on supporting foreign missions, county disaster aid, and community service. Its motto is "the church in the heart of town with the town at heart." (Above, courtesy Chris Gibbons collection.)

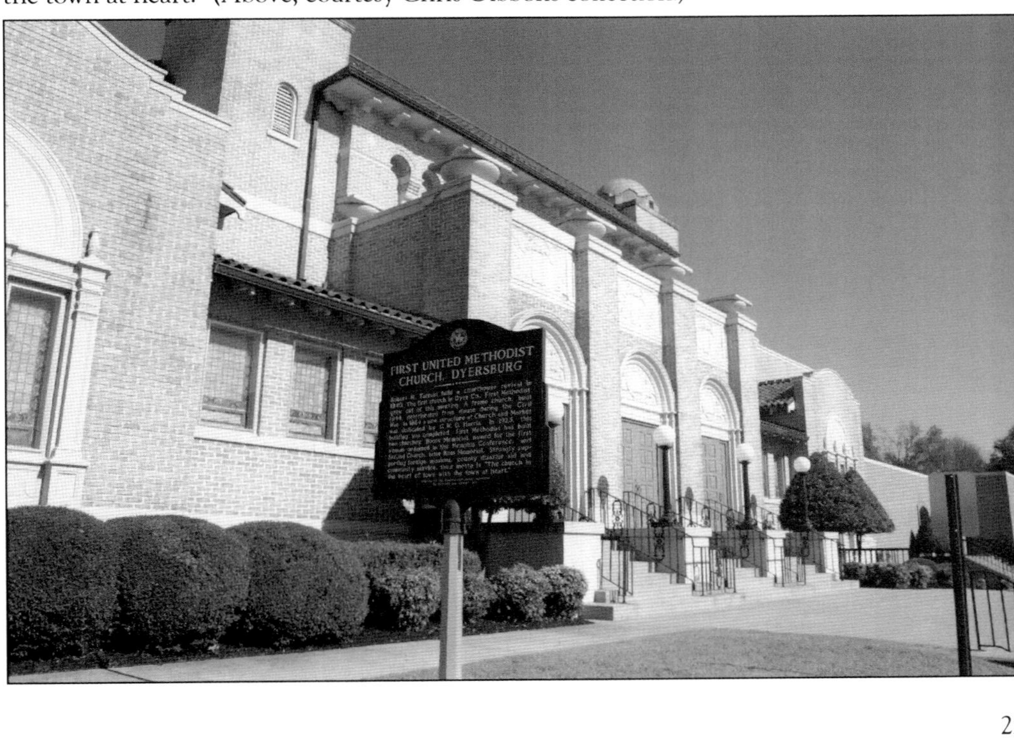

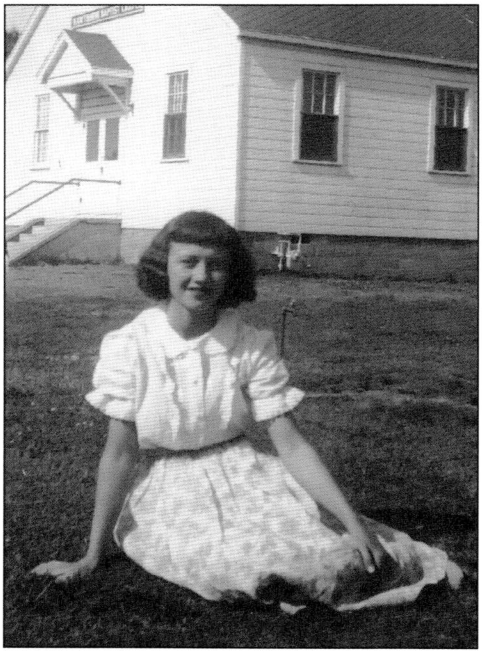

Rose Ray Hogue poses in a Sunday dress in front of the original Hawthorne Baptist Church in the mid-1950s. Rev. T.C. Thurman was pastor there for many years. A newer, larger building on the same site later replaced this one.

Rev. George B. Vernon and Mary Holland Vernon pose in front of East Dyersburg Methodist Church in 1953. Children of the congregation recall being asked to come forward on their birthdays, tell their age, and drop pennies in a jar—one penny for each year. (Courtesy Gaylon Reasons.)

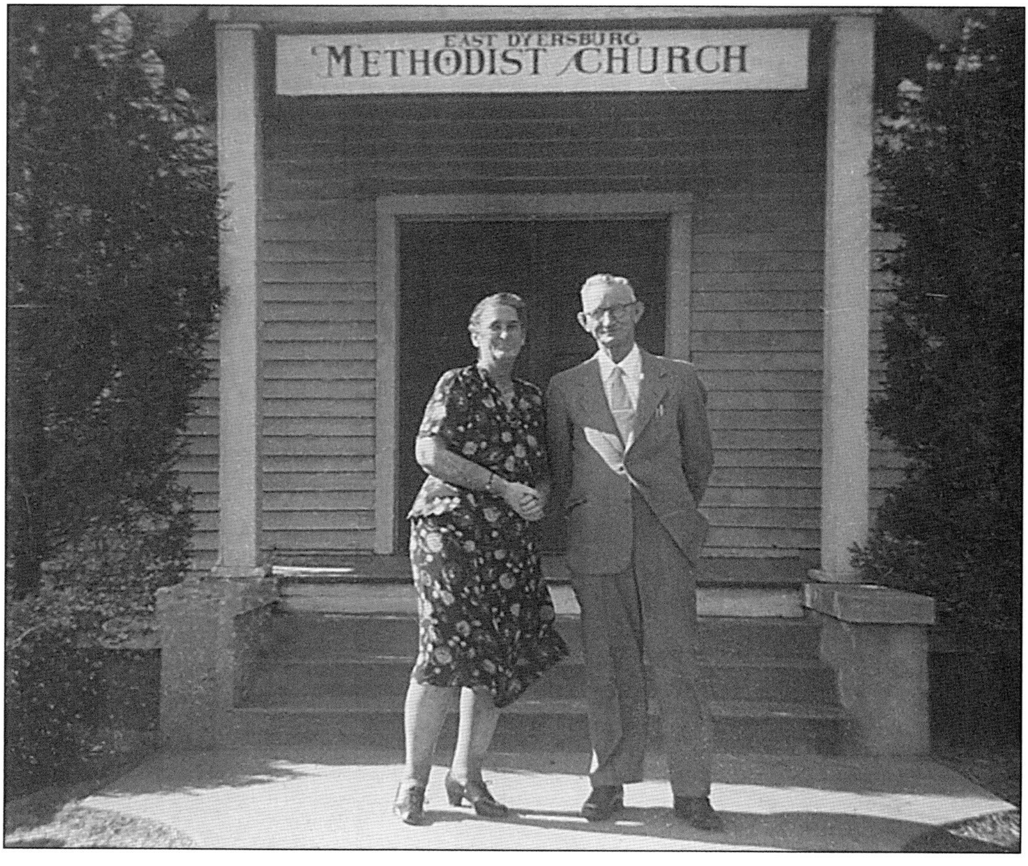

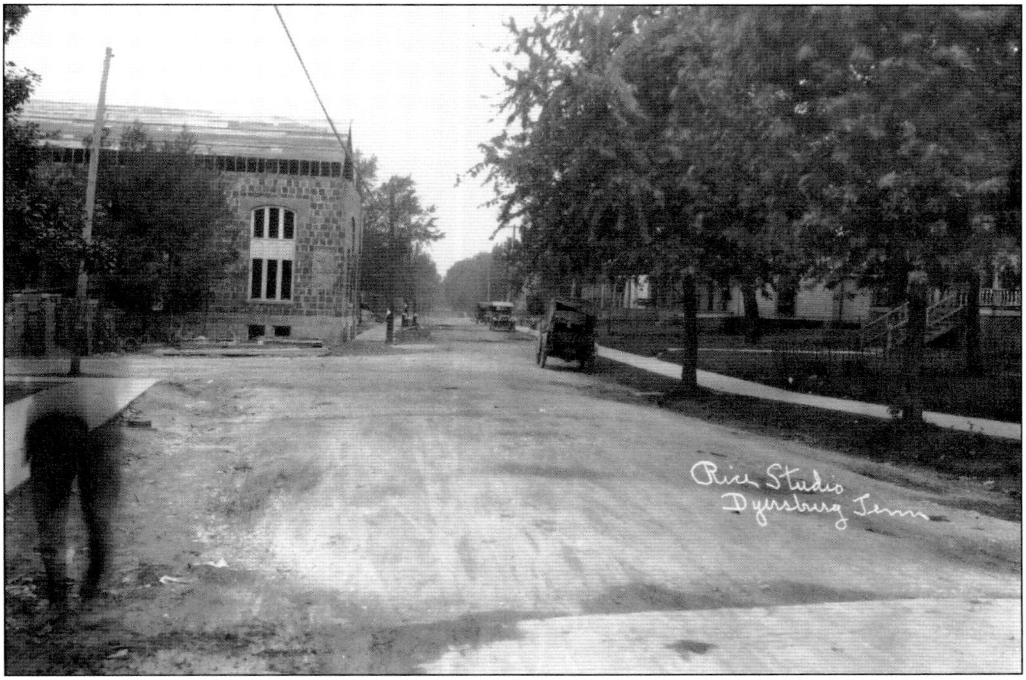

In these two views of McGaughey Street, looking west at Troy Avenue, the steps of the first Dyersburg Hospital can be seen on the far right. In the photograph above, First Presbyterian Church is under construction, and in the photograph below, some years later, the exterior has been renovated. That building is now gone.

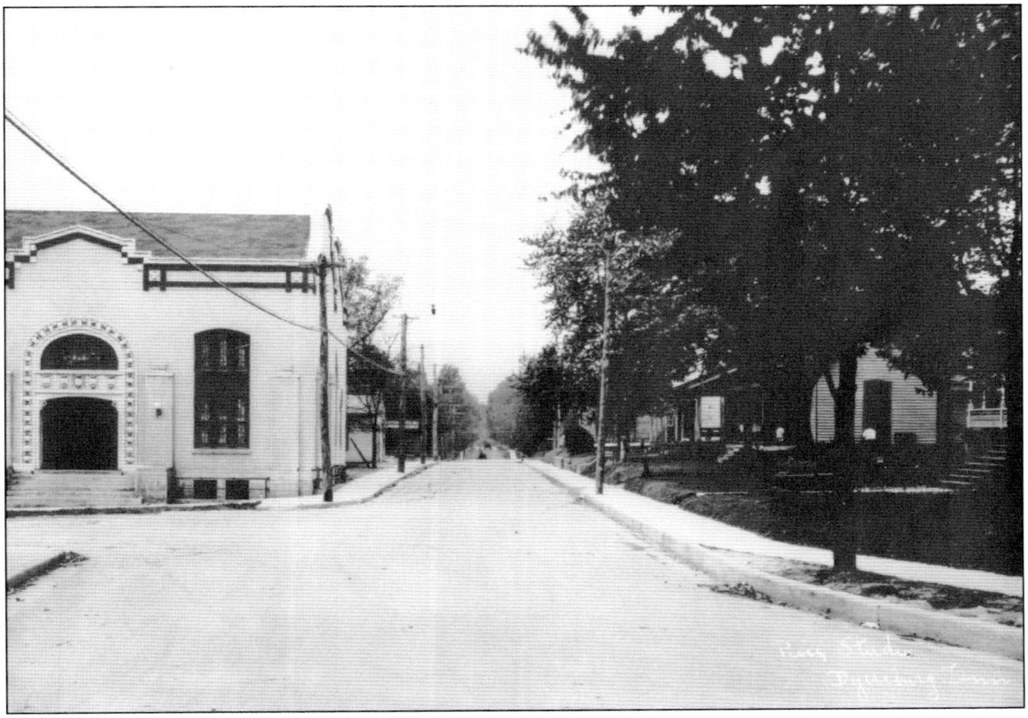

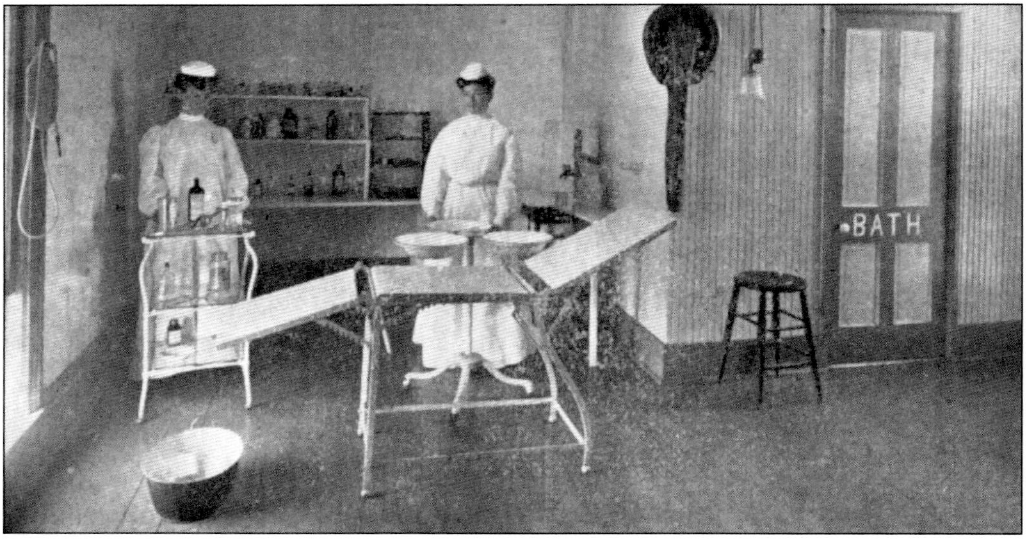

Dyersburg Hospital, the town's first, was founded by Dr. William P. Watson in his house. Its steps can be seen in photographs on the previous page. The name later became Dyersburg Sanitarium. Its operating rooms (above) and patients' rooms (below) were fitted with "the latest and most modern improvements," according to a promotional booklet from the early 20th century.

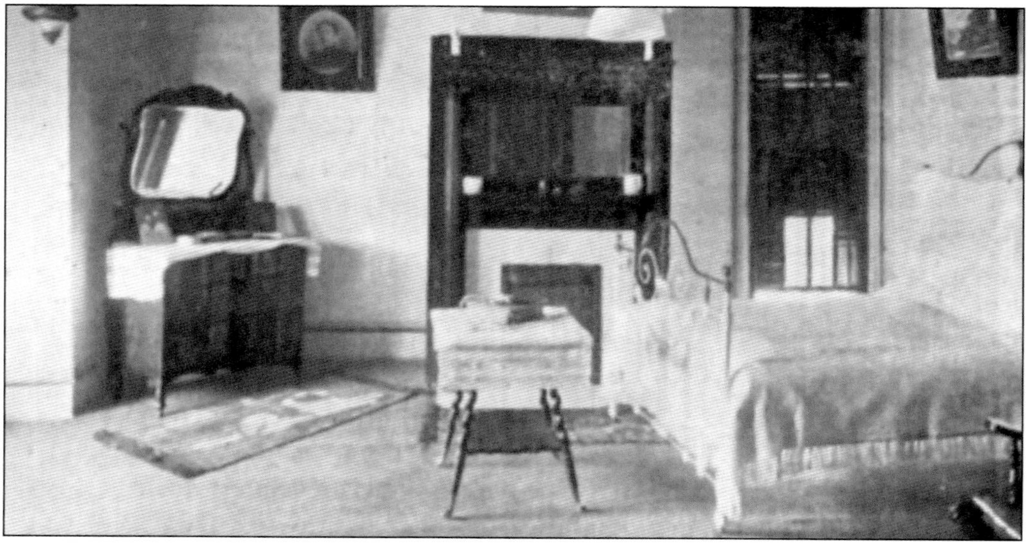

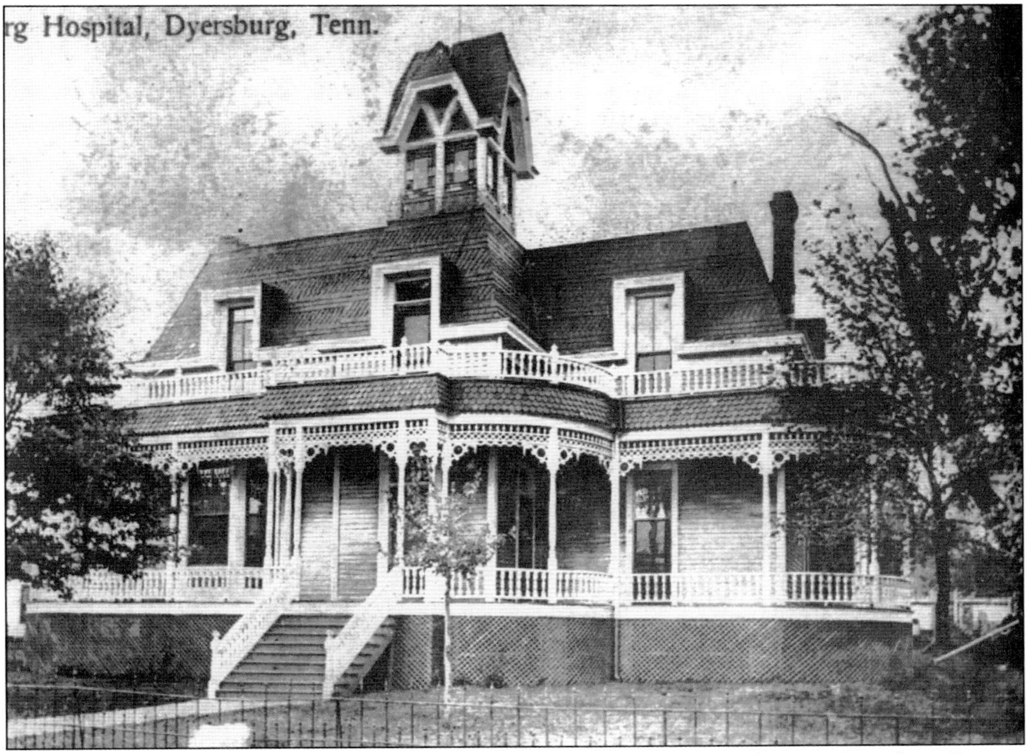

The Dyersburg Sanitarium is believed to have had the first indoor plumbing in Dyersburg. Room, board, and general nursing, day and night, could be had for $7 to $14 per week, not including doctors' charges. Surgical fees were an extra $1 to $5. In the 1920s, when pellagra became a problem, the hospital helped distribute brewer's yeast to combat the disease. However, it became necessary to run a newspaper item explaining that the yeast was not satisfactory for making "home brew" and should only be used to combat pellagra.

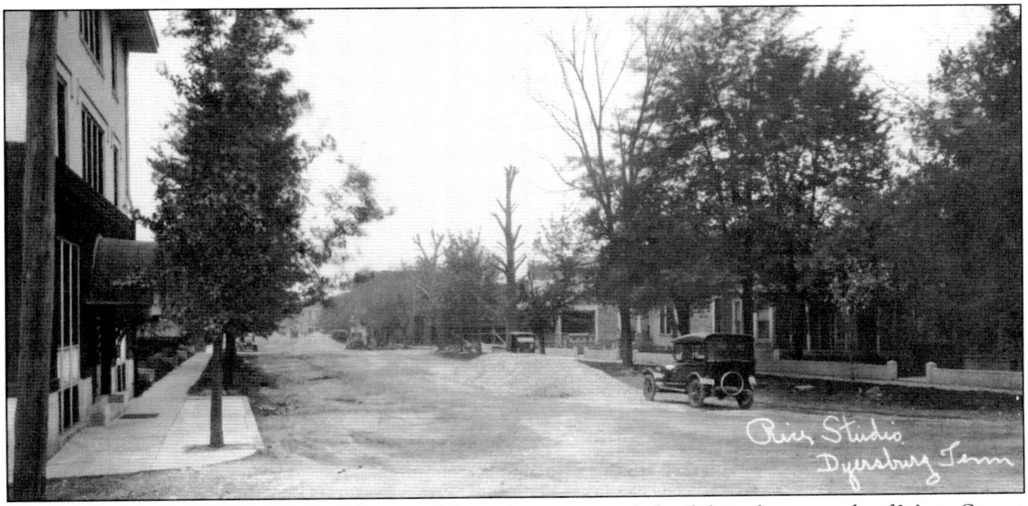

The Baird-Brewer Hospital's facade is visible at the extreme left of this photograph of Main Street looking south at McGaughey Street. The building, a renovated house once belonging to the Dulaney family, became the second medical facility in town after the Dyersburg Sanitarium.

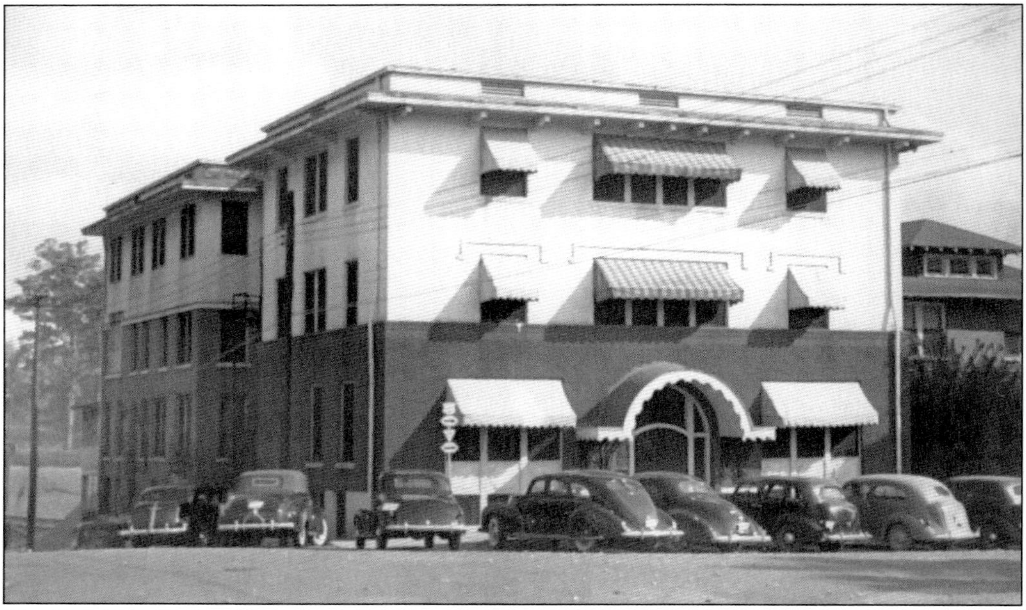

The Baird-Brewer building was originally called Baird-Dulaney because the structure had been the Dulaney home before it was remodeled into the hospital in 1914. The hospital was an early leader in the inpatient business. Emmett Kelly Junior—who has been dubbed "the World's Most Famous Clown"—was born in this building in 1923, the last day the circus was in town. His parents were circus performers; his father was the original "Weary Willie" clown character. Kelly, who would serve in World War II, died in 2006. (Below, courtesy University of Memphis Special Collections.)

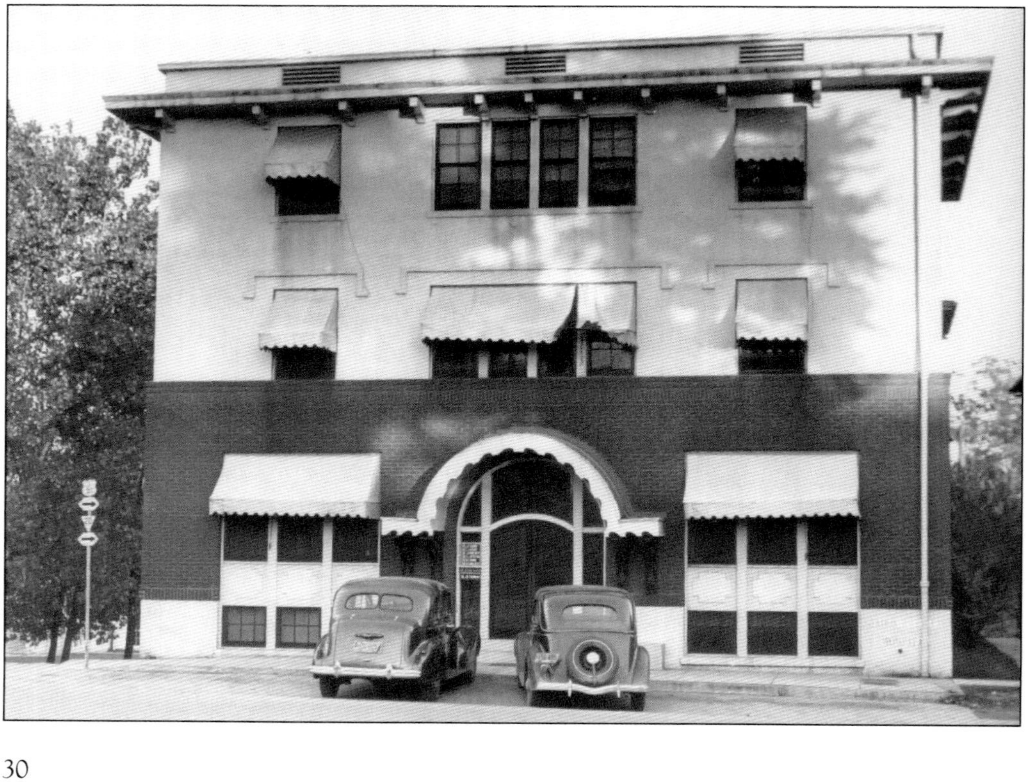

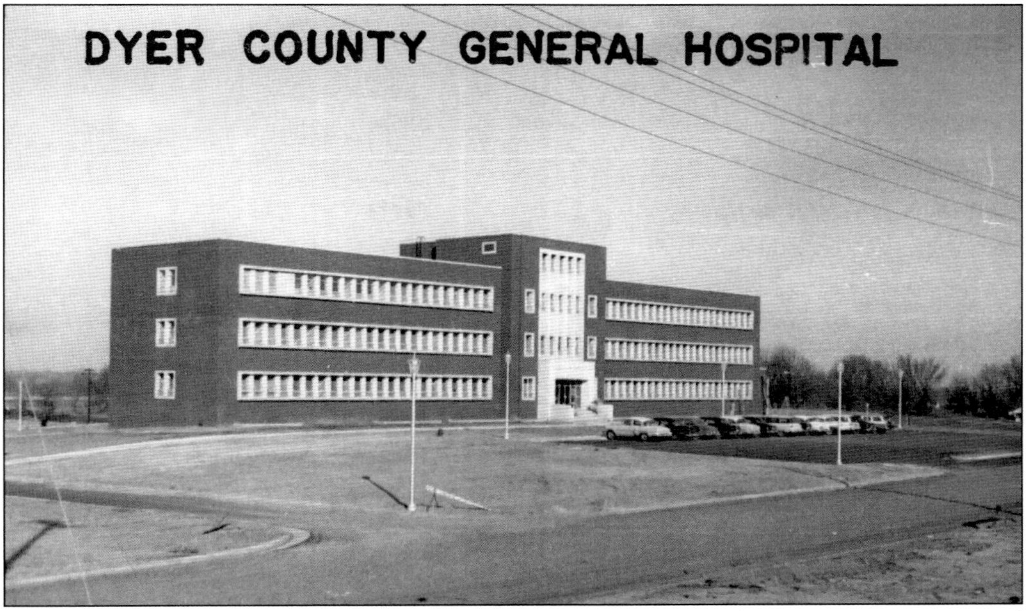

As Dyer County grew, so did its need for services and better medical facilities. Dyer County General Hospital (later renamed the Parkview) was built in 1956, and over the years, it was enlarged several times. A convalescent home and ambulance service were added. It is now the Dyersburg Regional Medical Center. (Above, courtesy Tennessee State Library and Archives.)

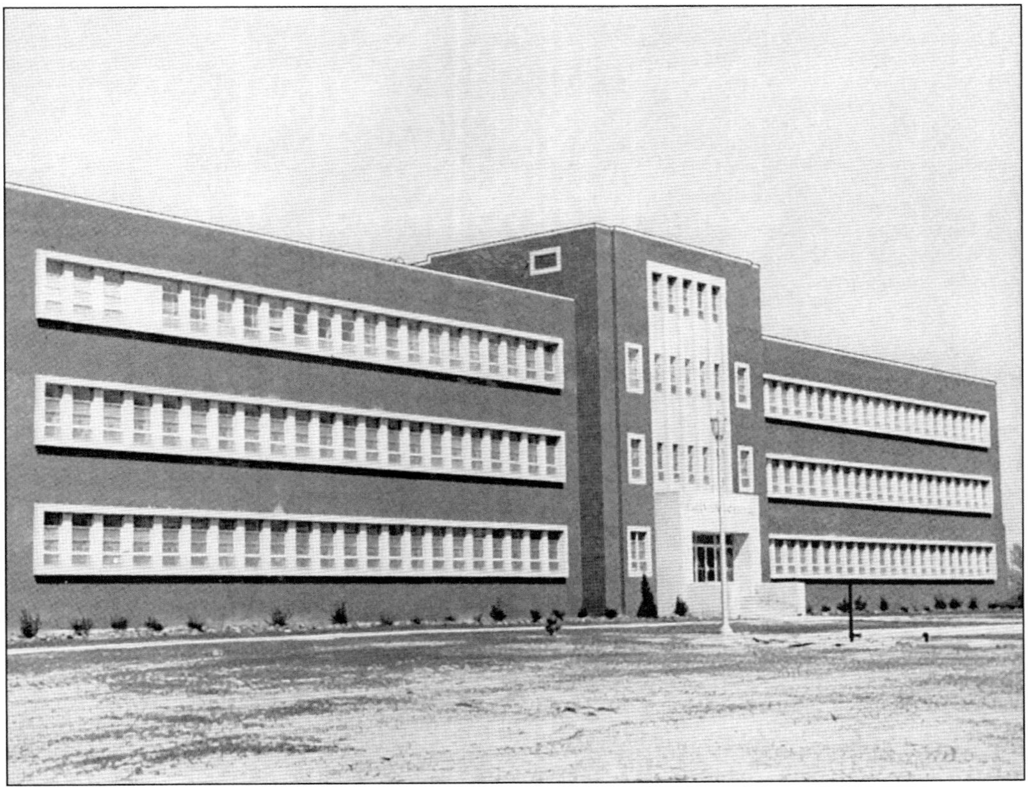

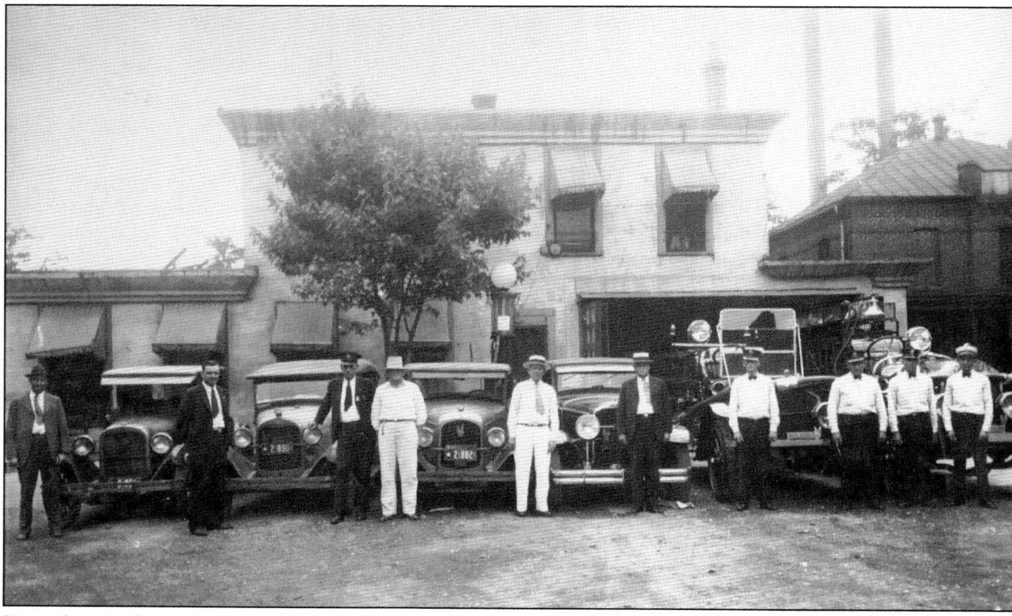

Dyersburg's fire company proudly shows off equipment in front of its fire station on Mill Avenue, with city hall visible in the background. The dark building was once the stable for the fire horses. Their harnesses hung from the ceiling, and when the fire alarm went off, the harnesses were dropped onto the horses so that they could be hitched up more quickly. (Courtesy Tennessee State Library and Archives.)

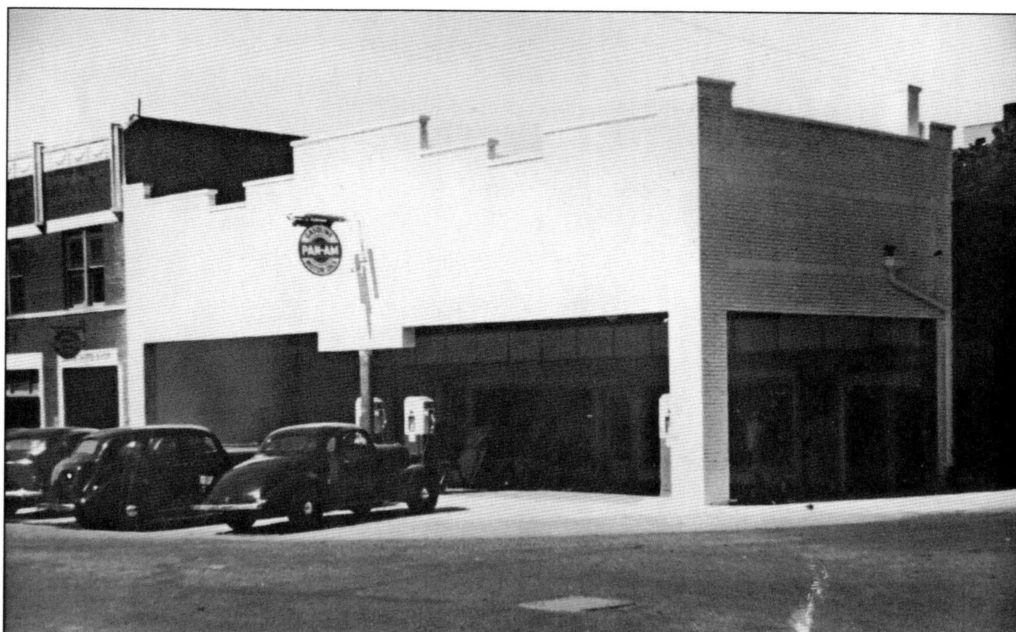

This building, at the corner of East Court and Church Streets and across from the bus station, once housed a busy taxi stand. Previously, it had been a gas station. The building still exists but has been completely enclosed and for many years was the site of the Cozy Kitchen restaurant. It now houses a law office. (Courtesy Chris Gibbons collection.)

Western Union had offices in the base of the Hotel Cordell Hull on the town square, which eventually became Security Bank. Local radio station WTRO was once located in an annex on the east side of this building. At the far left, a few windows of the post office are visible.

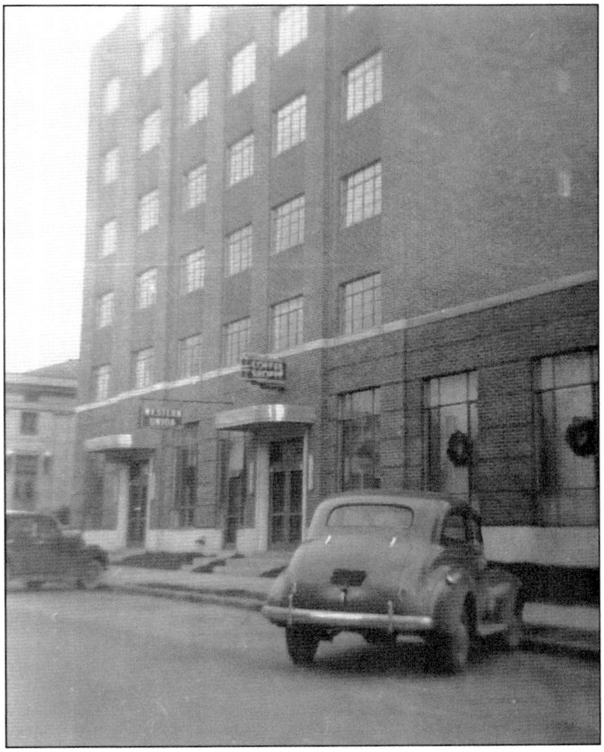

Seen here in the 1940s, the Greyhound Bus Station stood on Court Street in downtown Dyersburg. At the time, it had two waiting rooms, separated by race. Residents remember the calls that would come over the intercom: "Now boarding at Gate Two, northbound for Newbern, Trimble, Obion, Troy, Union City, Fulton, Wingo, and Paducah." The building, with its distinctive architecture, housed a pizza delivery establishment as of 2010.

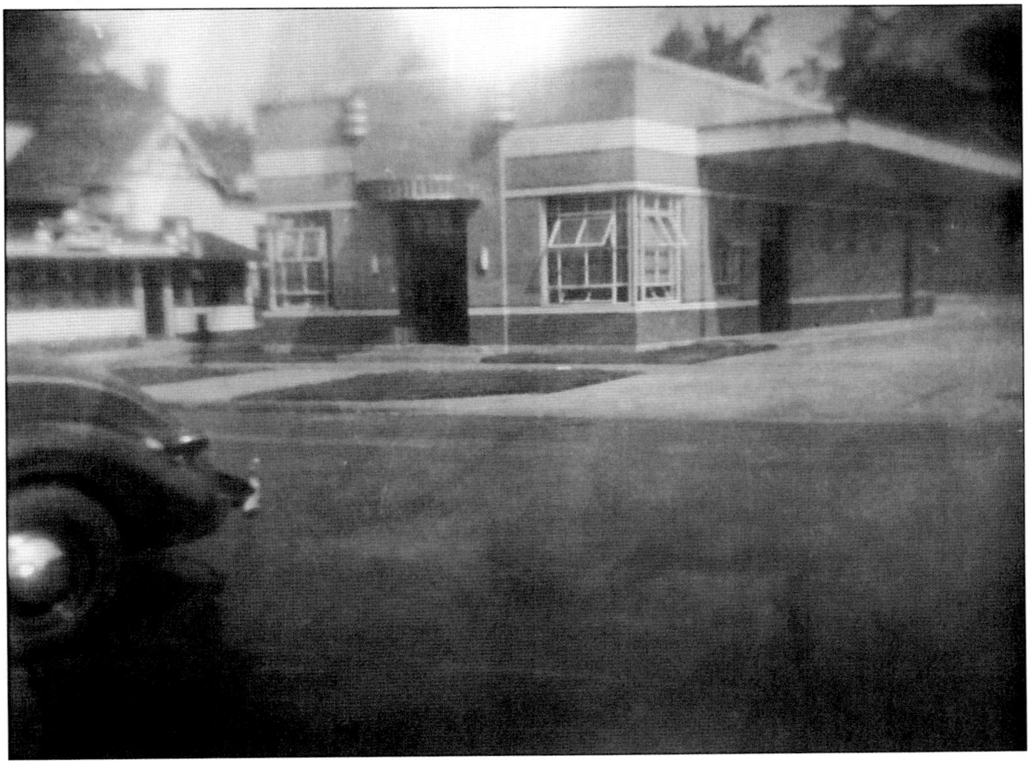

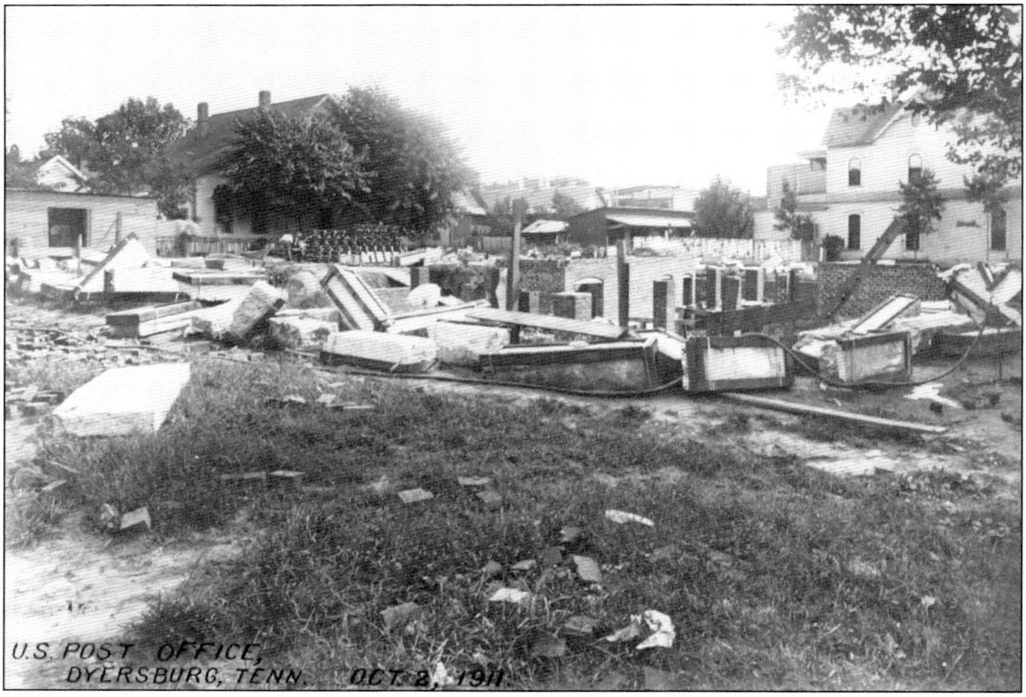

In the above photograph, the Dyersburg Post Office is seen under construction in the early 20th century at 204 North Mill Avenue. The vintage postcard below shows the completed building with its stately stone steps and imposing windows. In the 1960s, post office services moved to a new space, and this building became the library. A formal opening and dedication ceremony for the library were held on Sunday afternoon, April 17, 1966. (Above, courtesy Tennessee State Library and Archives.)

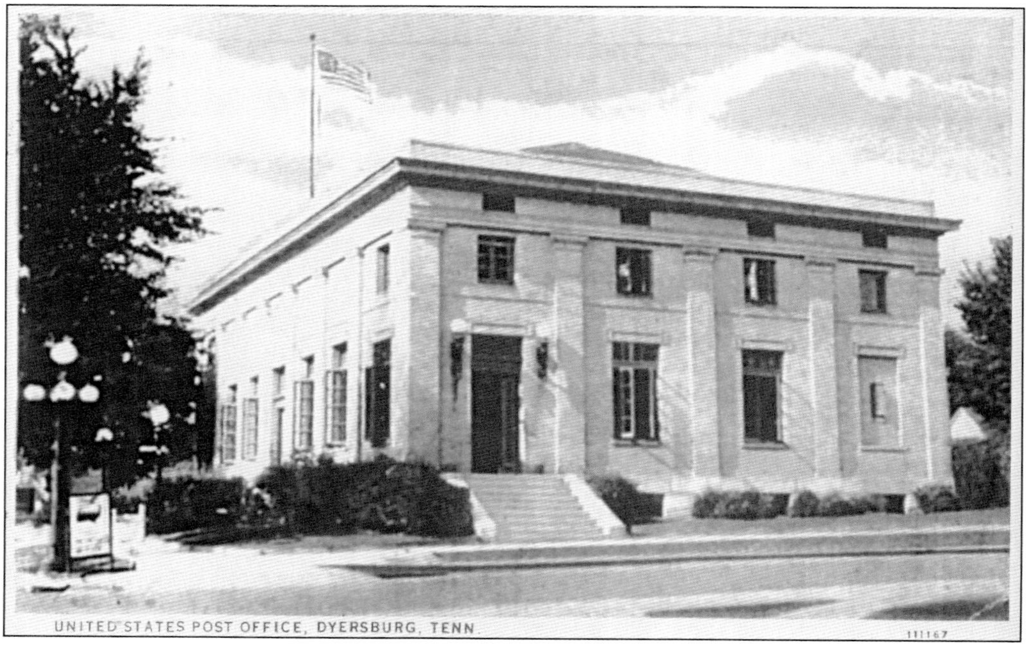

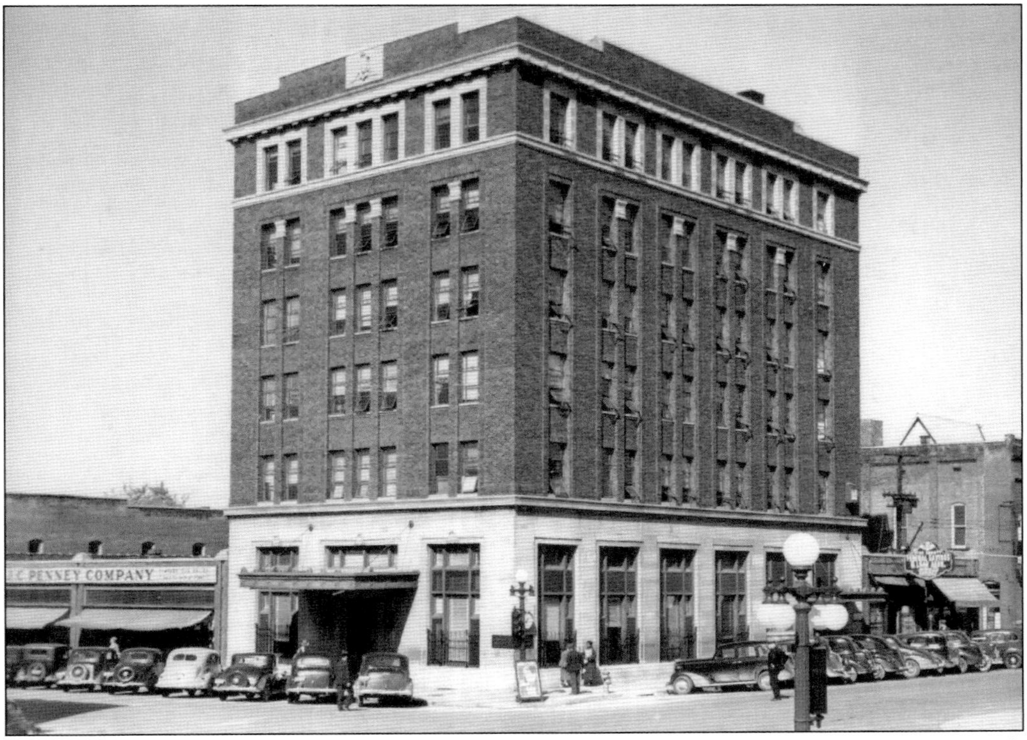

First National Citizens Bank is pictured in two views taken from the same spot. The photograph above, from the early 1940s, clearly shows the round white globe lights that used to decorate the town square. In the photograph below, from the 1950s, they have been replaced by modern light poles. City Drug Company, visible in the photograph below, first opened its doors in the 1880s.

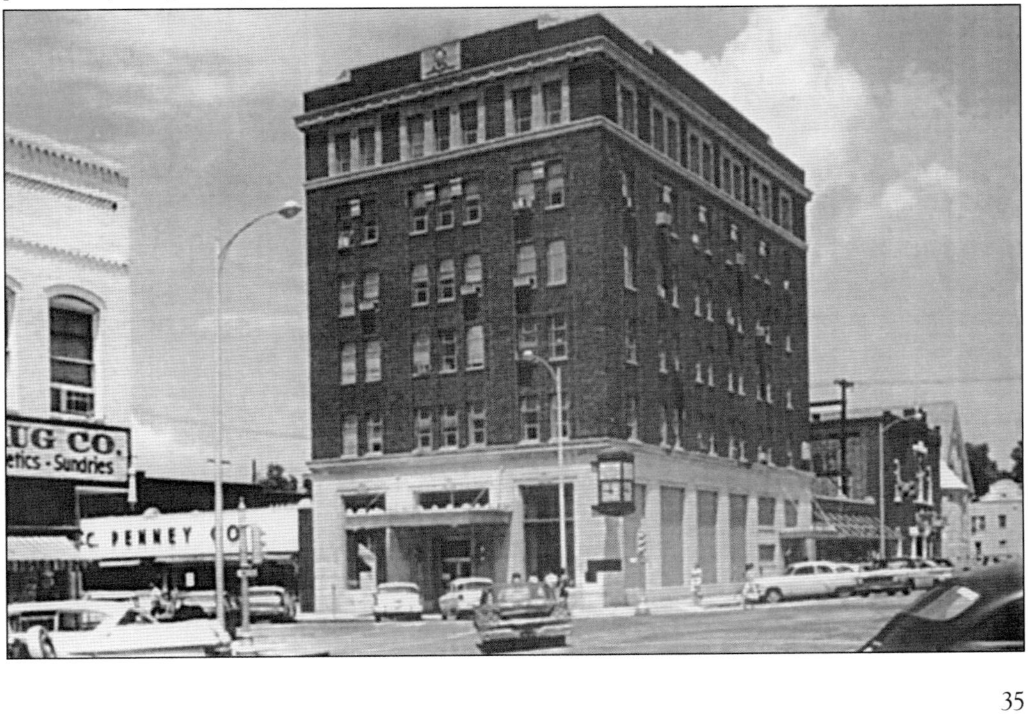

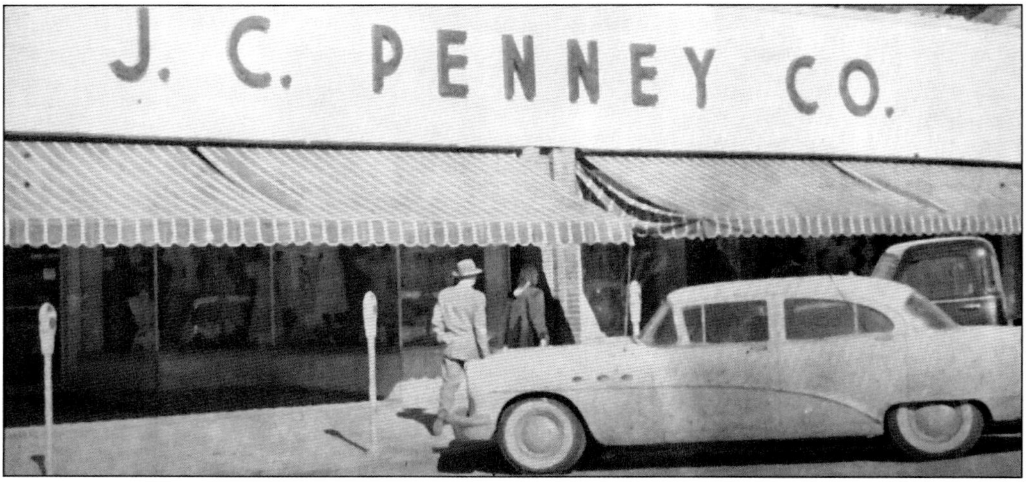

This photograph provides a closer view of the J.C. Penney facade (pictured on the previous page next to First National Citizens Bank). James Cash Penney opened his first store in 1902, and the chain quickly spread to many locations around the country, surviving and even thriving during the Great Depression. During World War II, customers could purchase war bonds in J.C. Penney stores.

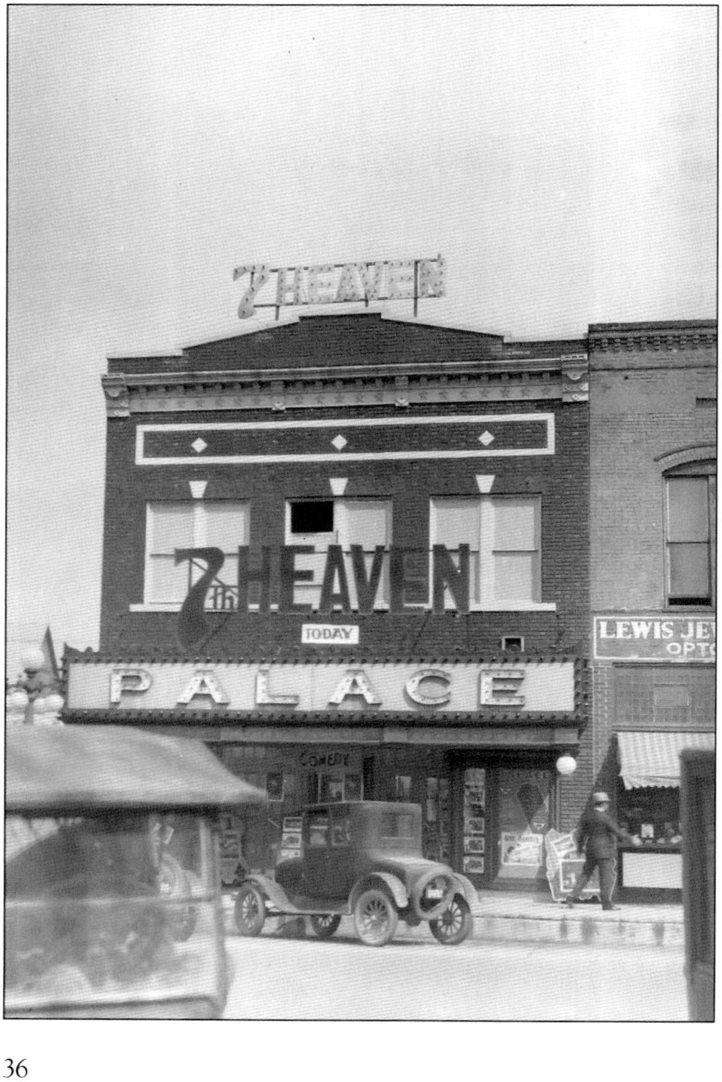

Dyersburg once had four different movie houses. This is the Palace, which began operation in the days of silent movies. On this day in 1927, the movie *Seventh Heaven* is showing, starring Janet Gaynor. This building later housed Reed's Drug store, owned by longtime pharmacist Dr. John Reed. He began his career in 1893 and did not retire until the 1960s.

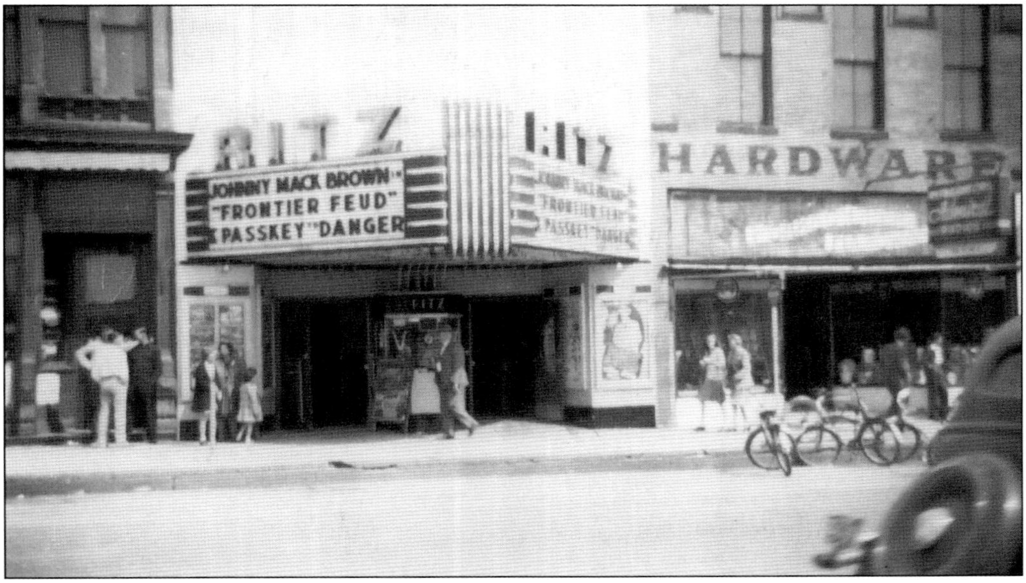

Bicycles are parked with no fear of theft in front of the Ritz Theatre in 1945. The Ritz building later became Dyer Drugs, then in the 1960s hosted at least one restaurant. The building burned in 2000, leaving an empty space next to Forked Deer Hardware, which for decades remained the oldest continually operating hardware store in the country. (Courtesy Sandy Deel.)

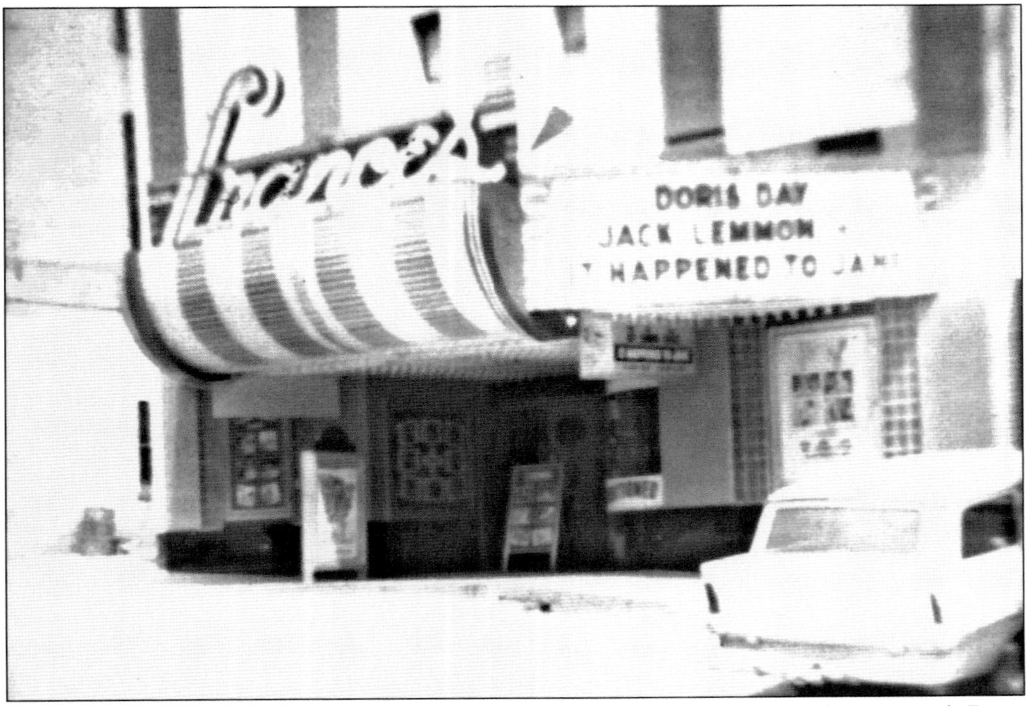

Around the corner from the Ritz, the Frances Theater is showing *It Happened to Jane* with Doris Day and Jack Lemmon on this day in 1959. This would surely have been a popular movie in Dyersburg, as the plot revolved around a railroad line. The building eventually ceased being a movie theater, later housing a shoe store. (Courtesy Gaylon Reasons.)

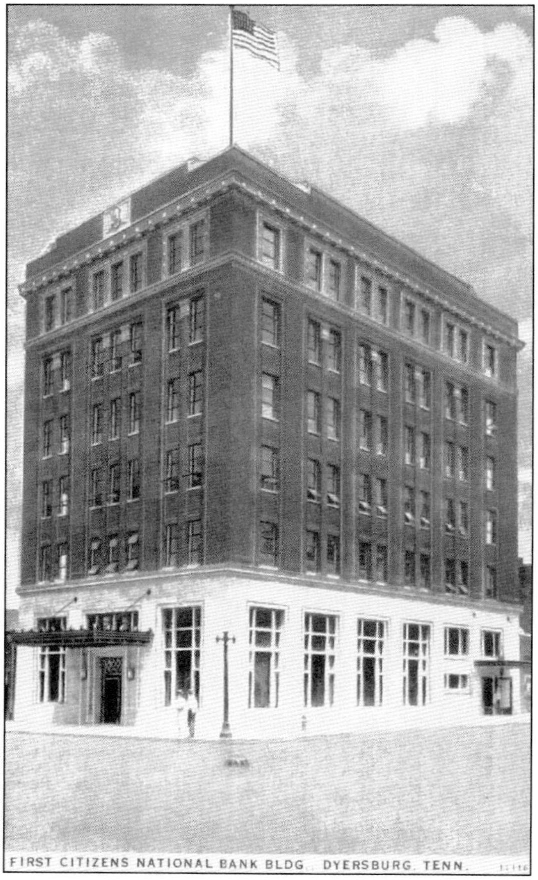

Vintage postcards provide similar views of First Citizens National Bank on the town square. In the photograph below, the edge of the historic courthouse can be seen. The grassy area in the foreground was a popular spot for concerts and performances, and a gazebo once stood in the general area. Citizens remember seeing country singer Roy Acuff performing there in 1948 during his unsuccessful run for Tennessee governor. Acuff, a Republican, lost to Democrat Gordon Browning.

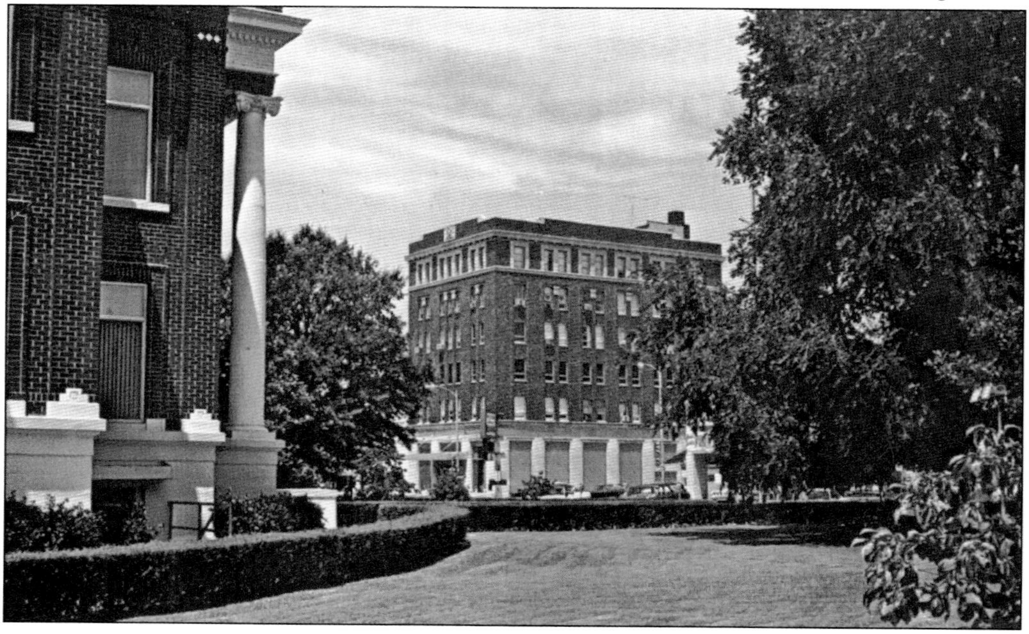

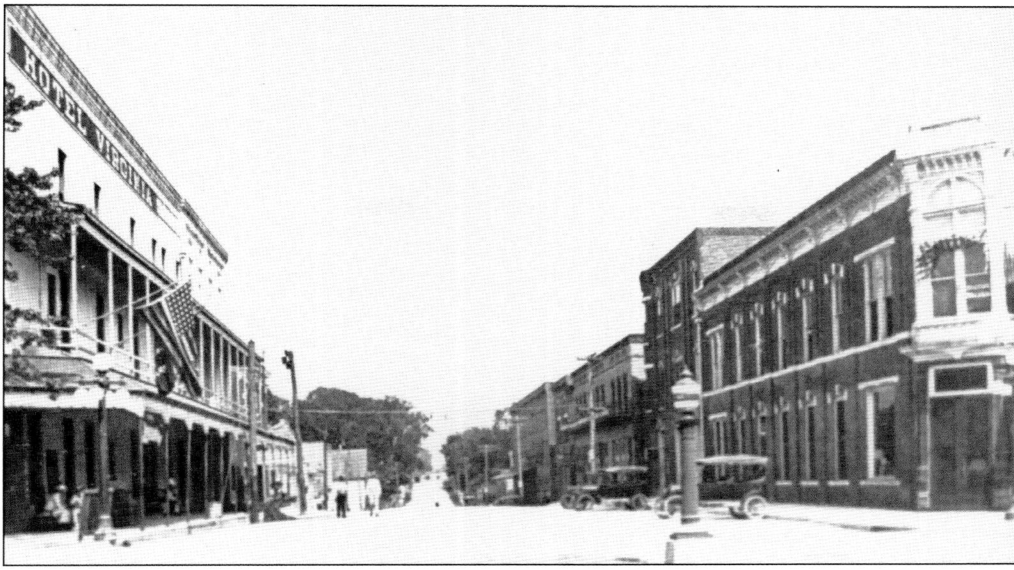

This image, shot from Main Street looking east on East Court Street, was taken in 1905. The Hotel Virginia, an early hotel for railroad travelers passing through, is on the left. It changed its name to Hotel Atwood in 1920 (below) and then later became the Forked Deer Hotel. Main Street runs left and right in the foreground of the photographs. Towns like Dyersburg, at the junction of river and rail traffic, greatly benefited from the business generated by passengers and workers from steamboats and railroad lines.

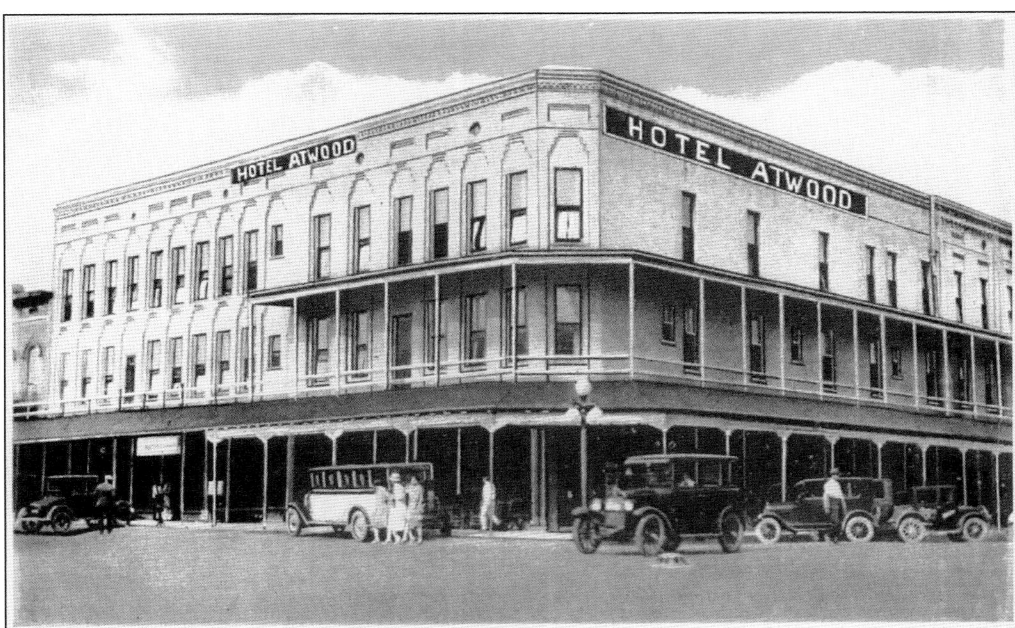

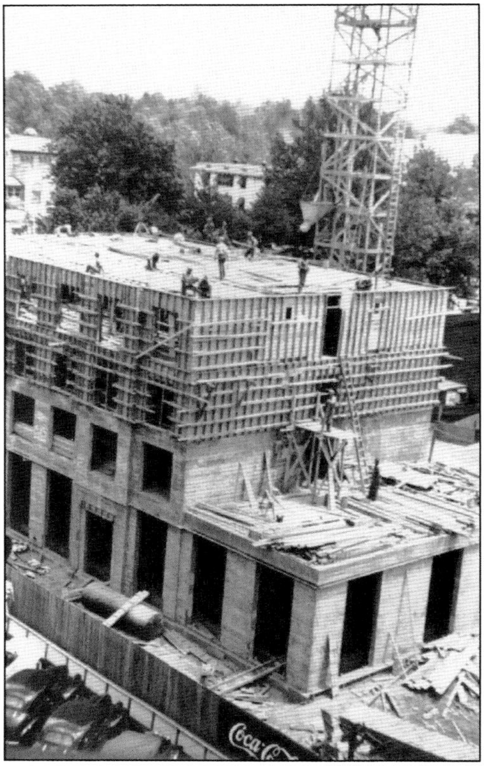

The Hotel Cordell Hull rises against the skyline in the photograph at left. The image below, a vintage postcard, shows it in its glory days. The Elizabeth Taylor movie *Raintree County* was shot in the Reelfoot Lake area in 1957, and crew members stayed here during filming. Actor Ward Bond was another famous visitor. The building became Security Bank in the 1970s.

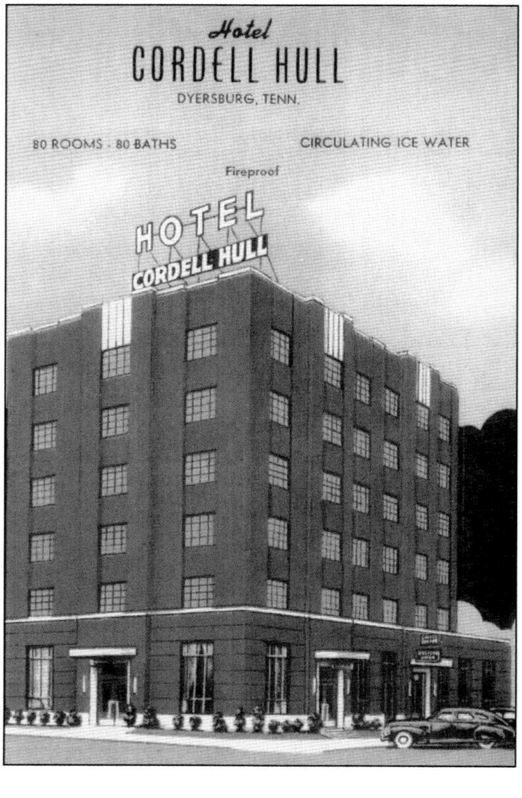

The Hotel Cordell Hull was one of many Southern buildings named in honor of statesman Cordell Hull. Born in a log cabin in Olympus, Tennessee, Hull (below) is best known as the longest serving secretary of state. He held the position for 11 years during the presidency of Franklin D. Roosevelt. In 1945, Hull received the Nobel Peace Prize for his role in establishing the United Nations. Previously, he served 11 terms in the House of Representatives, authoring the federal income tax laws of 1916 and the inheritance tax law of 1916. (Below, courtesy Library of Congress, Prints and Photographs Division; photograph by Harris & Ewing, reproduction number LC-DIG-hec-03390.)

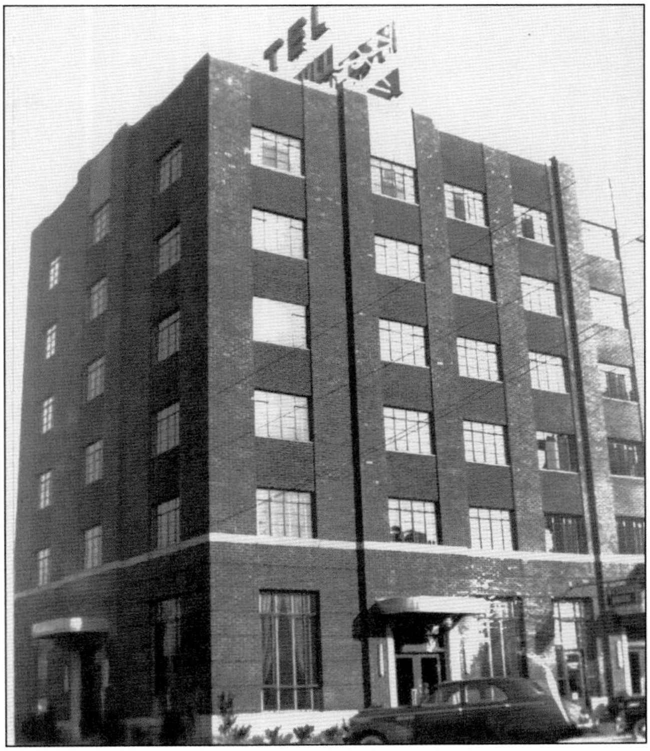

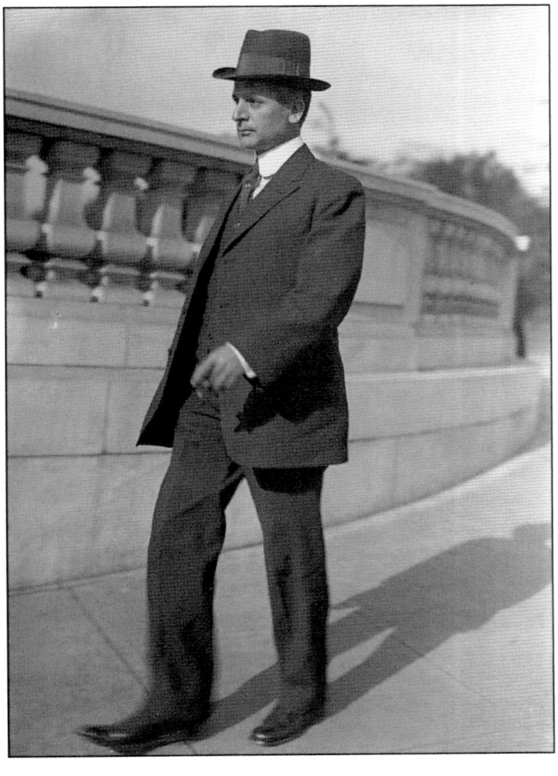

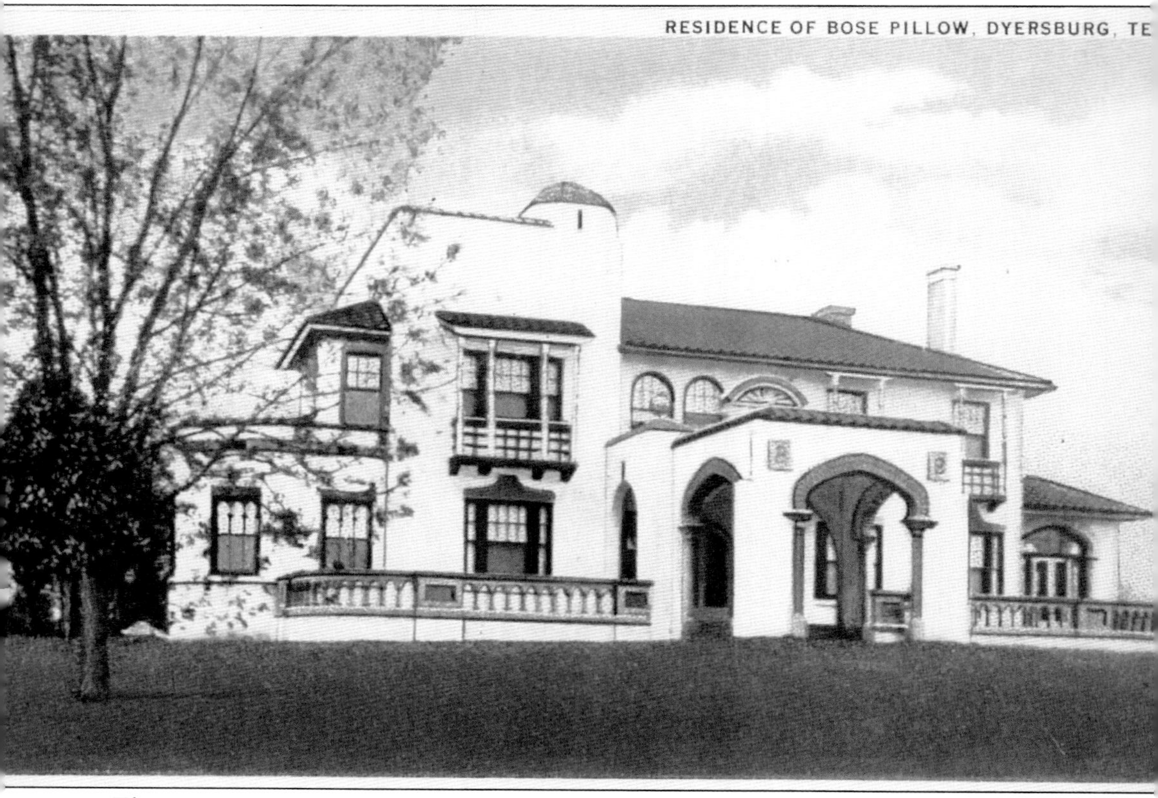

This vintage postcard of the Bose Pillow home shows a graceful mansion on Troy Avenue. It is rumored that Pillow, quite an infamous citizen in his time, won the money for this house while gambling. He died in 1929, and his tombstone can be seen in Fairview Cemetery. The house still stands and is privately owned.

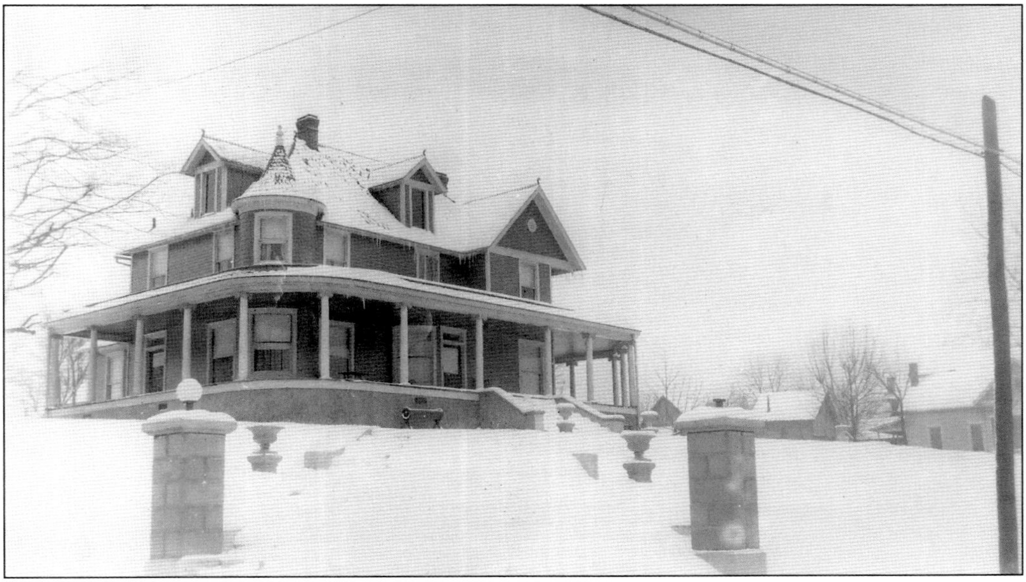

This lovely home was known in Dyersburg as the Reed Mansion. The sprawling Southern house stood at the corner of Sampson Avenue and East Court Street. Dr. John Reed purchased it in 1915 for $3,800, wired it himself for electricity, and completed extensive renovations. Some can be noted in the photograph below, including the concrete railing around the porch. (Both, courtesy John Reed.)

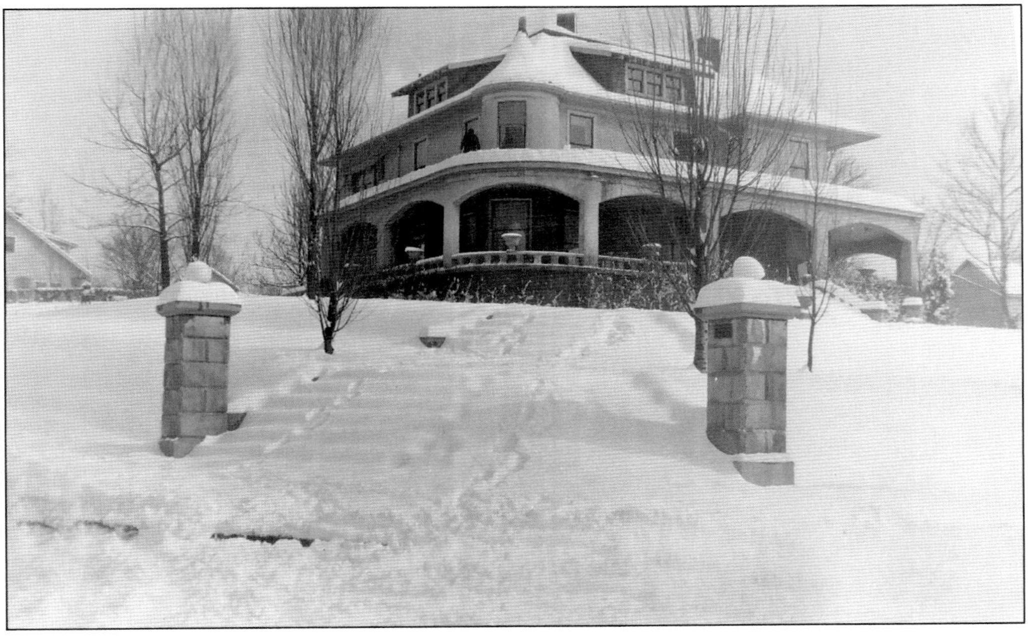

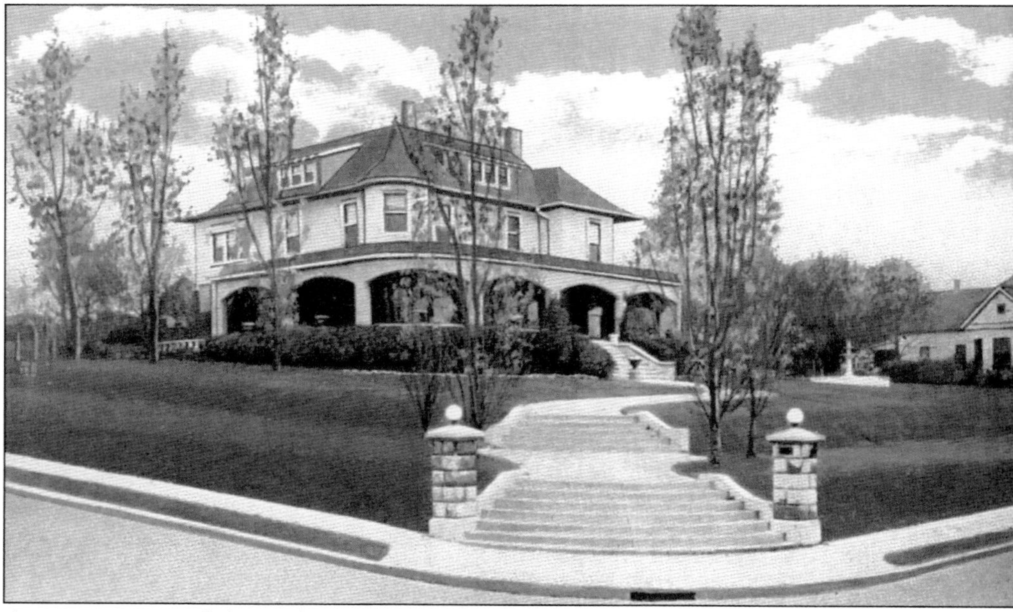

A vintage postcard shows the Reed Mansion in its glory days. The fountain on the right-hand lawn was one of the improvements and additions made by Dr. Reed to the home after he bought it. The stately home was a landmark in Dyersburg for decades. The bronze plaque, which can be seen on the small column to the right of the steps, was stolen when the house was demolished in the early 1970s. In 2010, it was found half buried at the edge of the town cemetery by a passerby and was given to Dr. Reed's grandson. (Courtesy John Reed.)

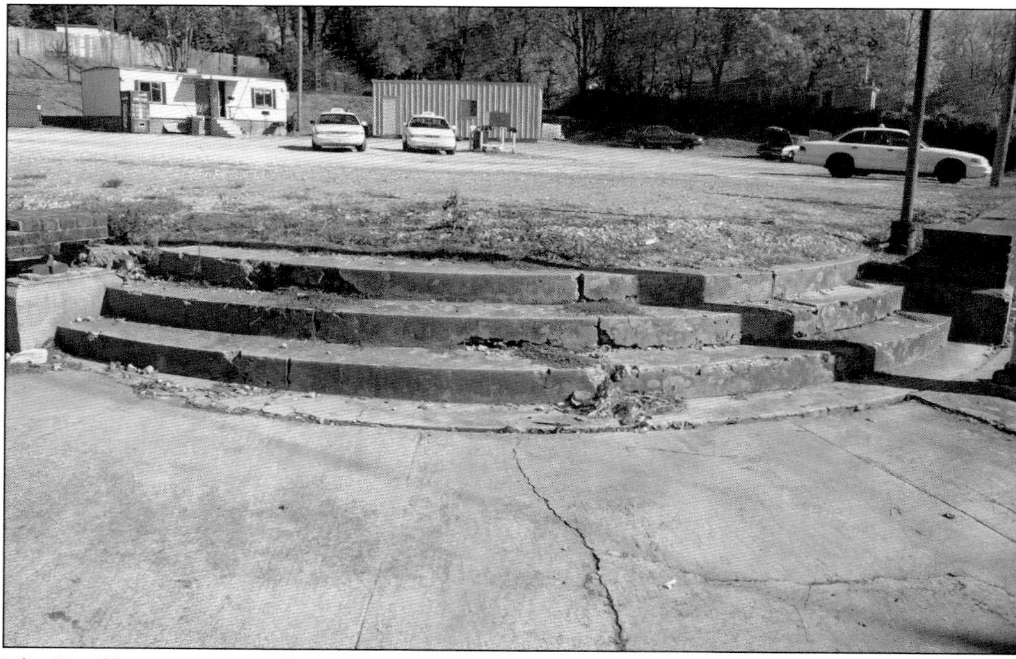

The Reed home was torn down about 1972 to make room for a nearby business to expand. Now, only the bottom three of its wide stone steps mark the spot where it once stood.

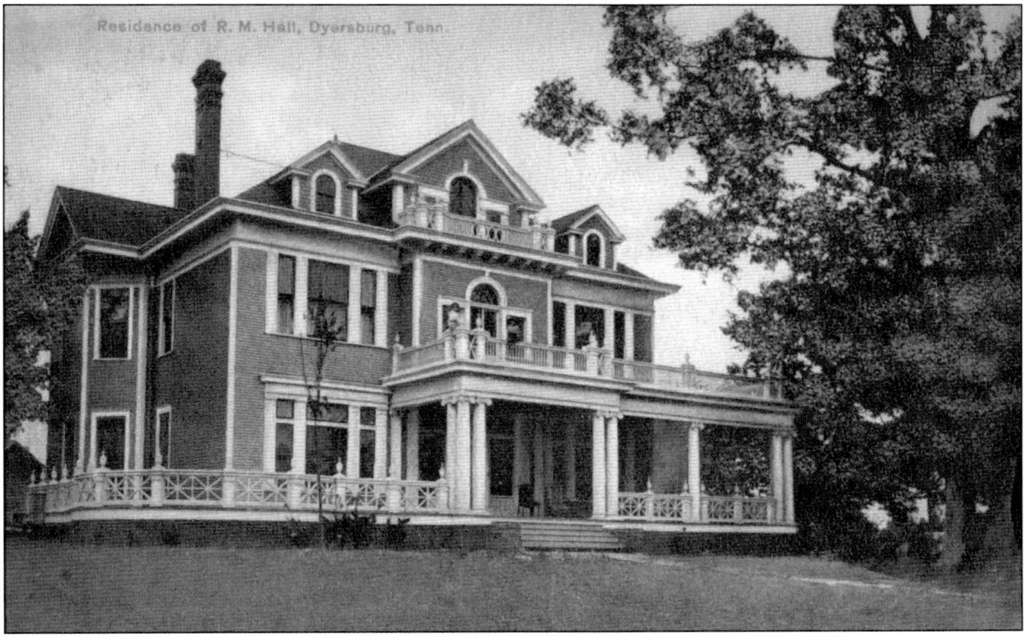

Robert M. Hall once owned this stately residence on Sampson Avenue. Hall was a railroad man who helped bring rail service to Dyersburg. He married the daughter of Col. Isaac Sampson, who owned the land on which this house was built. Legend holds that Sampson Avenue has received the same name twice, once before the Civil War, in honor of Colonel Sampson, until he switched his allegiance to the Union. It was then renamed Sampson Avenue in honor of his son, Capt. Franc G. Sampson, who remained loyal to the Confederacy. The house became Curry Funeral Home in 1881 and has remained in business ever since.

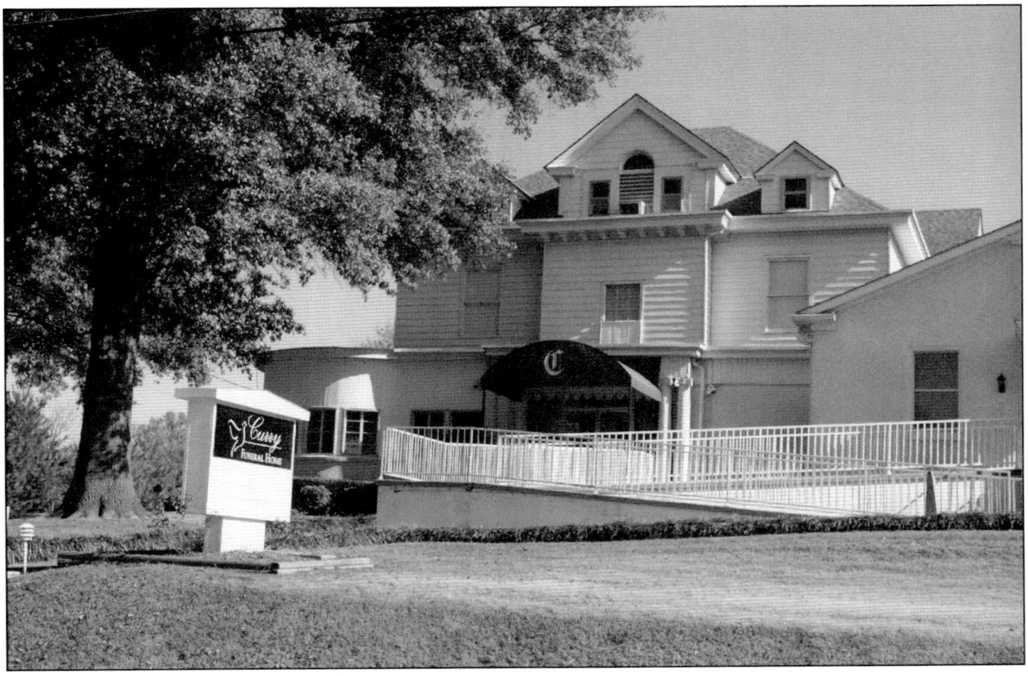

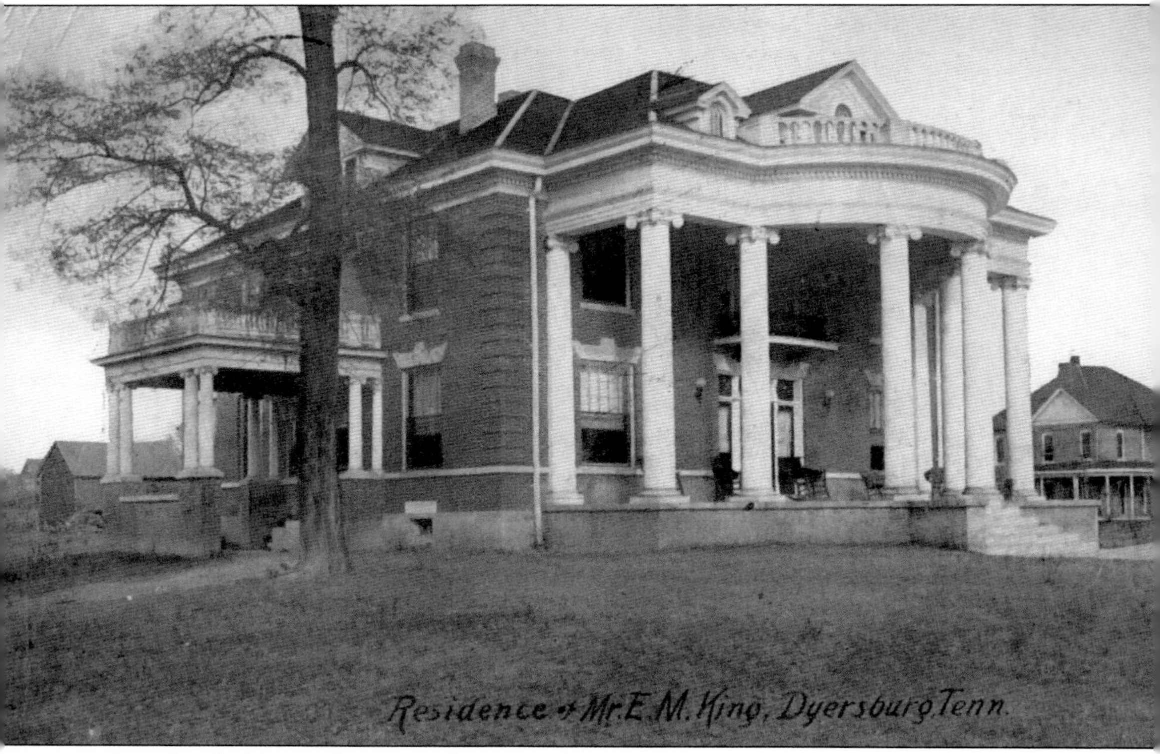

Listed in the National Register of Historic Places as the Edward Moody King House, the King home is a classic Colonial Revival structure. Architect George Mahan Jr. designed the home in 1904 for Edward King. At 9,897 square feet, the house includes a two-story portico entrance, 11 fireplaces, and 19 rooms, including a ballroom. It is privately owned and can be rented for events.

Three

BUSINESSES

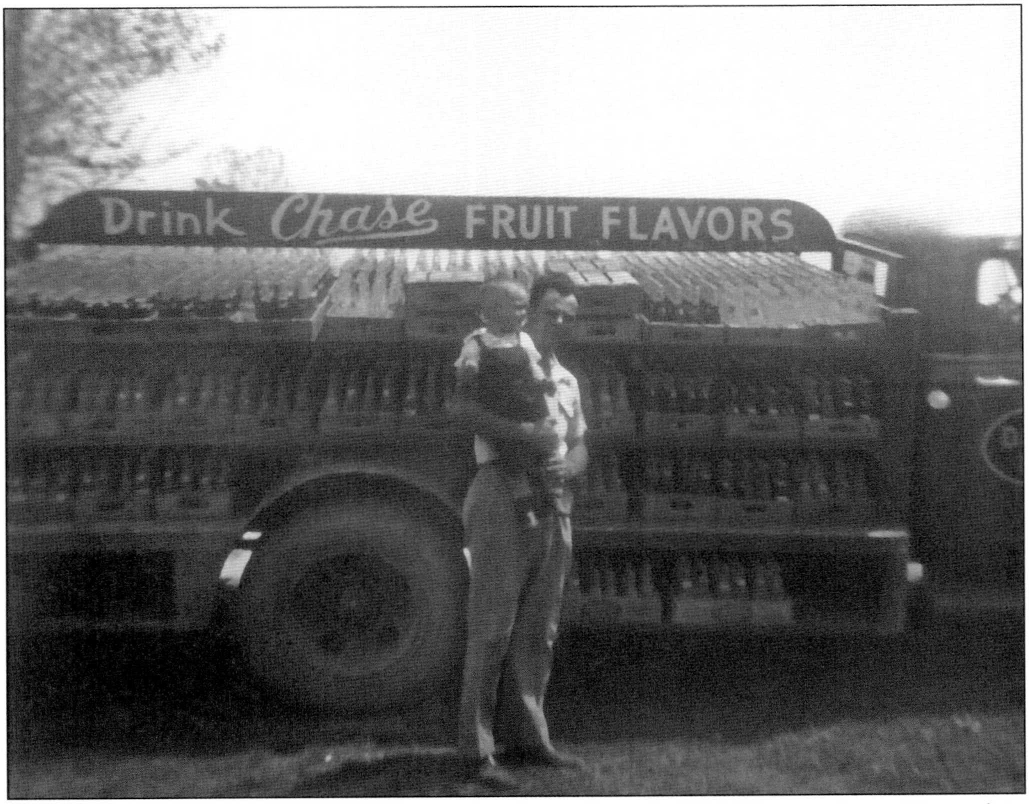

Thomas Reasons is pictured holding his nephew Larry Pease in 1954. Thomas drove this truck in the early 1950s for the Double Cola Bottling Plant at Harrell Avenue and Shelby Drive. "Doge" Evans and Homer Preslar owned the plant. It was one of five bottling companies that once existed in Dyersburg. The Chase fruit-flavored sodas were the product of a Memphian named Chase who had a history of bottling soft drinks in Memphis. (Courtesy Gaylon Reasons.)

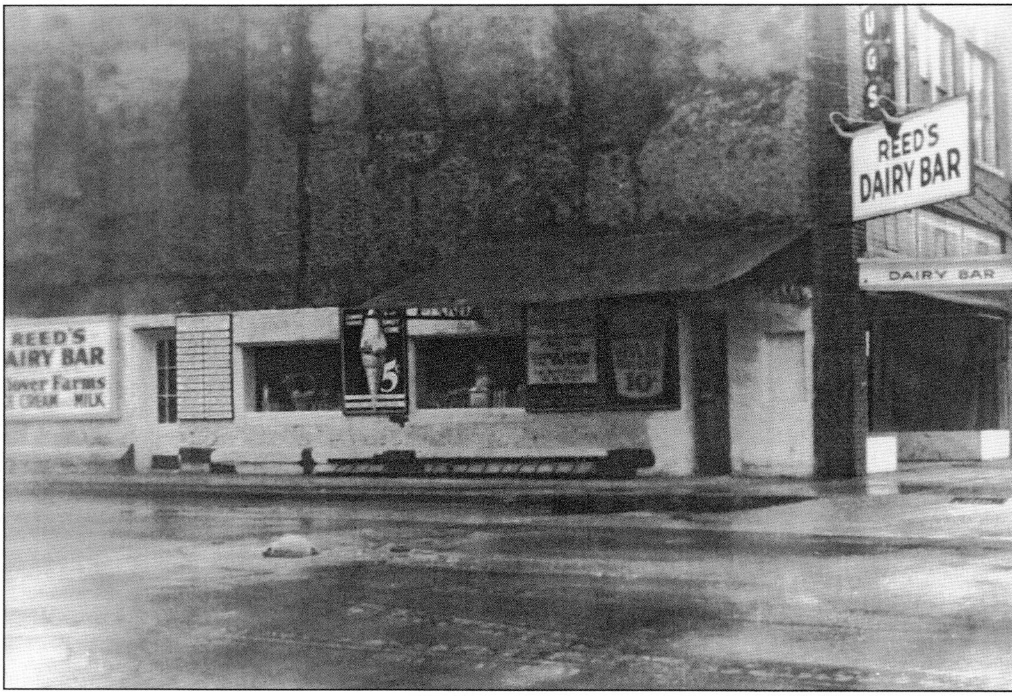

Dr. John Reed, owner of the Reed Mansion, ran this store on Harrell Avenue from 1933 to 1950. It had one of the last soda fountains in town. Previously, his drugstore was located on the town square.

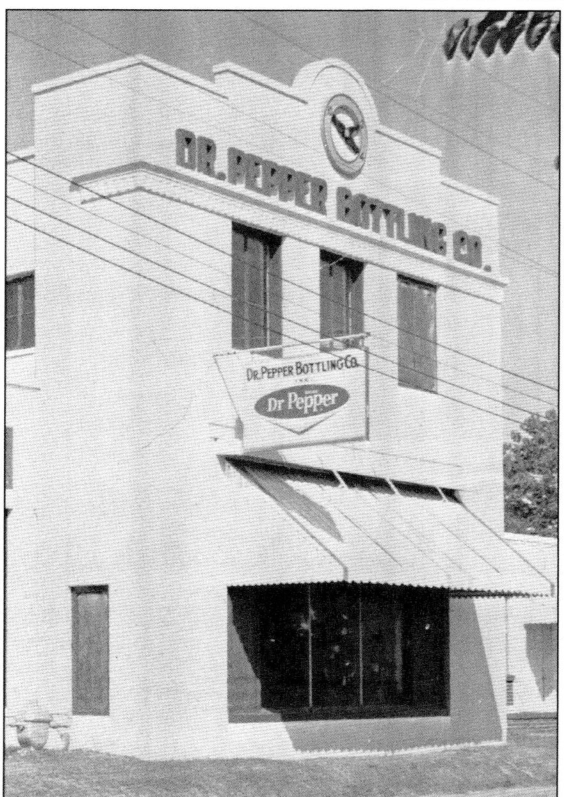

A.D. Burks founded the Dr. Pepper Bottling Company of Dyersburg in the 1930s. The tall building stood on Phillips Street, just around the corner from the cotton mill. Dyersburg residents recall that if Burks ran into a youngster anywhere in town drinking a Dr. Pepper, he would hand the child a silver dollar.

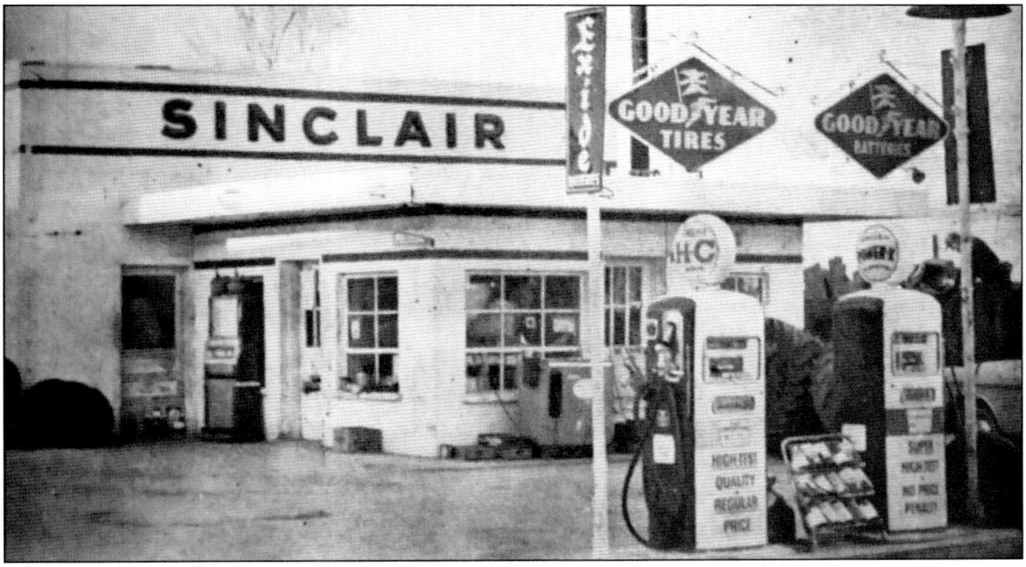

This popular Sinclair gas station (above) once stood at Church Avenue and Court Street. Located across from the bus station and the General Appliance store, it stayed busy year-round. The Texaco station (below) once stood at the corner of McGaughey Street and Mill Avenue. The buildings no longer exist. At the time these photographs were taken in the mid-1950s, gasoline was 21¢ a gallon and workers checked the car's fluids and tires for free each time.

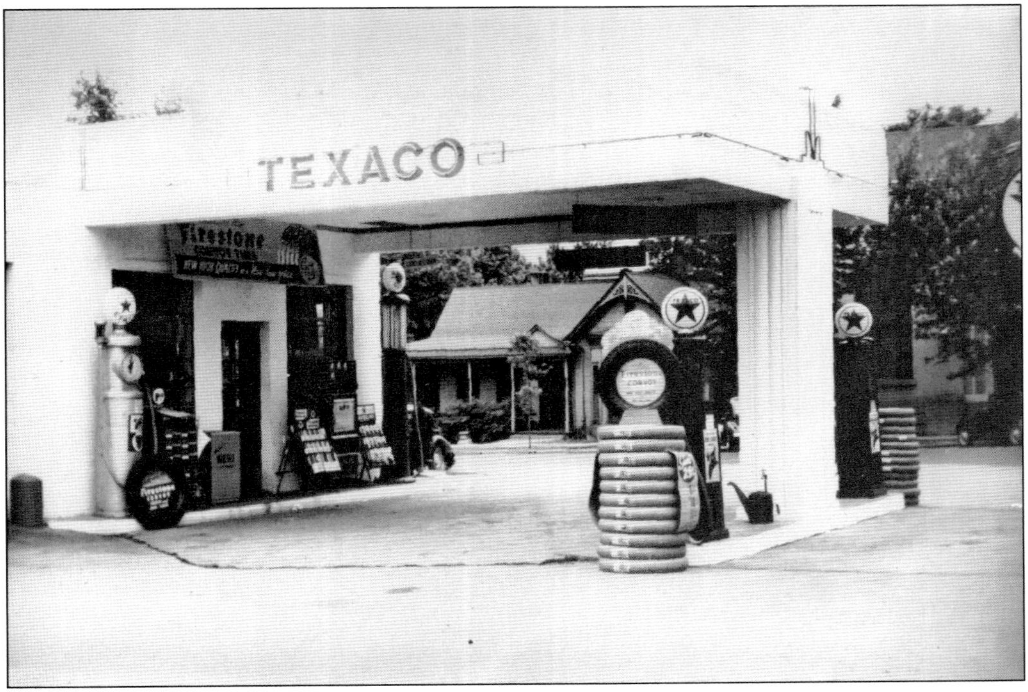

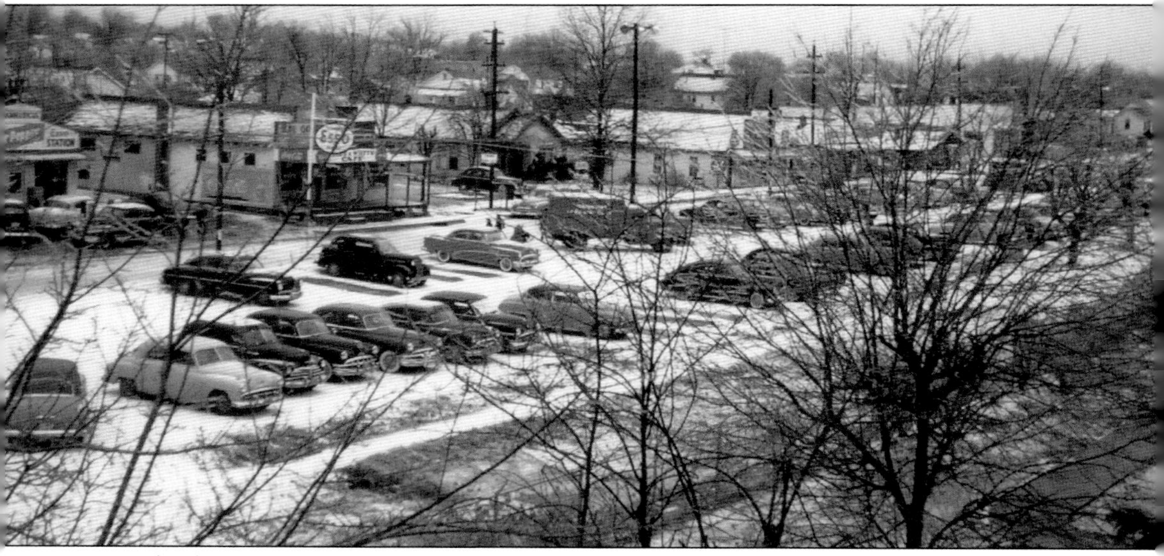

In this beautiful wintertime view, taken from a window in the cotton mill in 1953, Ted "Buck" Dycus's Esso station can be seen. It once stood on Harrell Avenue across from one of the mill entrances. To the right is the Blue Goose Café, which later became Bob Smith's Café, a popular spot for pinball-machine players. (Courtesy R.L. Summar family.)

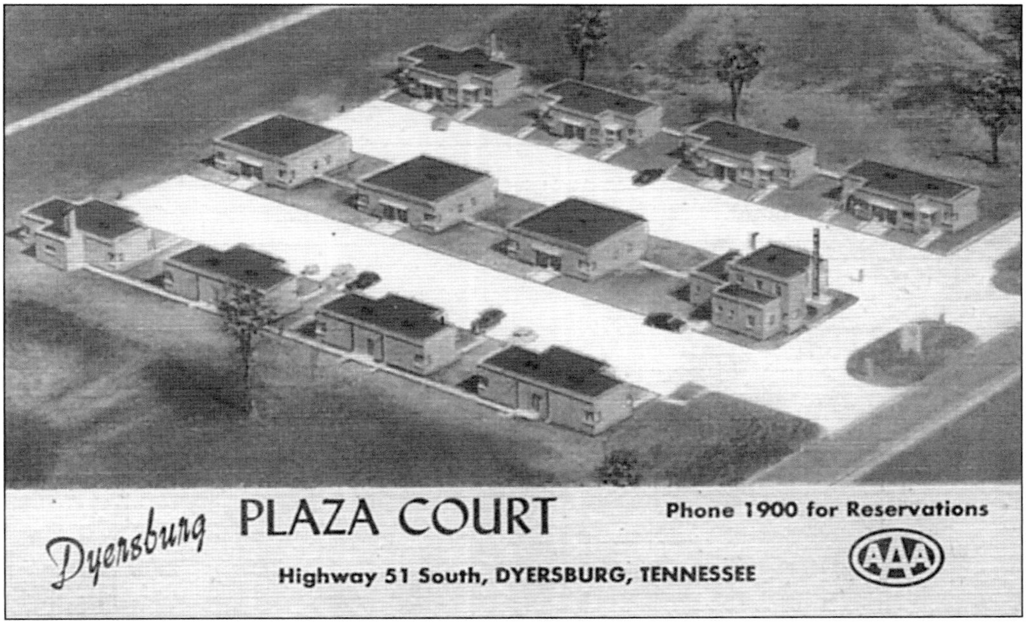

The Dyersburg Plaza Court was one of the first motels ("motor hotels") in Dyer County. The units were scattered like cabins, with an adjacent restaurant and a grocery store. They were located at Southtown, the nickname for the part of town closest to Highway 51. This vintage postcard shows the Plaza Court when it was still a fairly new attraction on the road into Dyersburg. (Courtesy Gaylon Reasons.)

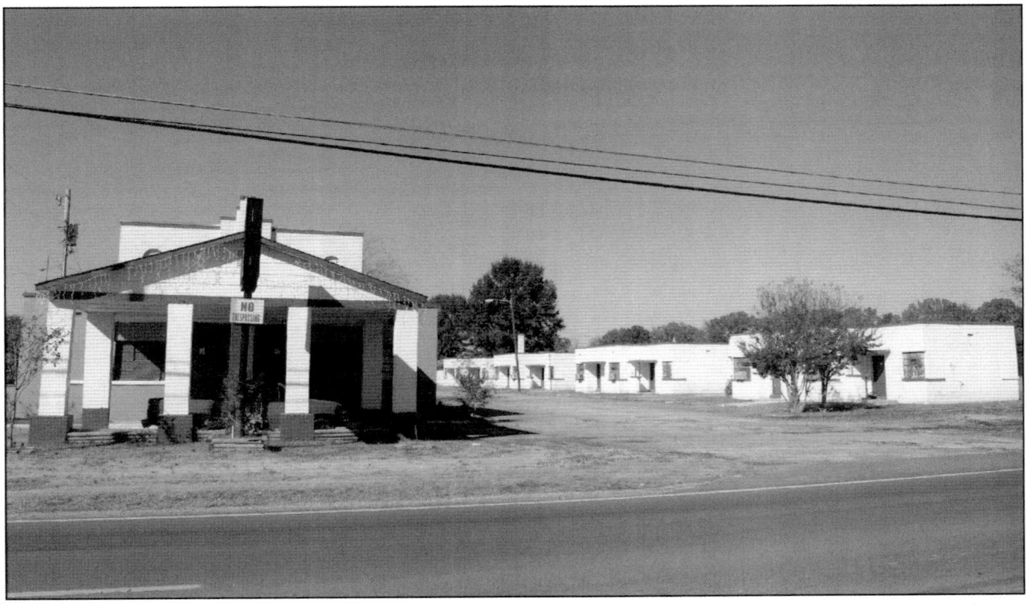

The Plaza Court boasted of having "44 deluxe units, air conditioning, an excellent café, a telephone in each unit" and "circulating ice water." But Southtown has always been susceptible to flooding. The area experienced damaging floods in the mid-1930s, mid-1950s, and mid-1960s. The buildings of Plaza Court survived those, but they were heavily damaged by floodwaters in 2010 and 2011, and at that time their future remained uncertain.

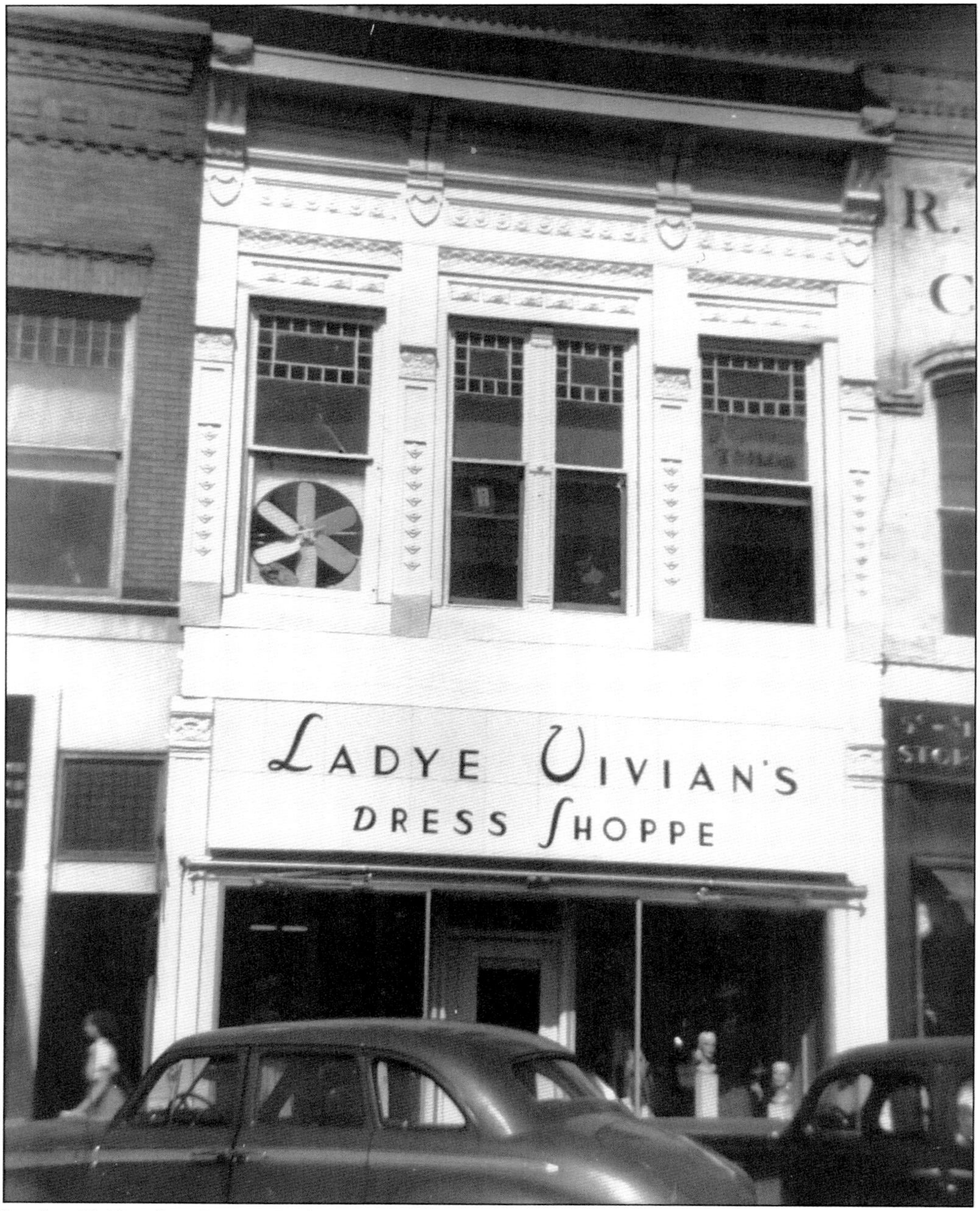

In the 1940s, the elegant Ladye Vivian's Dress Shoppe, with its extraneous Es, occupied 216 Court Street on the north side of the town square. By the 1960s, the business had transitioned to Ladye Vivian's Hat Shop and moved to West Market Street. This building changed hands, becoming an insurance company at one point and then a Tempe's clothing store. The windows were eventually covered with a solid facade.

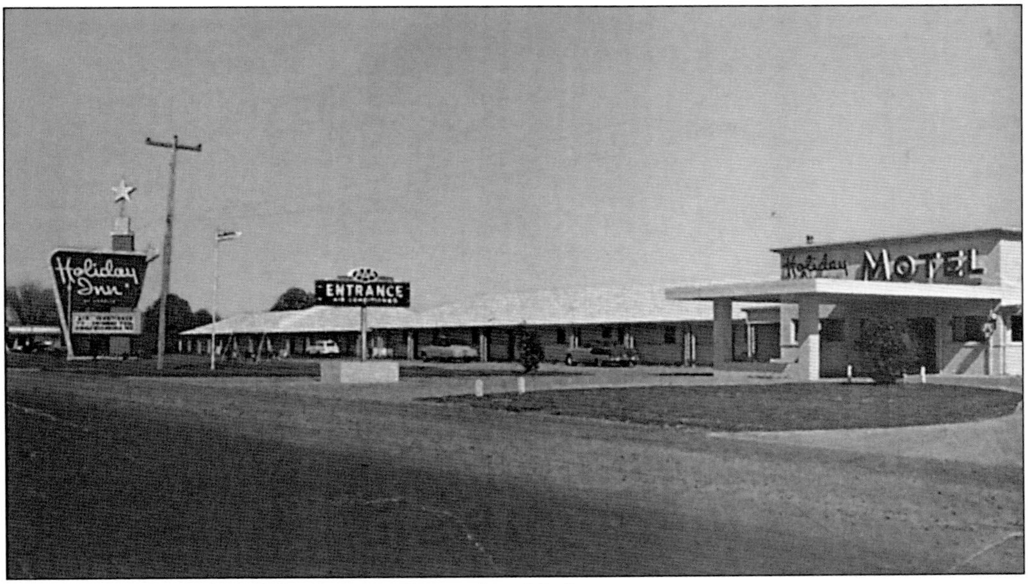

Dyersburg's original Holiday Inn was located on Highway 51 North, slightly outside of town. The chain was invented just down the road in Memphis by entrepreneur Kemmons Wilson, who was disappointed by the unpredictable quality of motels his family encountered during a 1951 road trip. The name was chosen by the chain's original architect, a fan of the Bing Crosby movie of the same name. This Dyersburg Holiday Inn, originally the site of the Plantation Motel, is now gone—Frank Maynard Boulevard runs straight through where it once stood. (Both, courtesy Gaylon Reasons.)

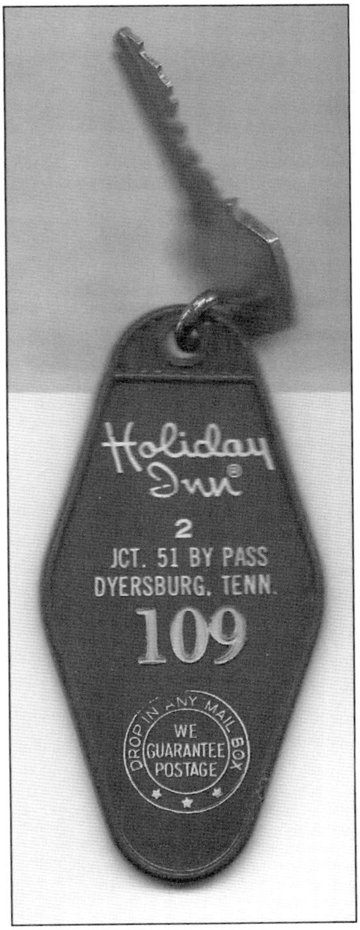

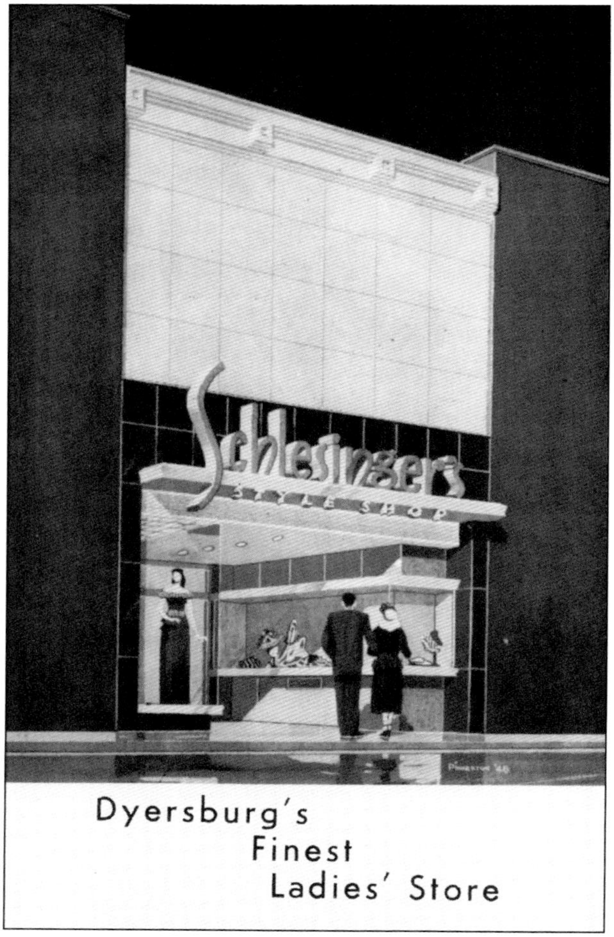

Schlesinger's Style Shop, pictured in advertisements from the mid-1950s, was a very fashionable place to shop. It was located on Court Street between the Dyersburg State Bank and Latimer's Drug Store. In the image below, young ladies admire the display of the latest clothing styles. The ensemble costume was very popular at that time, usually consisting of a two-piece suit or a matching coat and dress, and a well-groomed woman would usually accessorize her outfit with gloves, stockings, a hat, and a top-quality handbag.

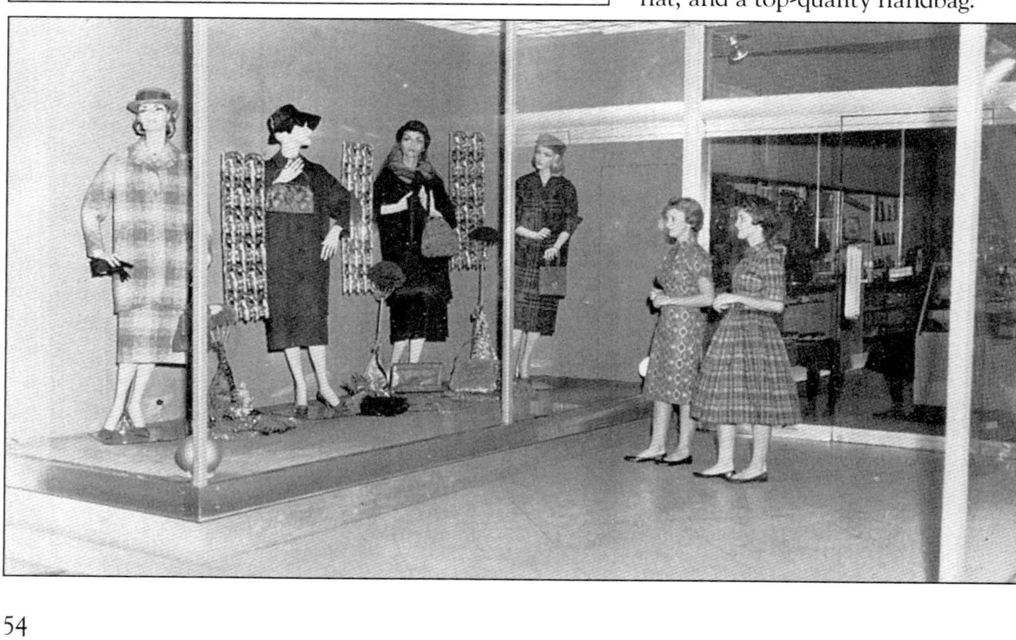

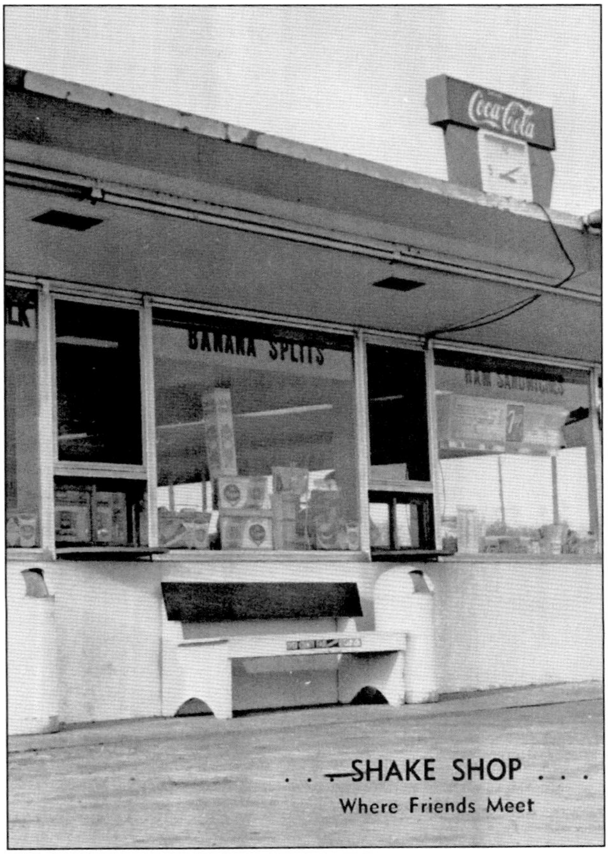

The Shake Shop, a very popular teenage hangout, once stood across Highway 51 from the old Plantation Motel (later the Holiday Inn). Pictured in scans from Dyersburg High School yearbooks, the Shake Shop was the "cruising" spot for Dyersburg teens in the 1950s and 1960s, when a Wottaburger could be purchased for 35¢ and a regular hamburger for 25¢.

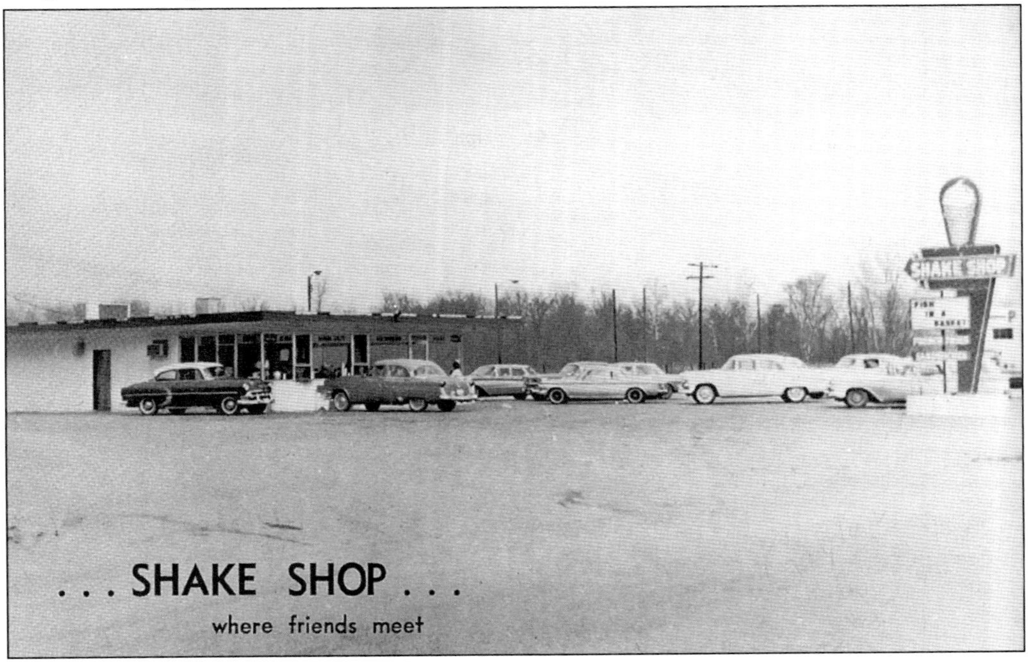

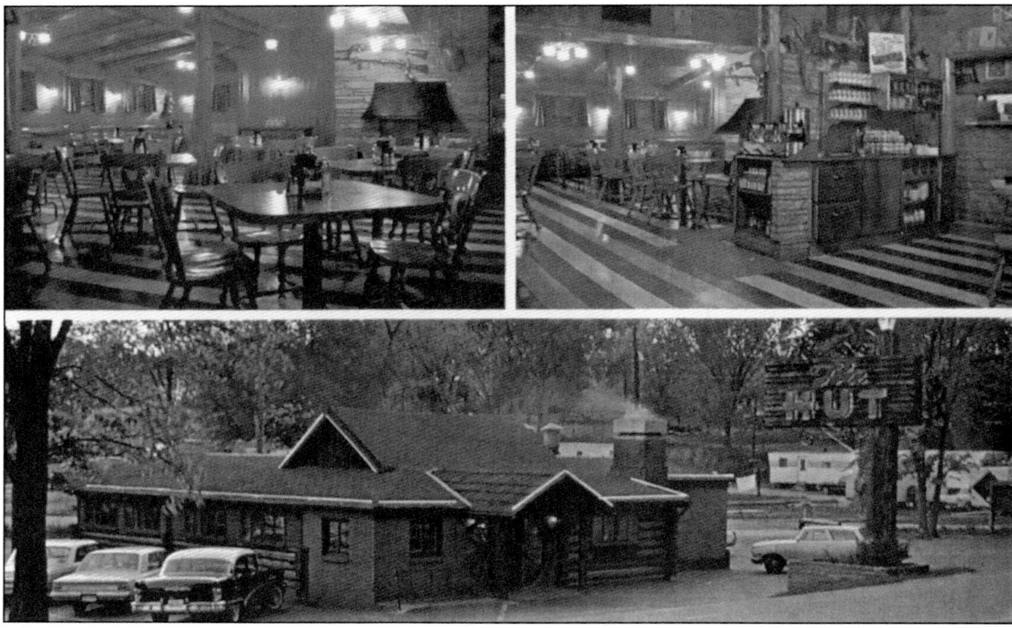

The Hut, pictured in the mid-1950s, was an unassuming but popular steak house located on Lake Road (formerly known as Nichols and now US 78), about a mile south of Okeena Park and swimming pool. Paper menus from the 1940s proclaimed "Service Men Welcome," as it was a popular spot for young airmen who trained at the nearby Dyersburg Army Air Base. The Hut was owned by Jimmy Noonan. The site is now the location of Maple Ridge, an assisted-living facility.

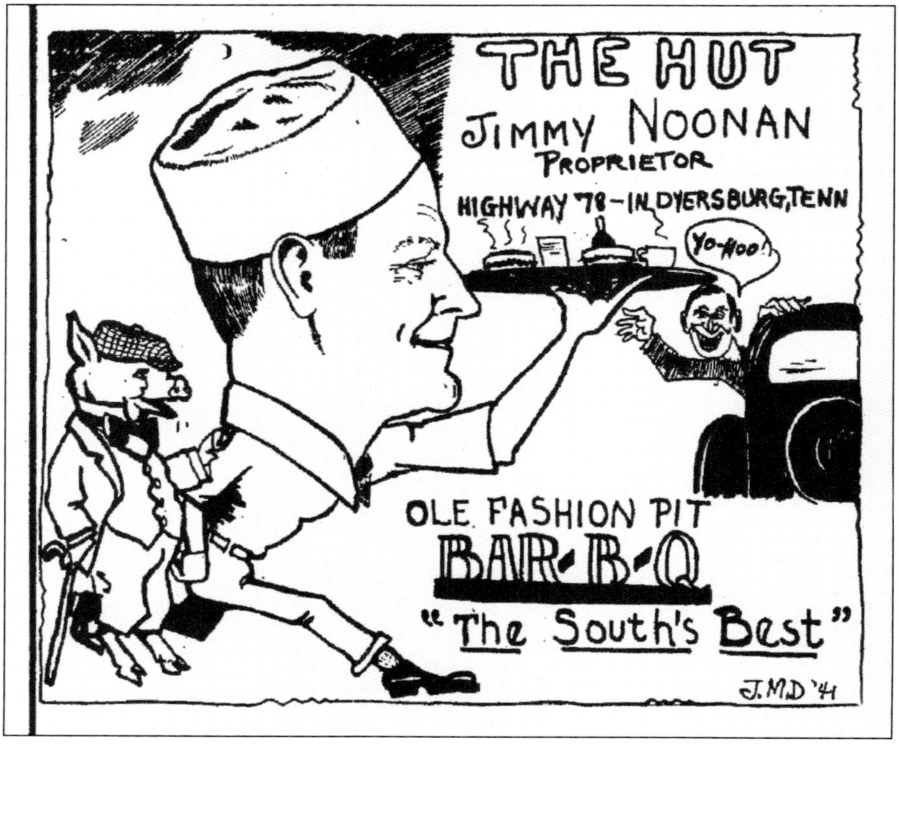

Four

STREET SCENES

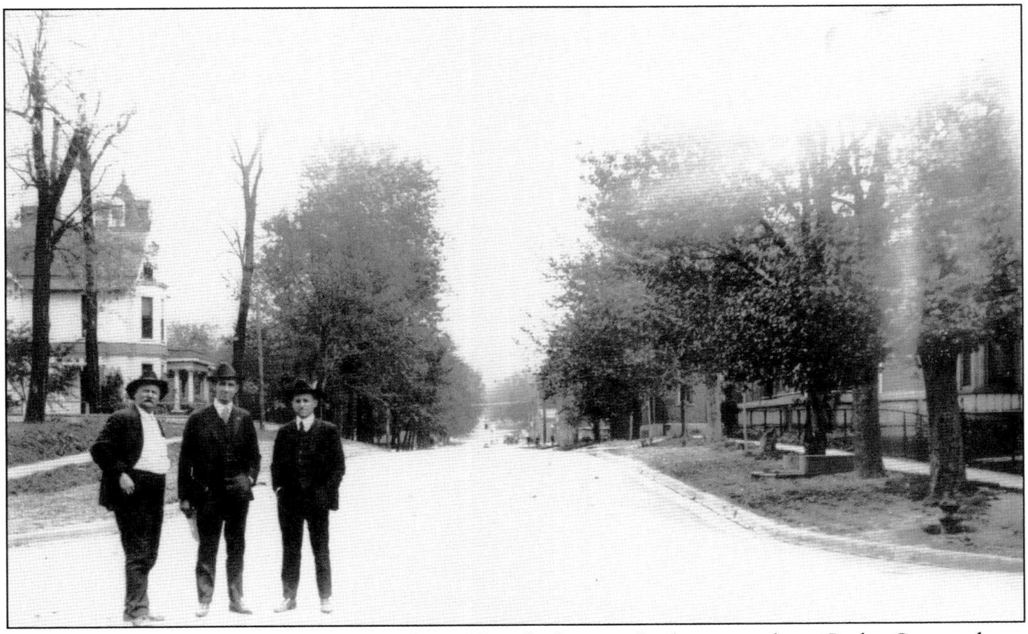

Three neighborhood men are pictured on Church Avenue looking north at Cedar Street about 1915. Posing for this photograph are, from left to right, unidentified, S.R. Blackman, and L.O. Brayton, a civil engineer. Rice Studios of Dyersburg, now defunct, documented the paving of many city streets, which began in earnest in 1920. Rice was originally located downtown before moving to the outskirts of town where it operated for many years. Numerous Rice Studios photographs can be seen in this chapter.

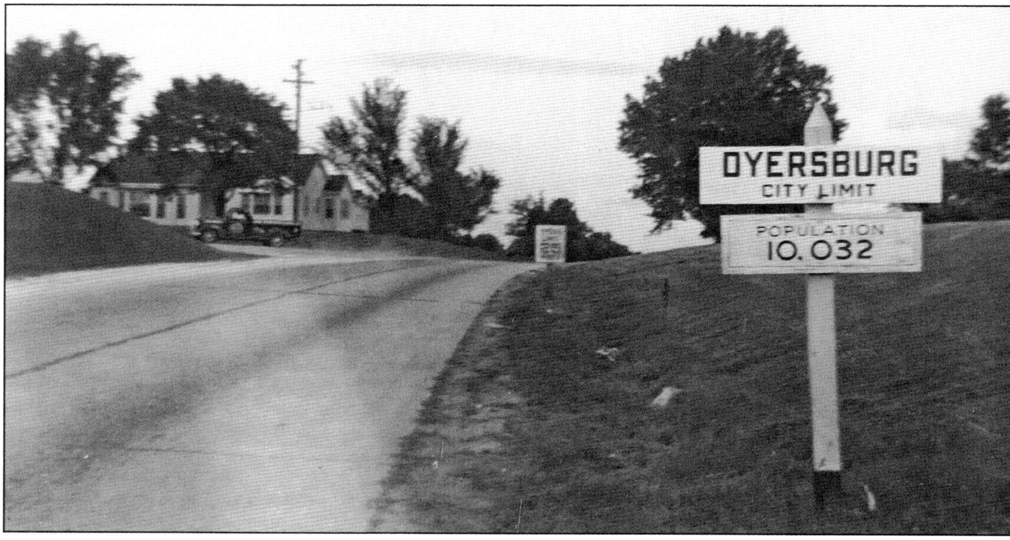

Dyersburg marked its city limit in the World War II years with this sign on Lake Road (now US 78). The hill to the left was then part of the 18-hole Okeena Golf Club course, designed in 1924 by a Canadian pro. It is now the site of Dyersburg State Community College. In the years of World War II, Dyersburg evolved from a town to a city, gaining 3,000 in population when family members needed a place to stay to be near airmen at the Dyersburg Army Air Base a few miles away.

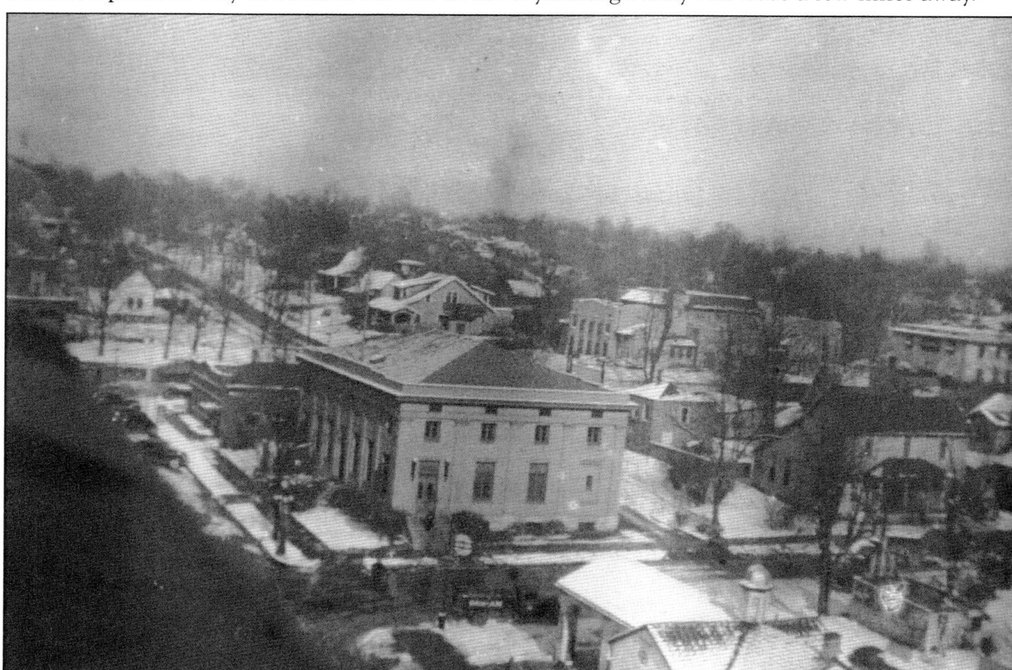

A wintertime street view is captured from an upper floor of the First Citizens Bank on a snowy day in the early 20th century. The post office, now the library, dominates the center of the photograph. Just above it and to the right is the First Methodist Church. The Baird-Brewer Hospital can be seen to the far right. The Hotel Cordell Hull would later be built in the empty spot next to the bright white roof.

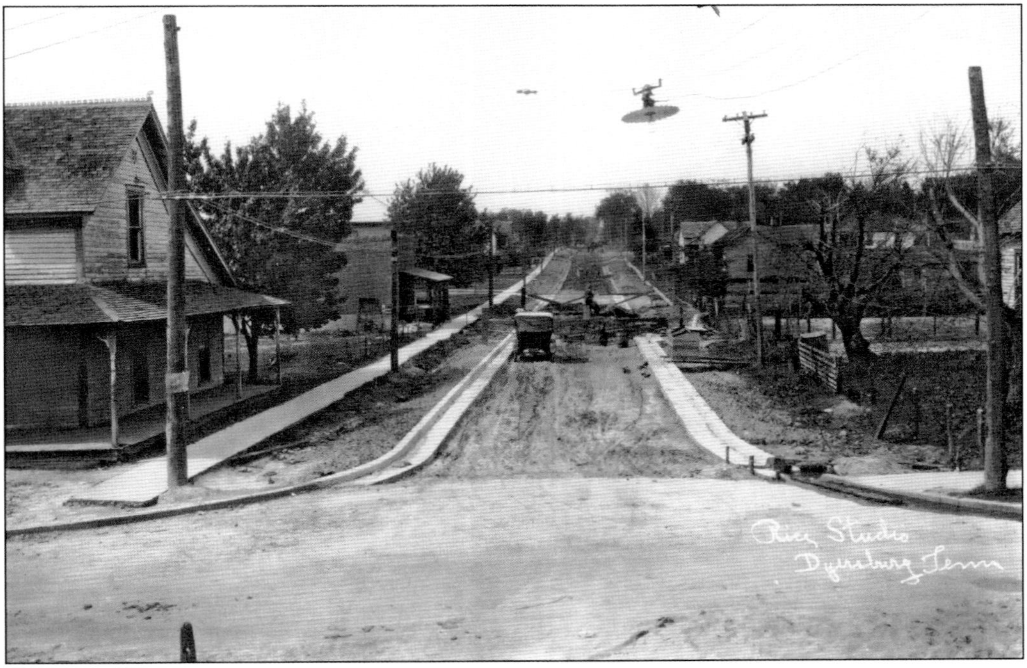

Two views of Nichols, looking north at Tucker Street, show some changes. Nichols, now Lake Road (US 78), is the route leading from Dyersburg to Reelfoot Lake. The view is looking toward Reelfoot. Rice Studios documented the paving process in the mid-1920s. At that time, Nichols dead-ended into Tucker, and the photograph was taken from the front yard of the house standing there. Highway 78 now runs straight through, and the house is gone.

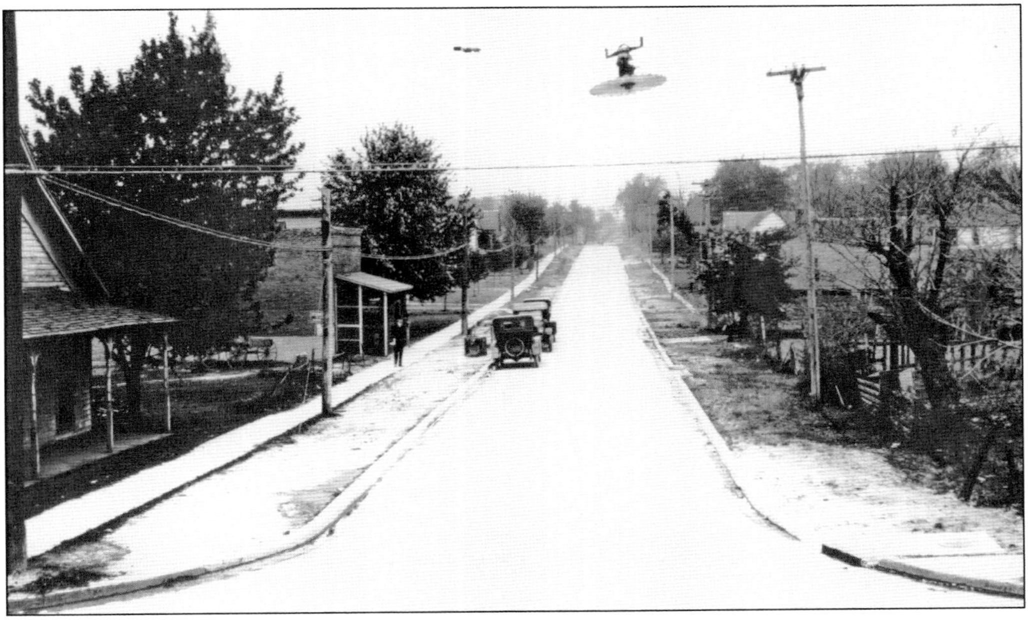

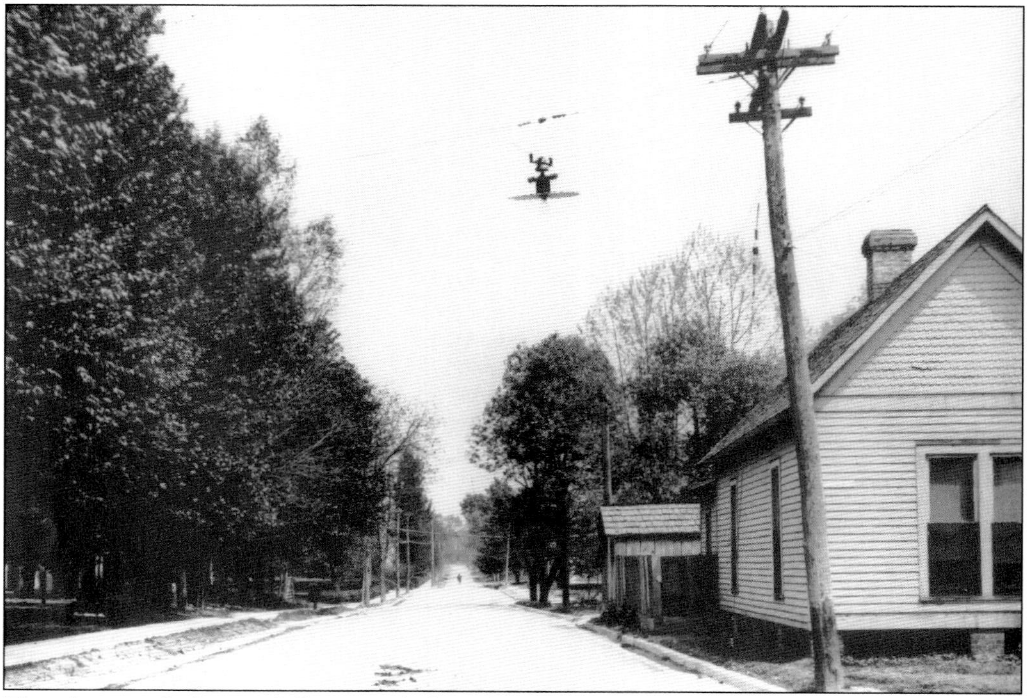

This photograph shows a different angle from the photographs on the previous page. It is of Tucker Street looking west at Nichols, and it portrays a scene now greatly changed. The frame house at right became a business, a grocery store named Baker's Weona.

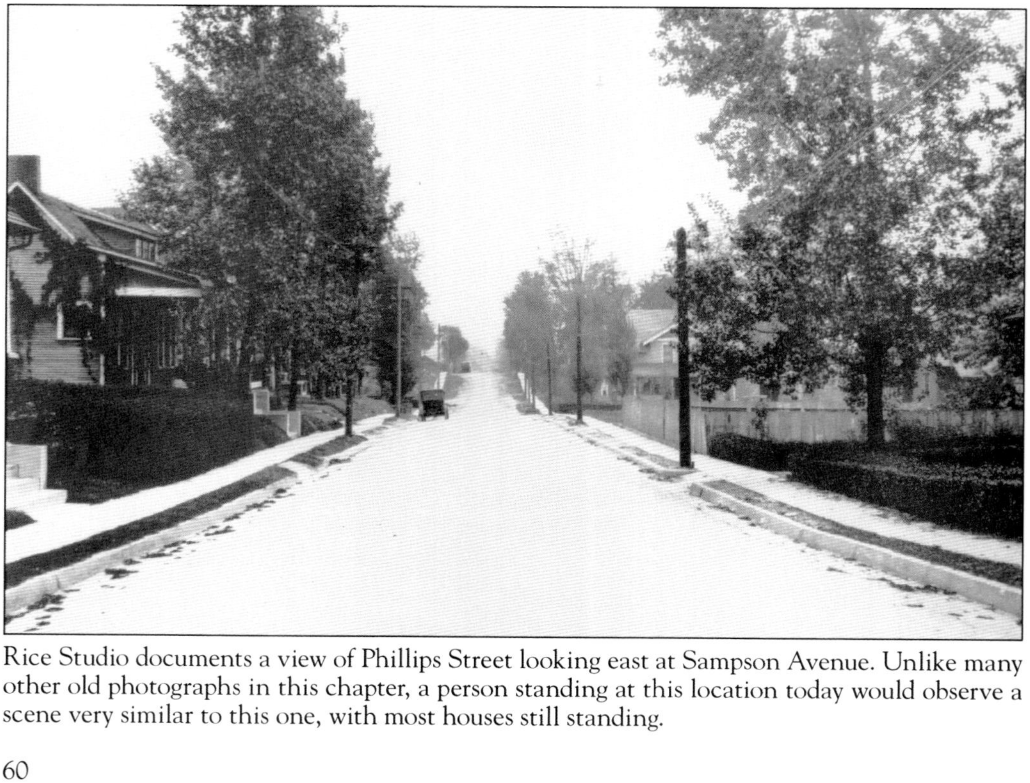

Rice Studio documents a view of Phillips Street looking east at Sampson Avenue. Unlike many other old photographs in this chapter, a person standing at this location today would observe a scene very similar to this one, with most houses still standing.

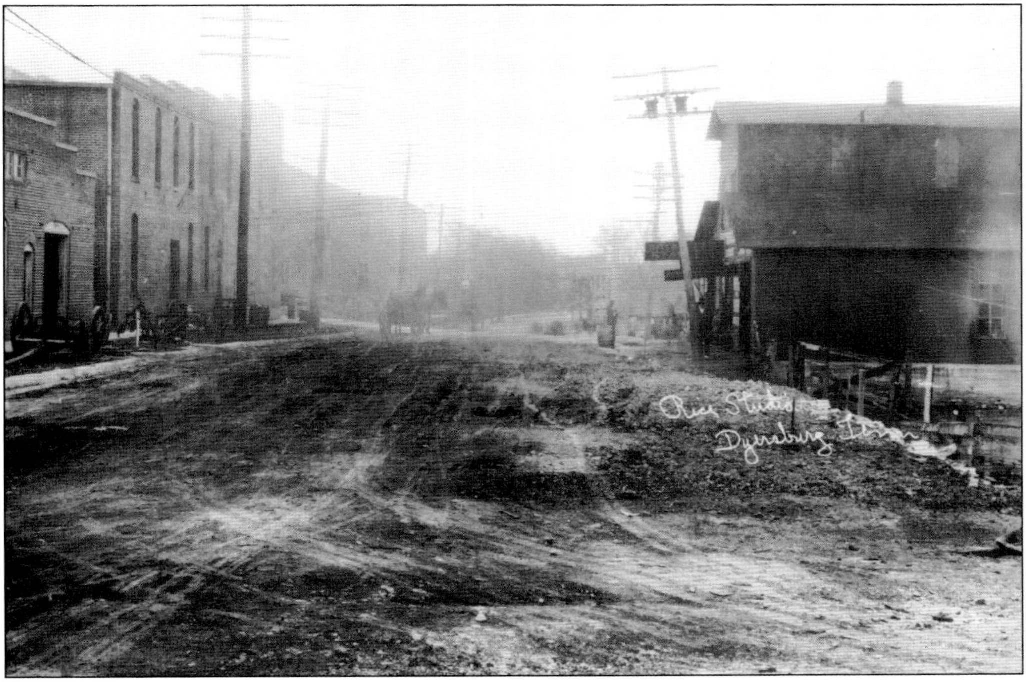

Two views of Cedar Street, looking east at Mill Avenue, document the paving process in the 1920s. Rhea Wholesalers stood at the far end of this street (just out of sight). The building at the left with the staggered roofline was demolished around 2000, and the antique bricks were sold to townspeople. The large building to the right was once the barn for the city's horses and mules.

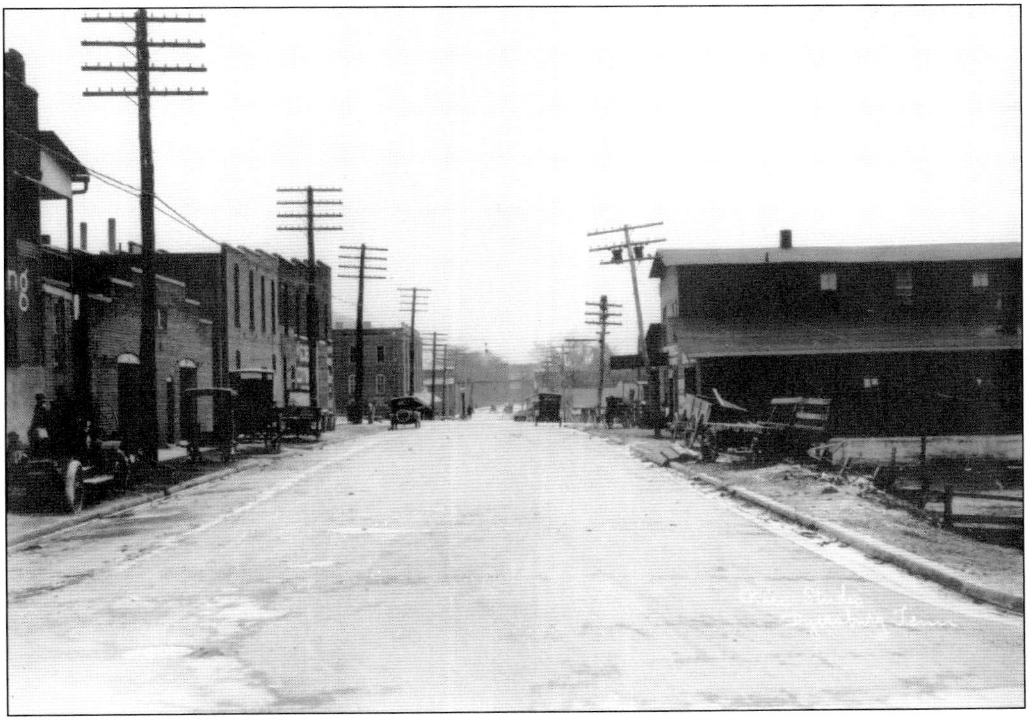

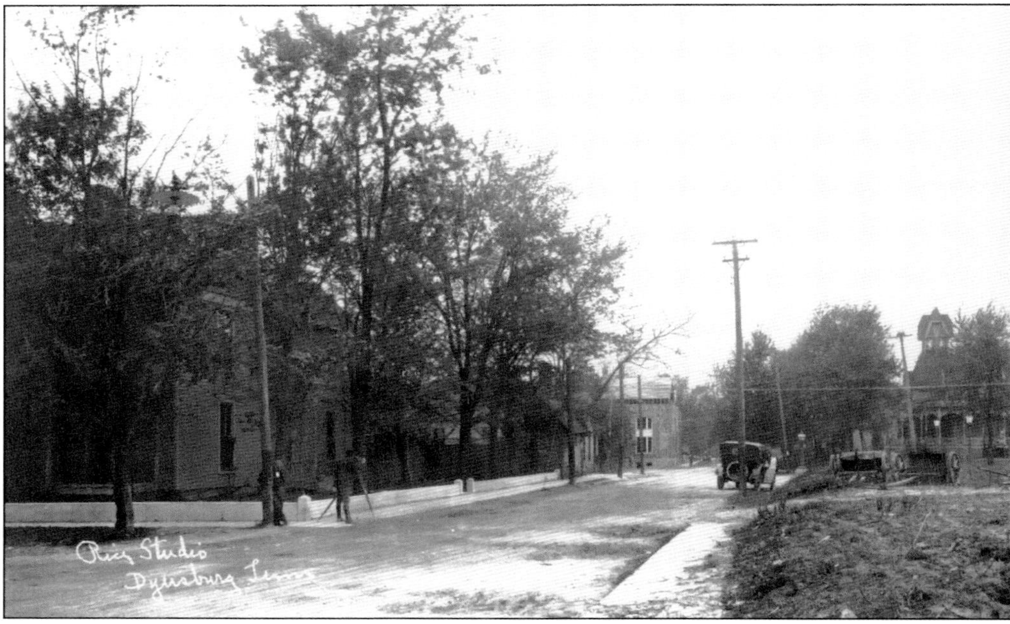

Two views of McGaughey Street, looking west at Main Street, reveal the changes in the mid-1920s. In the photograph above, another photographer from Rice Studios can be seen documenting the view from a different direction. In that photograph, to the far upper right, the old pergola of the first Dyersburg Hospital (the former house of Dr. William P. Watson) can clearly be seen. The pergola was designed to let hot air escape from the building. In the photograph below, curious but well-behaved Dyersburg children are captured by the photographer. The pergola was removed at some point in the early 20th century.

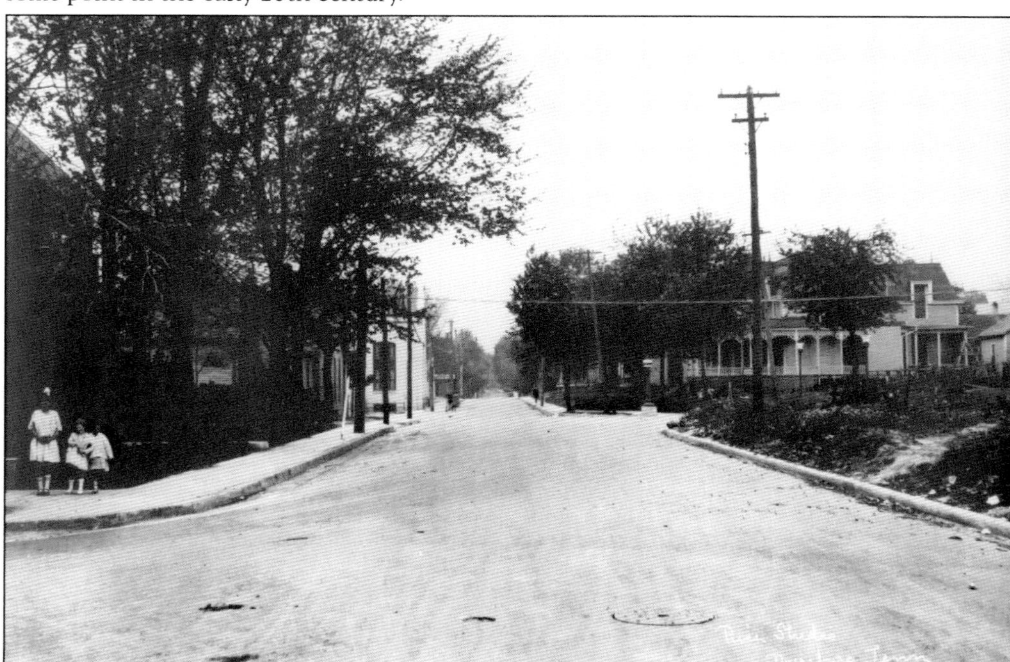

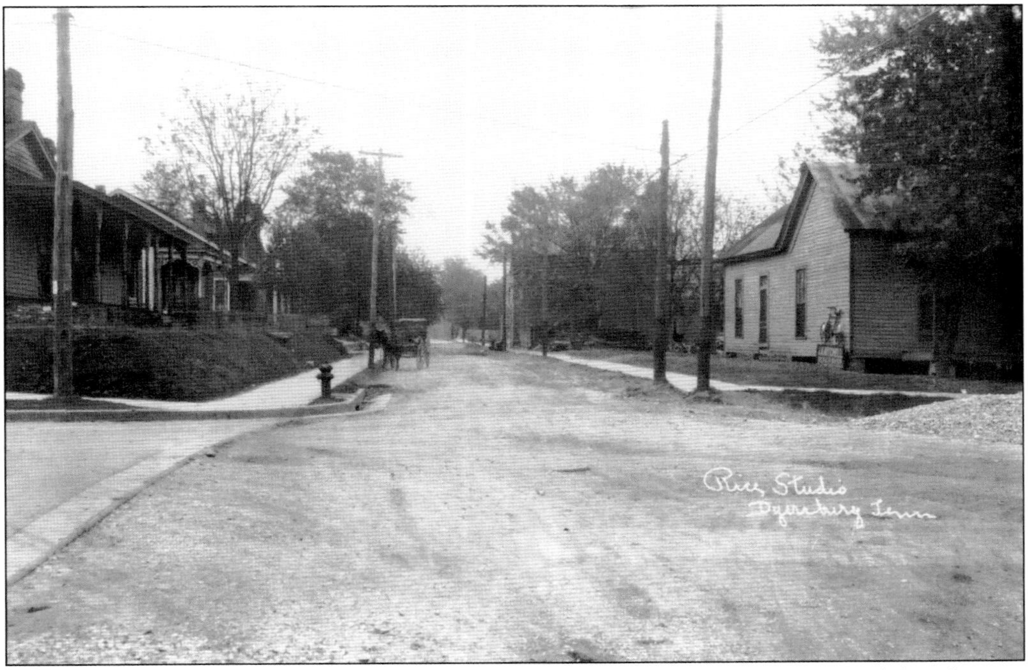

Two excellent views of McGaughey Street, looking east at Church Avenue, reveal few changes in the quiet neighborhood other than a few more telephone poles in place. Eventually, however, all the buildings seen here were demolished and replaced by parking lots.

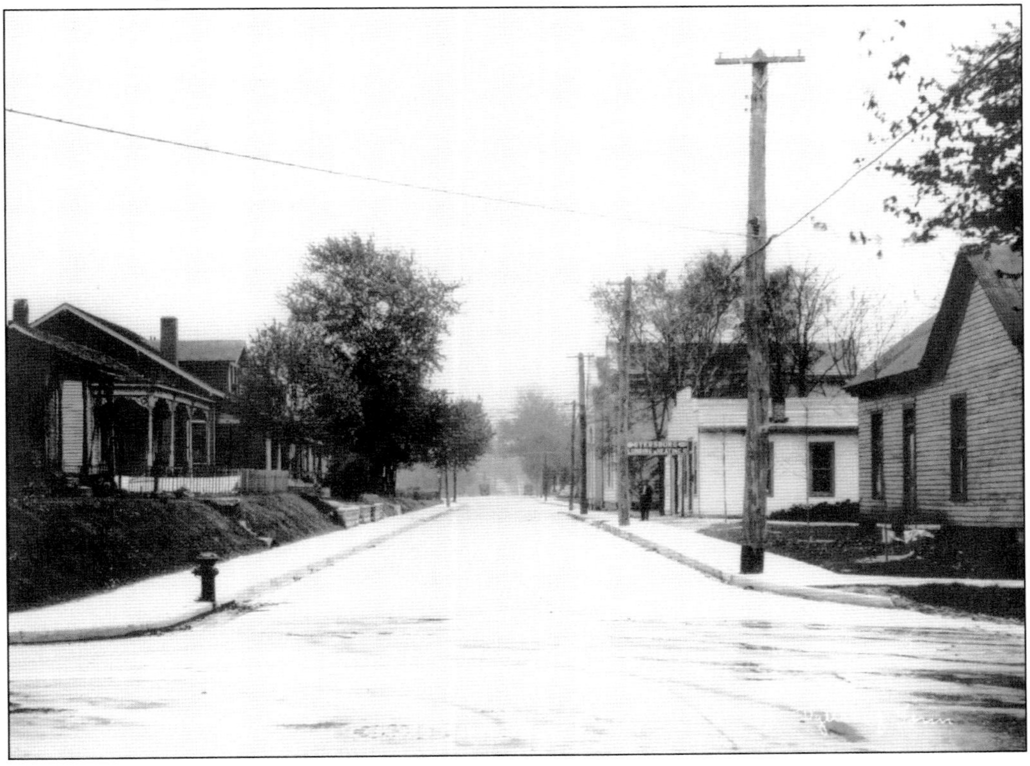

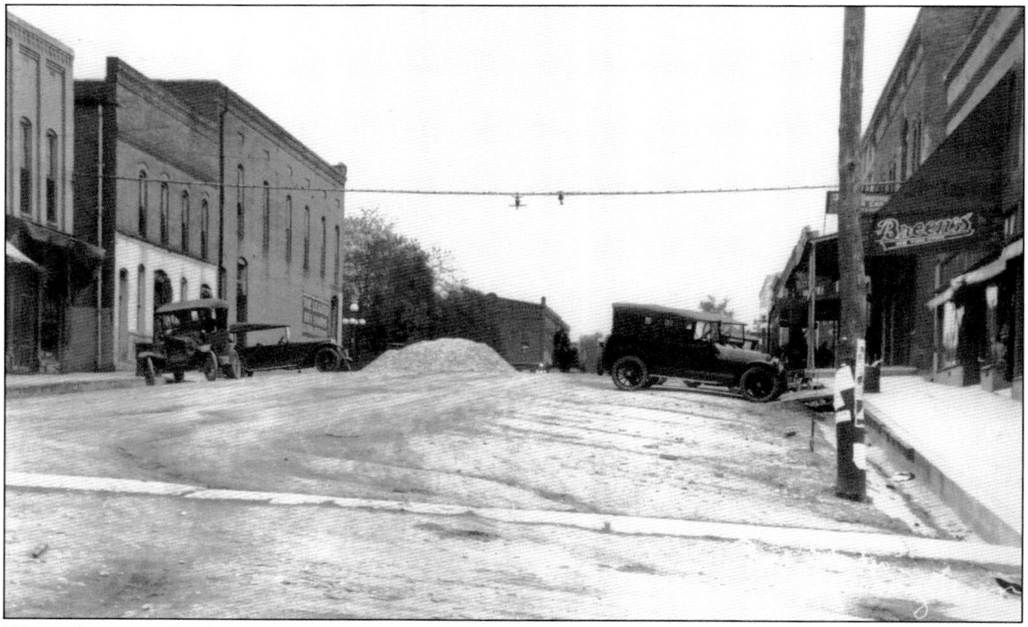

This photograph shows Main Street looking north at Cedar Street, which is the entrance to the town square when approaching from Highway 51. This was the part of town once known as Whiskey Shoot, which was a red-light district in the early days of Dyersburg. Young airmen from the nearby Dyersburg Army Air Base were warned not to get into trouble here.

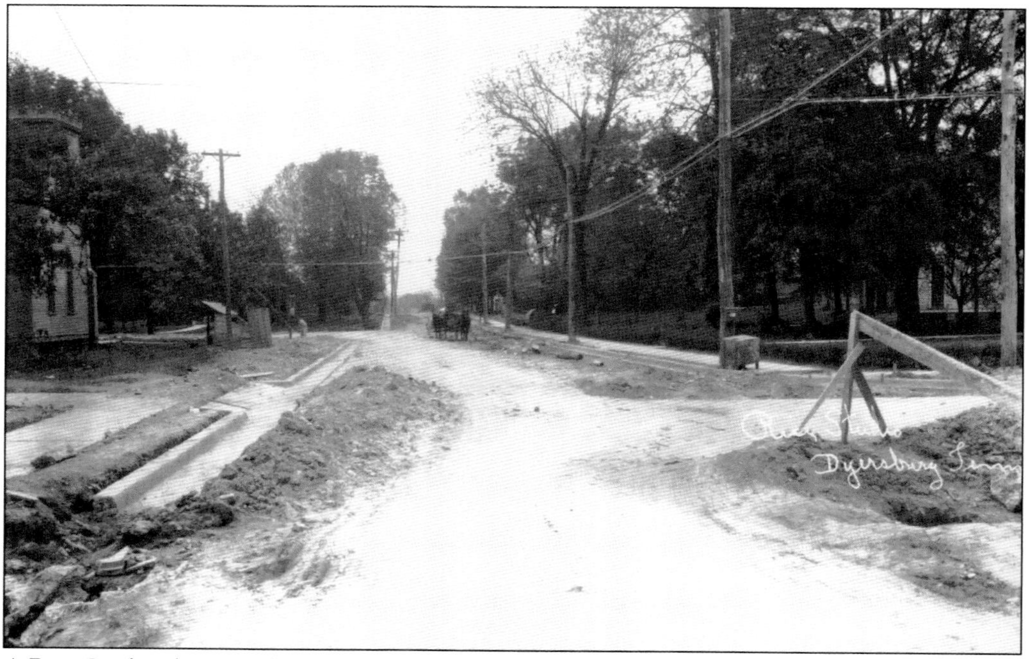

A Rice Studio photographer captures King Avenue at Finley Street, looking south, in the 1920s. The lovely King mansion is at the far right, just out of sight in this photograph. A bit of the original St. Mary's Church can be seen to the left. It was demolished and replaced by a new building in 1945.

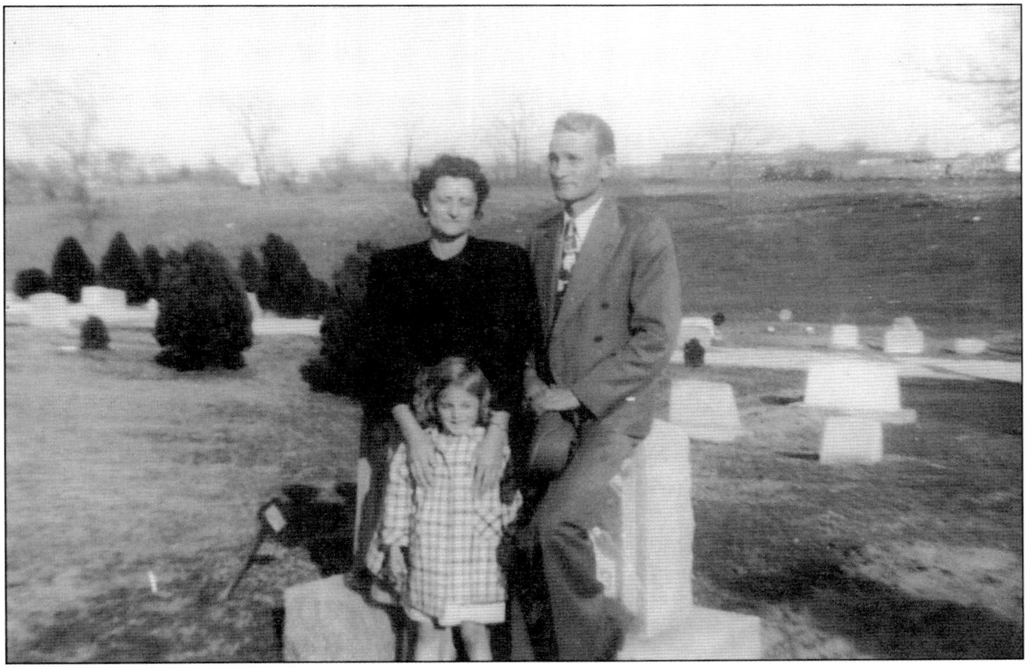

C.R. Stephens; his wife, Callie; and their daughter Brenda visit a gravesite at Fairview Cemetery in the early 1950s. The view is looking east toward Burnham Field—the long, low building is the grandstand.

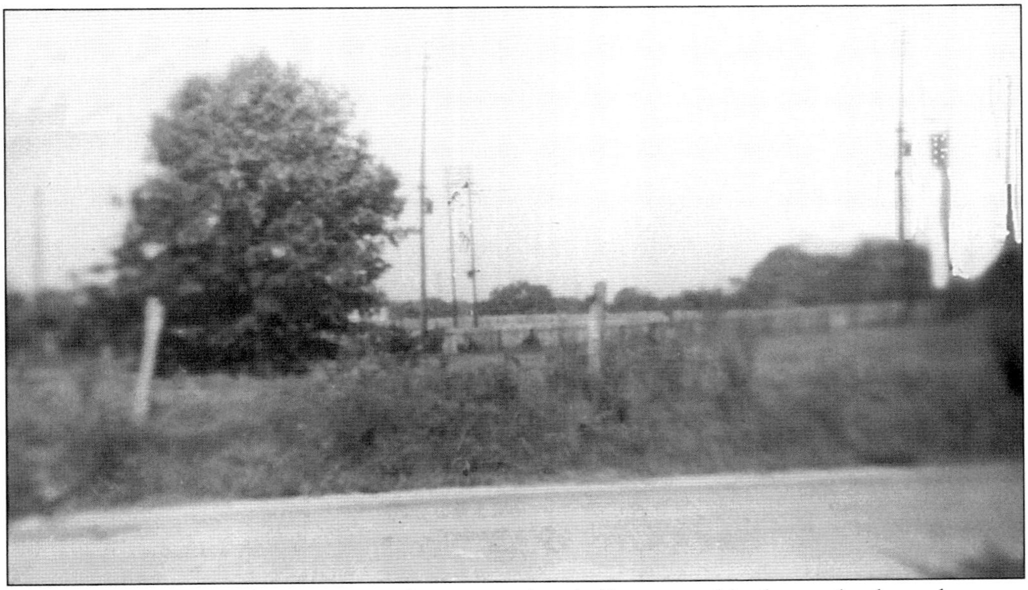

Dyersburg Cotton Products sponsored a semipro baseball team and built a park where the team could play. Part of the funding came from W.H. Burnham of Adrian, Michigan, one of the early members of the board of directors. Burnham Field was named for him. It was dedicated on May 23, 1941. Three players left the company for professional baseball, two to play in the major leagues. The team folded in 1949, and Burnham Field was donated to the City of Dyersburg for its youth baseball program. (Courtesy Gaylon Reasons.)

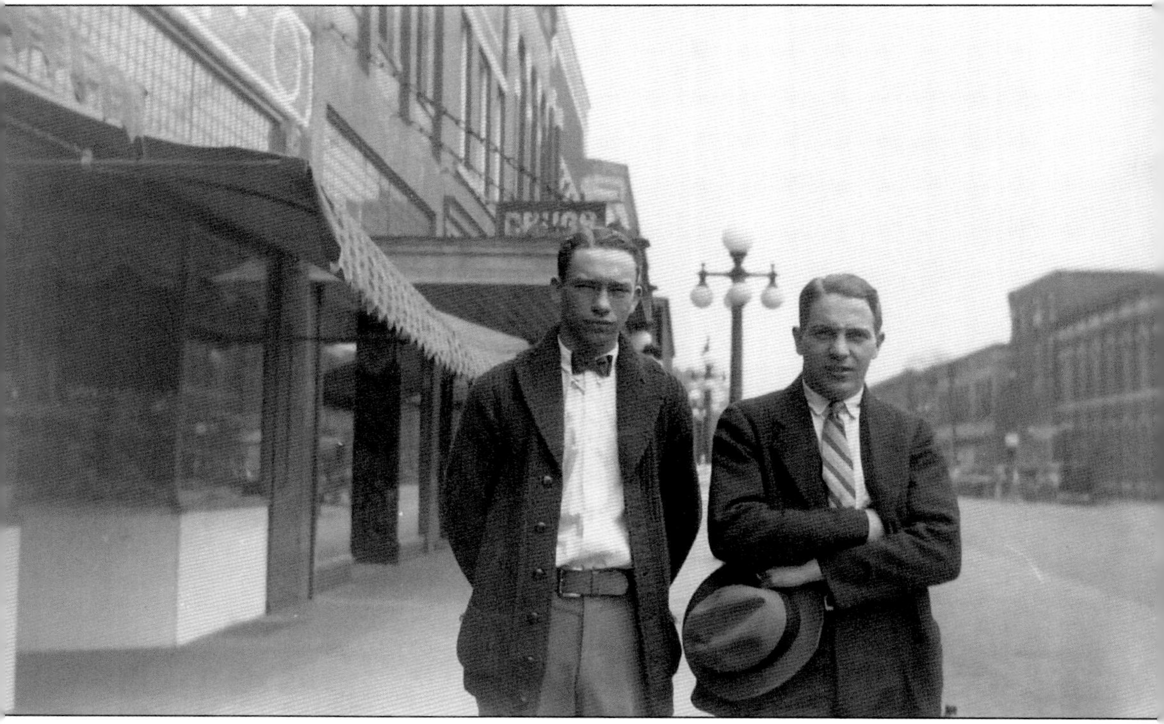

Two young men pose for the camera in the late 1920s. They are standing on the north side of the town square with Reed's Drug store in the background. This photograph provides a good view of some of the distinctive white globe lights that once decorated Dyersburg's downtown. (Courtesy John Reed.)

Five

SCHOOL DAYS

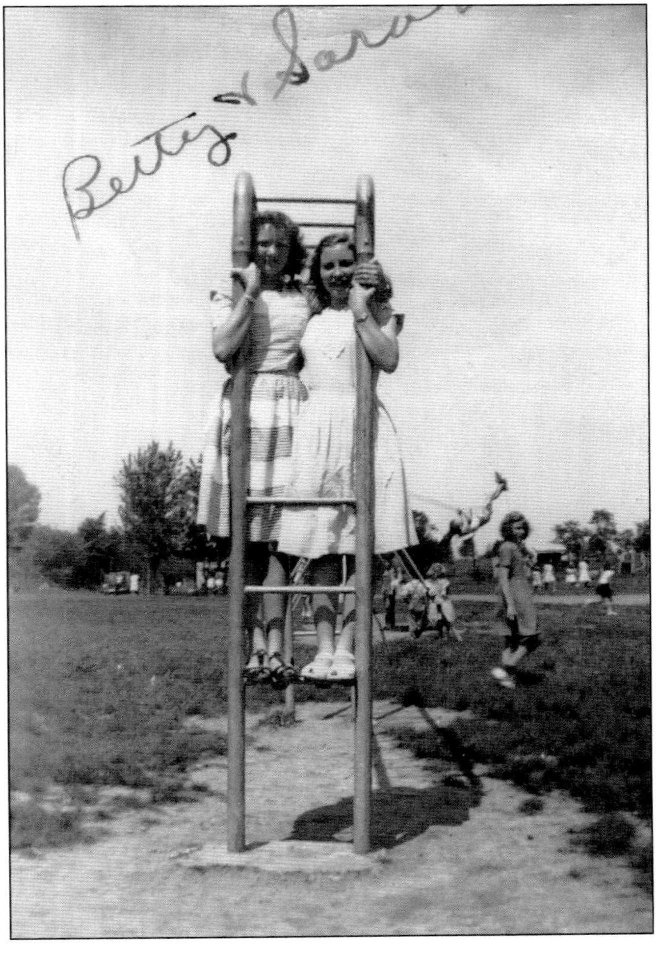

Betty and Sarah (last names unknown) pose for the camera in the early 1950s on the monkey bars at Jennie Bell Elementary School. For many years, the large playground, with its metal swings, old merry-go-round, and monkey bars, was a favorite hangout for Dyersburg children. About 1950, American educators nationwide had begun to study ways to make playgrounds safer and more enjoyable for children.

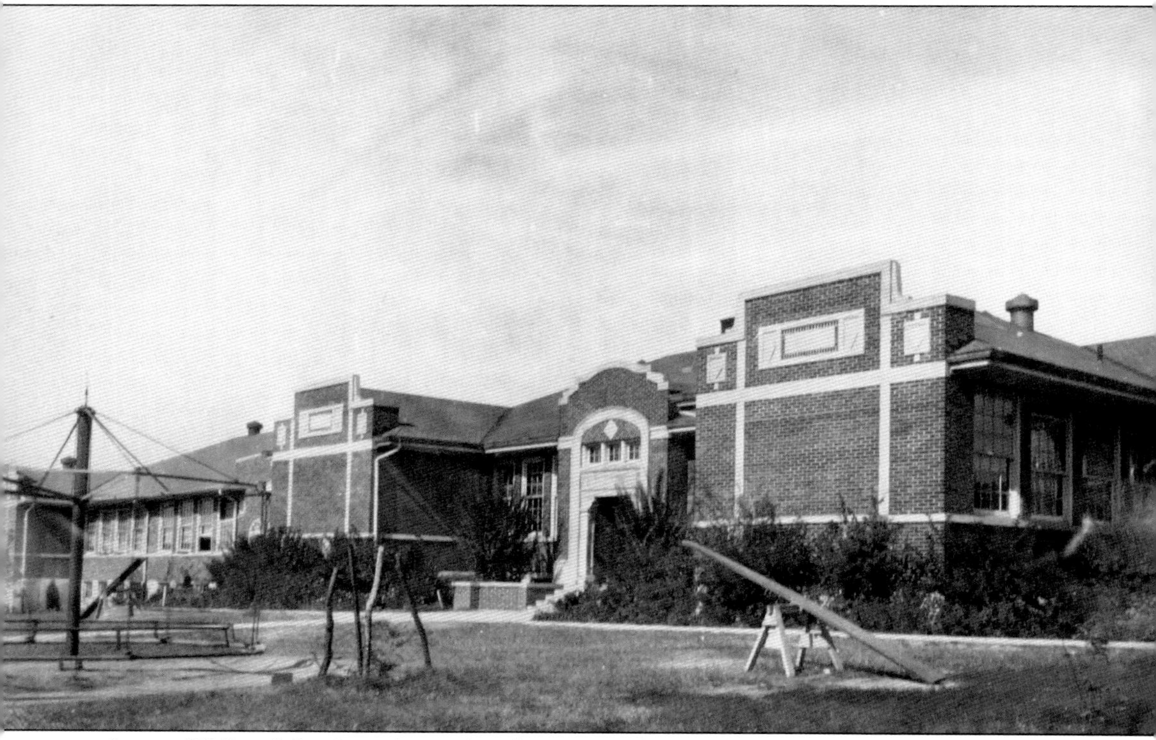

Jennie Walker School was located at the corner of Sugg Place and Watkins Street. The virtually identical Alice Thurmond School was built on Pate Street. Both schools housed elementary grades in the Dyersburg City Schools system. (Courtesy Tennessee State Library and Archives.)

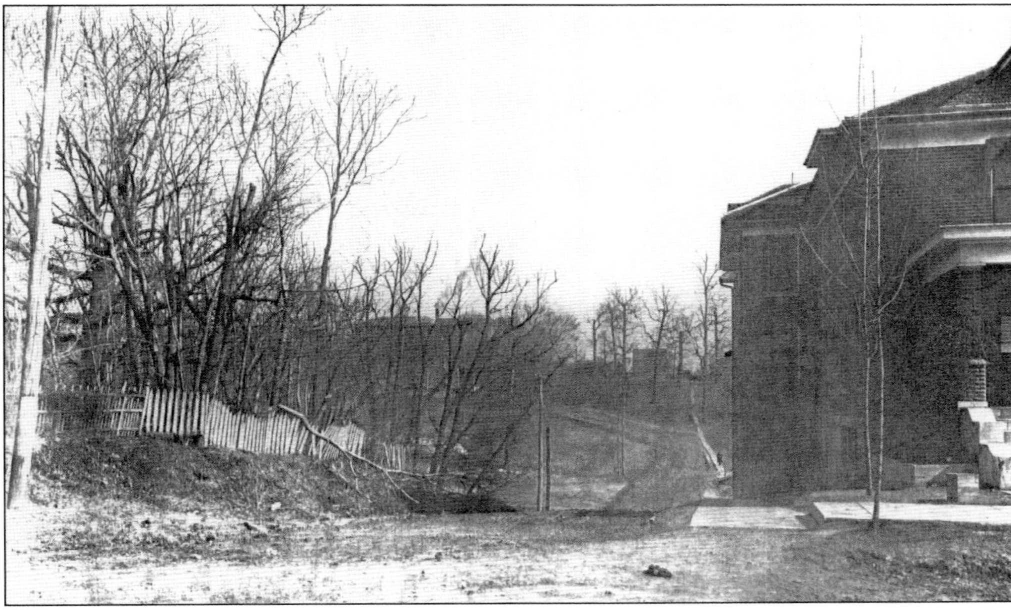

This rare old photograph (above) was shot looking east from the corner of Main and McGaughey Streets at Old College Hill. The residence at right is the Dulaney home, which was remodeled and became the Baird-Dulaney Hospital and then the Baird-Brewer Hospital. The fence and trees at left mark the property of Col. Tom H. Neal. The property, called Tanglewood, was sold to First Methodist Church in the early 1920s and became the site of its new building. The first Dyersburg High School was built on the hill—College Hill—seen above the old fence, and a football field was created at the foot of the hill. The image below shows the same spot as it appeared in 2010, with the Baird-Brewer building and First Methodist Church in place.

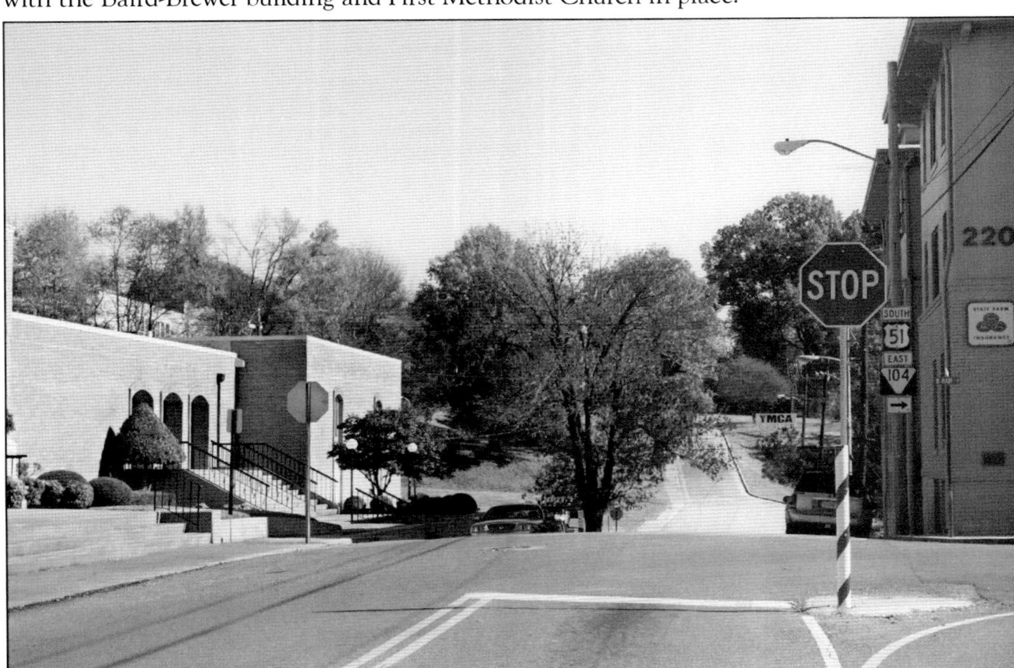

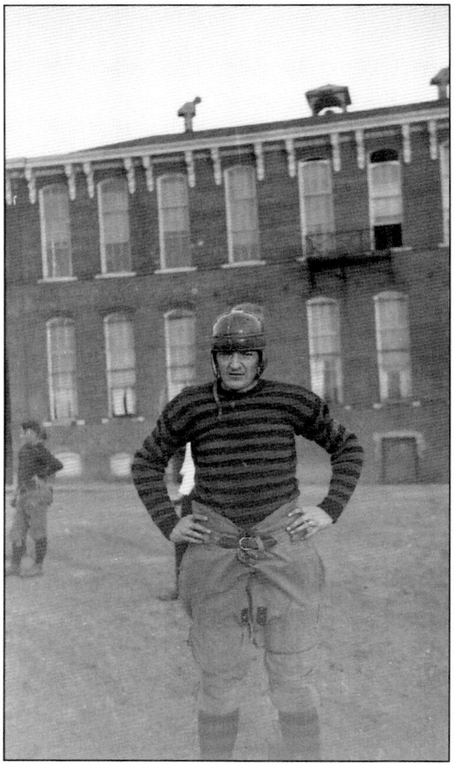

These unidentified young football players—friends of Jewell Reed, son of pharmacist Dr. John Reed—practice behind the first Dyersburg High School in the 1920s. Note the leather football helmets. Dyersburg's first high school, or the Male and Female College, as it was called, was the first building to house older students in Dyersburg. It was a four-year institution that received students from the city and those who might have graduated from the two-year high schools in surrounding communities such as RoEllen, Newbern, Tatumville, and Navoo. The cornerstone of the building still exists, near where the Dyersburg City Schools central office stands today. (Courtesy John Reed.)

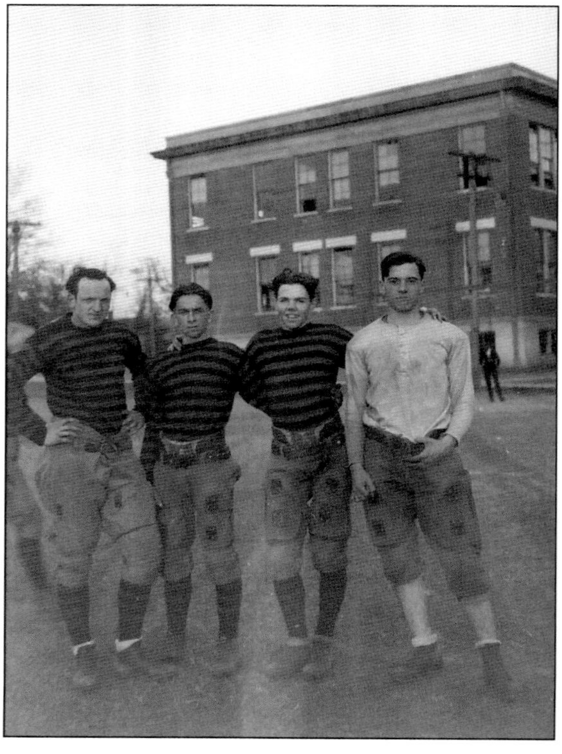

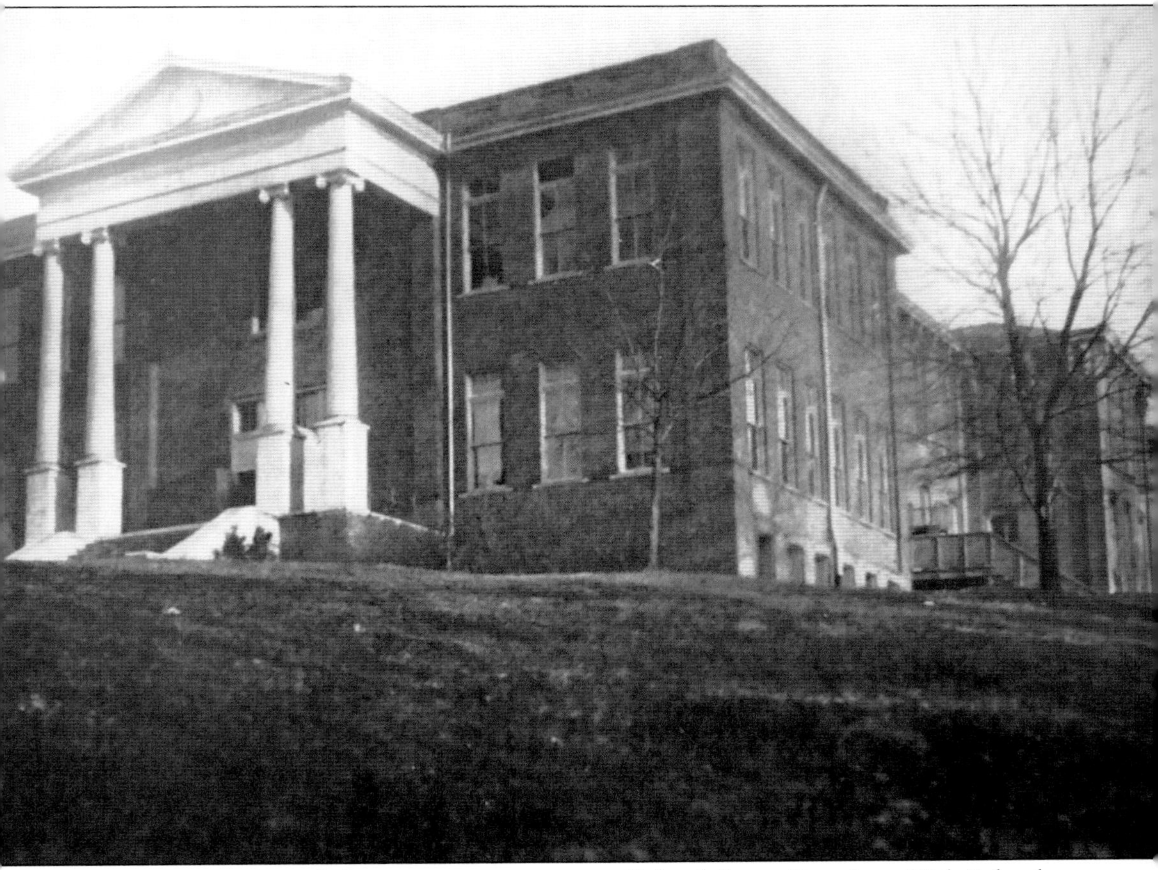

This photograph is the only known image to capture all the different Dyersburg High Schools in their places on College Hill while they were still standing. The first was the building in the middle (originally the Male and Female College). The second was the building in the foreground, constructed in 1886. At the rear is the third building, which later became Central Grammar School. All the buildings pictured were eventually demolished, and the city schools' central office was built in 1977 on the location in the rear.

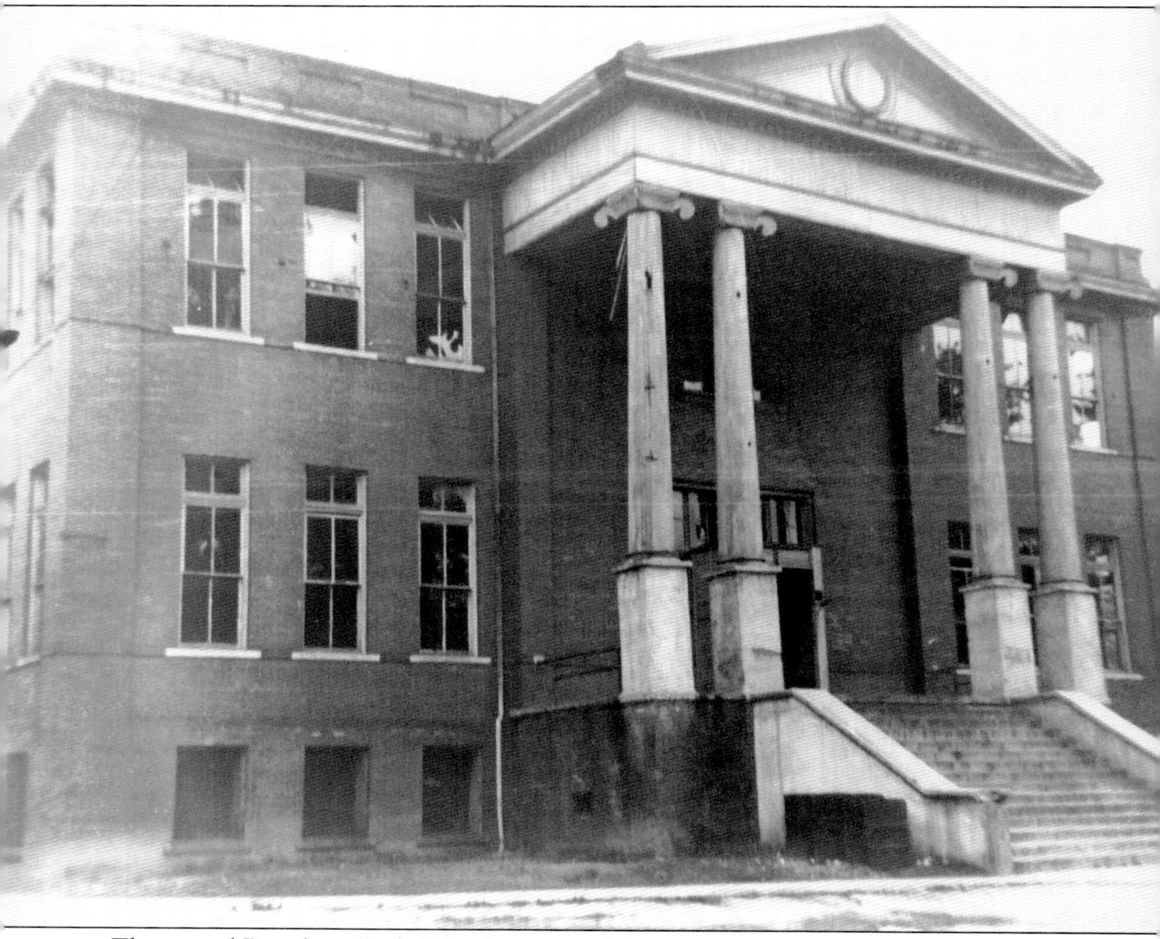

The second Dyersburg High School is pictured shortly before its demolition. Beginning in 1903, the campus was the site of the West Tennessee Track and Field Meet for many years. This was the only school in the county at that time that graduated students after four years; 11 other high schools in the city and county graduated students after just two years, so those who wanted a full four-year diploma had to come to Dyersburg to get it.

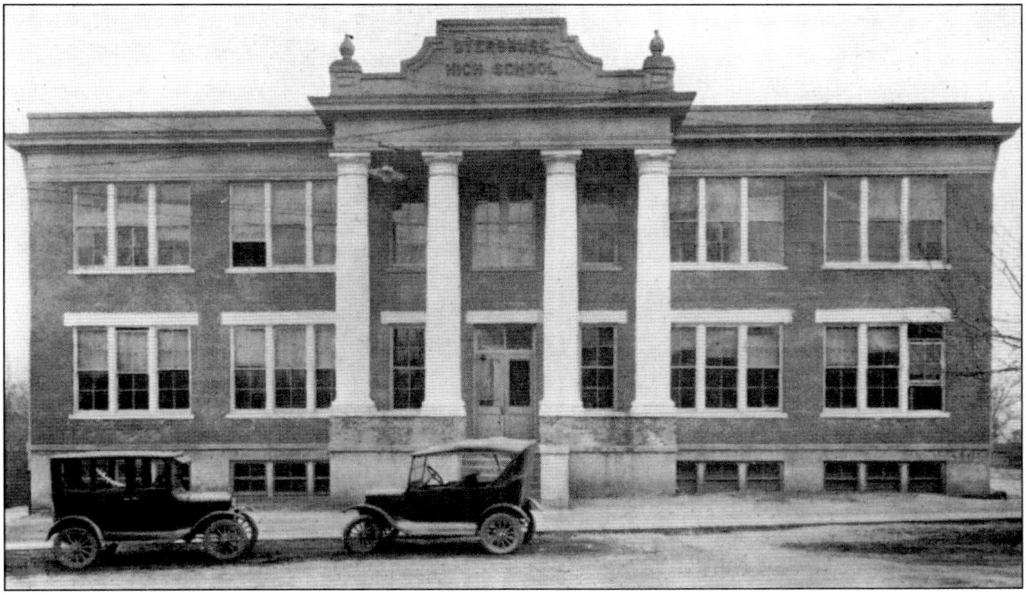

This imposing structure, with its distinctive pointed decorations on top, was the third Dyersburg High School. Built in the 1920s, it was accompanied by a separate gymnasium that was constructed down the hill. The two buildings were connected by a long flight of concrete steps, left intact after both buildings were gone.

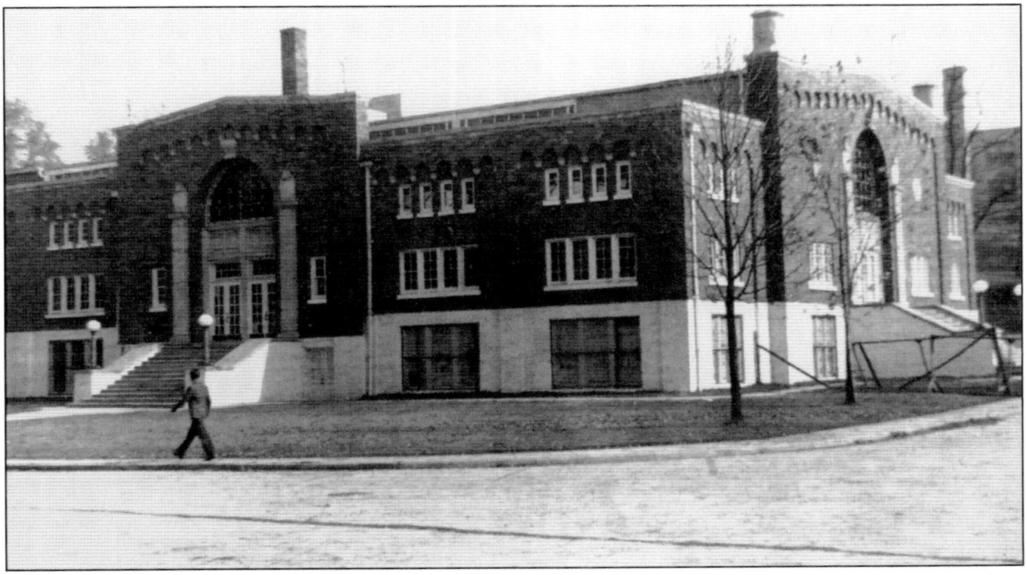

In 1927, the new gymnasium was constructed along with the third Dyersburg High School. It boasted the latest comforts that the era could offer, and it had a wading pool on the grounds. Generations of students played basketball on its polished hardwood floor. The space was also used for large events, including religious revivals. This photograph was taken from McGaughey Street, looking northwest, soon after the building was completed.

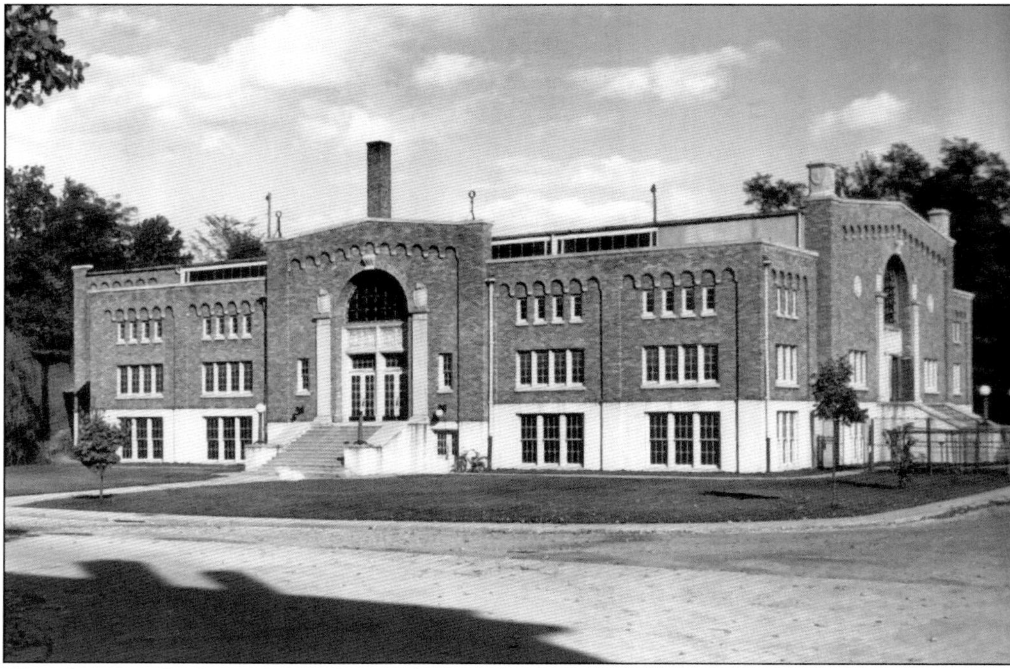

The photograph above shows the newly completed Dyersburg High School Gymnasium in the late 1920s. Note the distinctive white globe lights at the entrance, which match the those that decorated the town square. In the photograph below, taken some 30 years later, the trees have grown tall. The building was demolished in 1993, and its wood floor was cut into small sections and sold to townspeople as a fundraising effort. A parking lot now occupies the exact footprint of the building. (Above, courtesy University of Memphis Special Collections.)

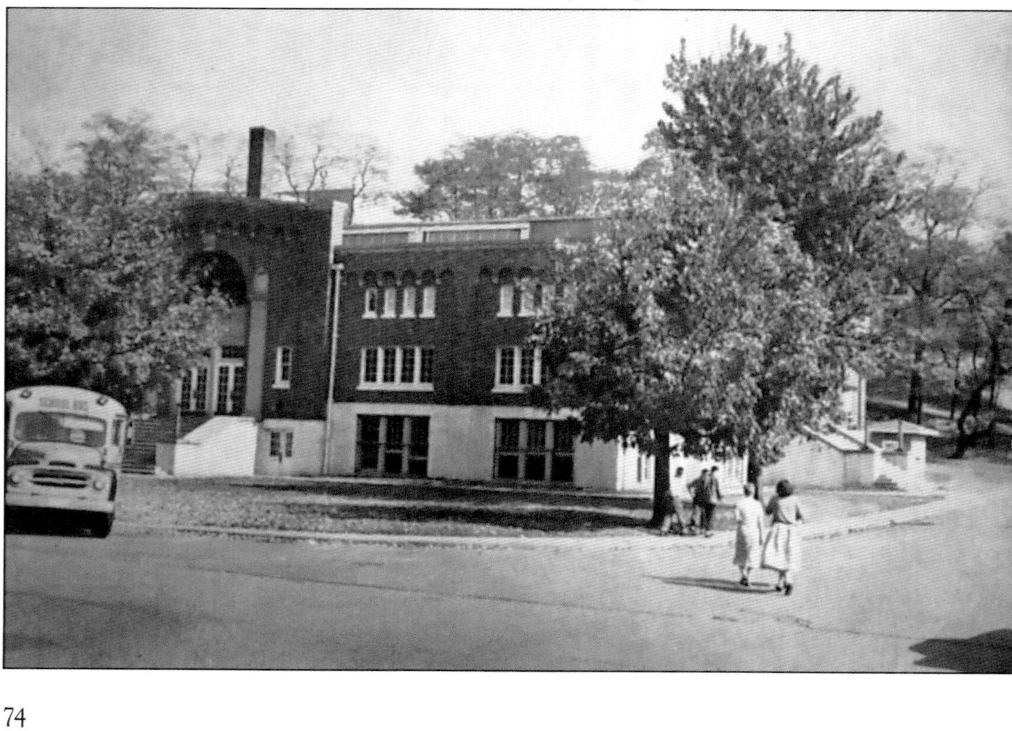

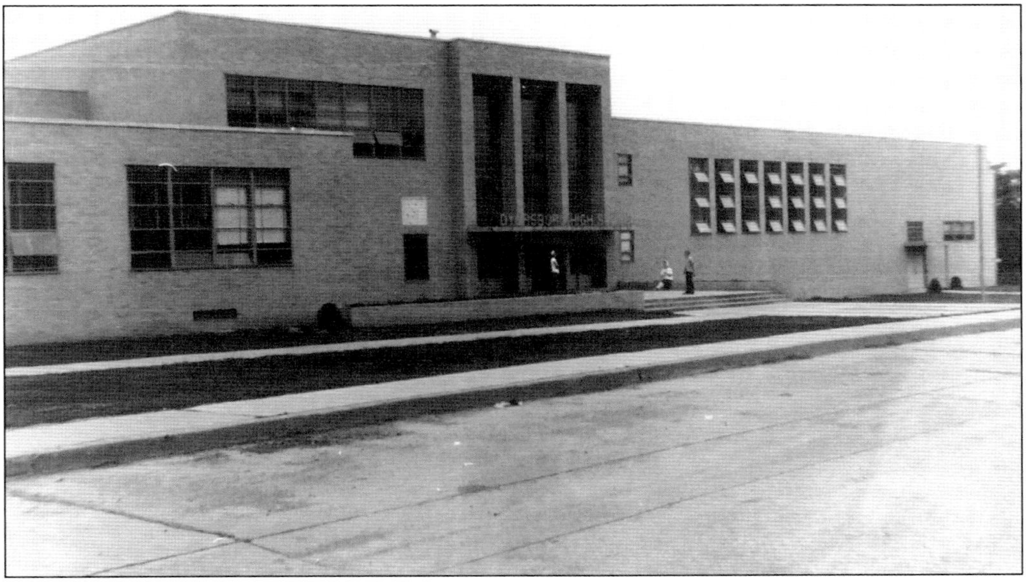

The Great Depression of the 1930s brought hard times to Dyersburg, but one benefit was a new, updated high school. Completed in 1939 with labor from Franklin D. Roosevelt's Works Progress Administration (WPA), the low, rambling building boasted Art Deco details on the exterior walls and inside its front entrance. A spacious auditorium and a large library with a fireplace were included. Many children rode their bicycles the short distance to school, so sturdy metal bike racks stood outside the entrances. (Above, courtesy Tennessee State Library and Archives.)

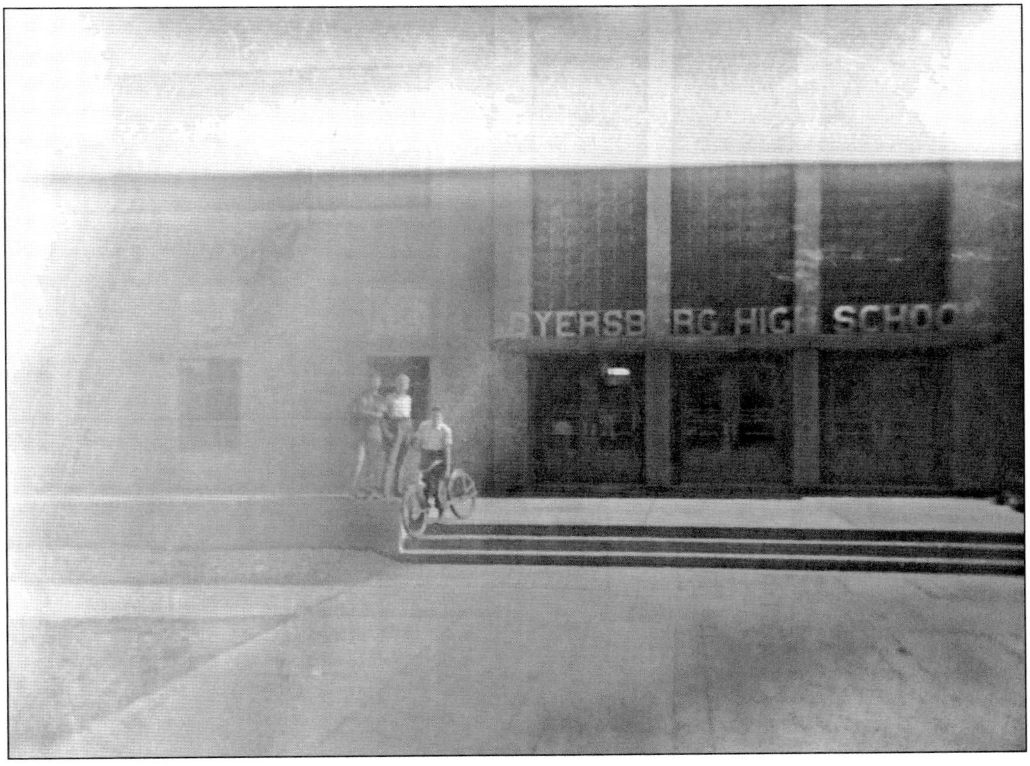

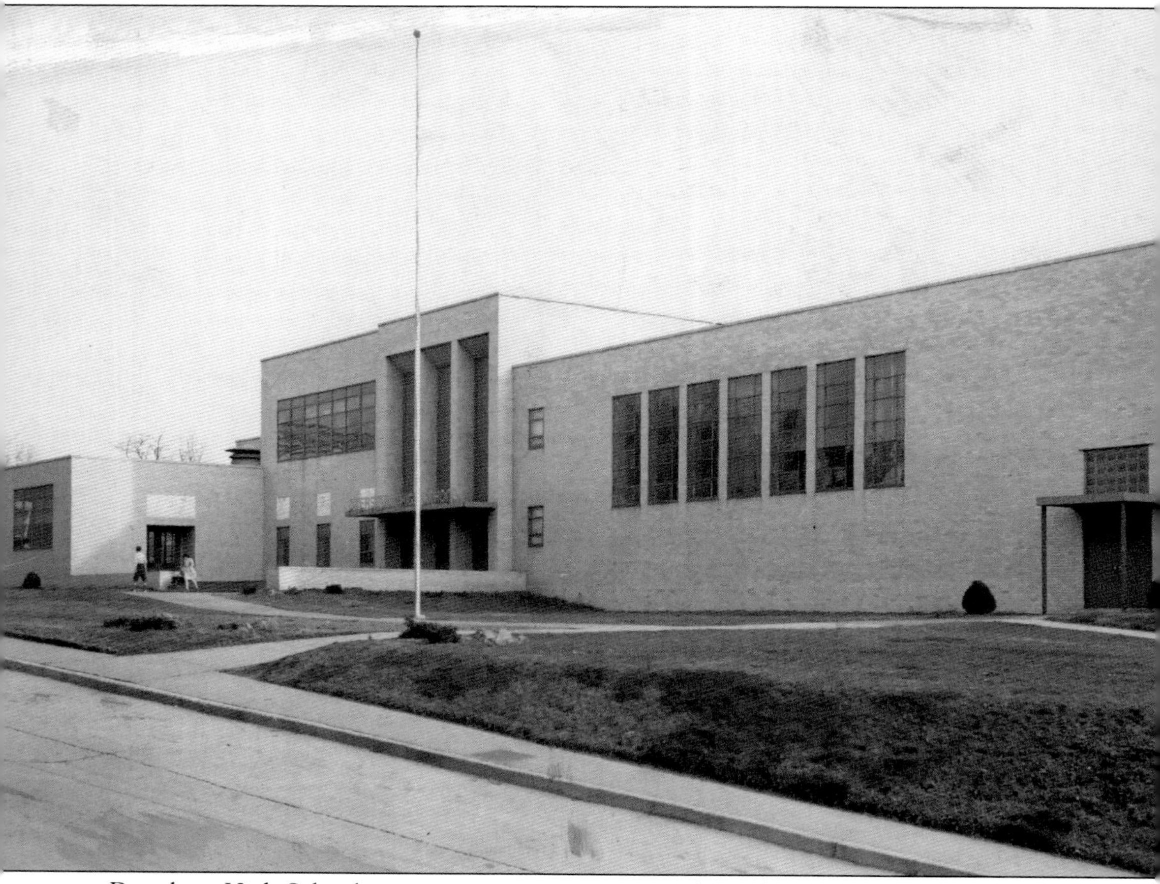

Dyersburg High School is seen on a quiet morning in the early 1950s. Eventually, this 1939 Art Deco building was supplanted by a larger high school, built on the Highway 51 Bypass in 1971. Unlike its predecessors, however, this building in the photograph was not demolished. It was preserved and became the home of a community center, a YMCA, and a museum operated by the Dyer County Historical Society.

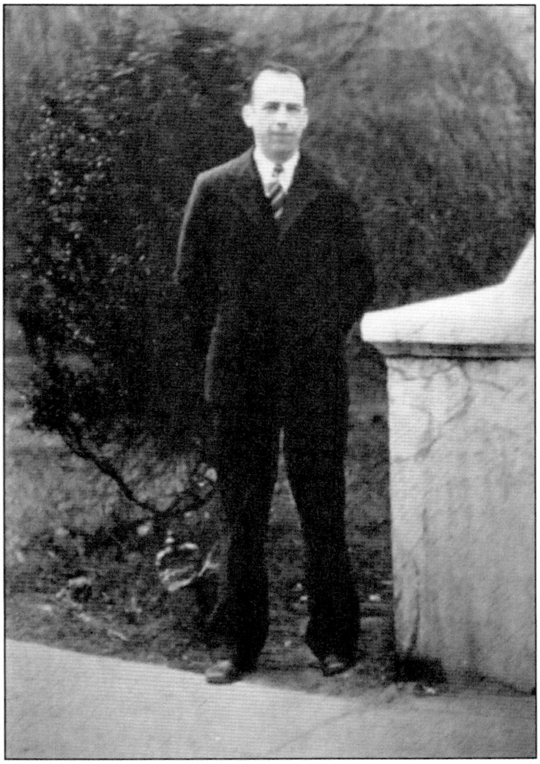

J.C. Sawyers began his career at Dyersburg High School in 1928, coaching football and basketball. Eventually, he worked his way up to become principal of the school, and he held that position until he retired in 1970. When a new high school was constructed in 1971, its football stadium was named after him.

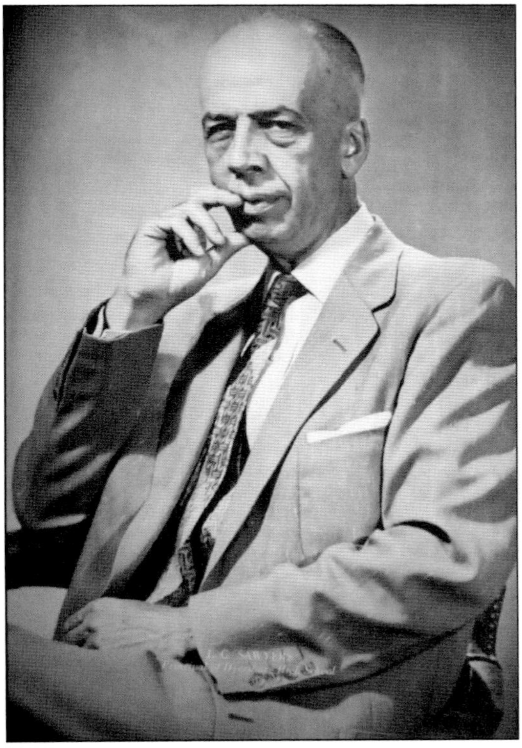

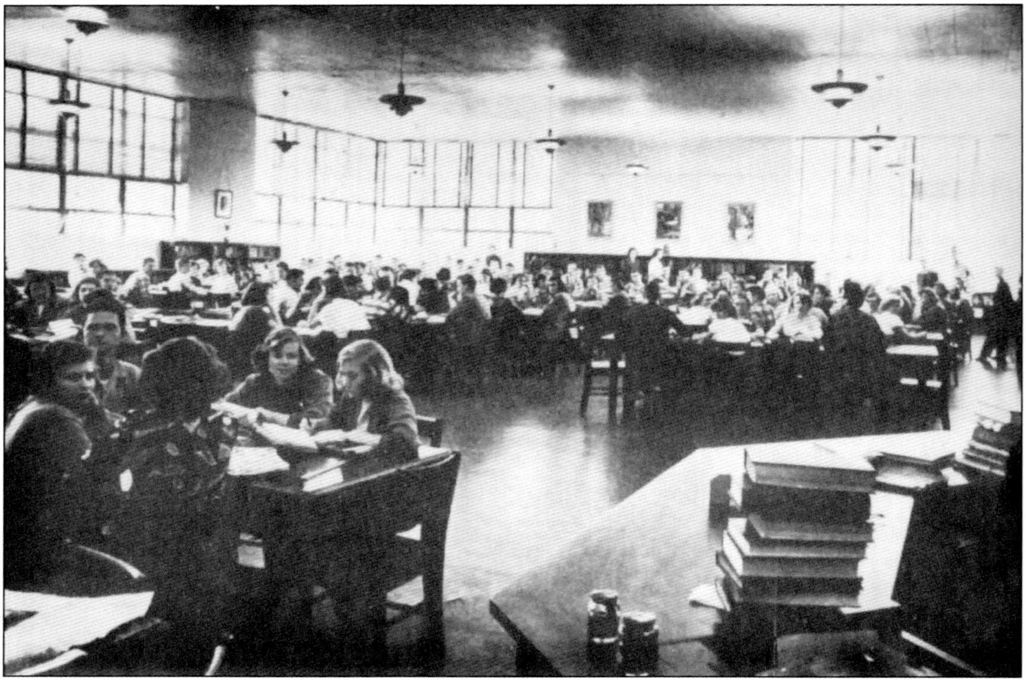

Dyersburg High School students in 1952 crowd into the library to study. The huge windows let so much natural light into the room that very little extra illumination was needed. When a new high school was built in 1971, this building became a community center, and eventually computer-training classes were held in this room. To reduce glare on the computer screens, nearly all of the enormous windows had to be covered.

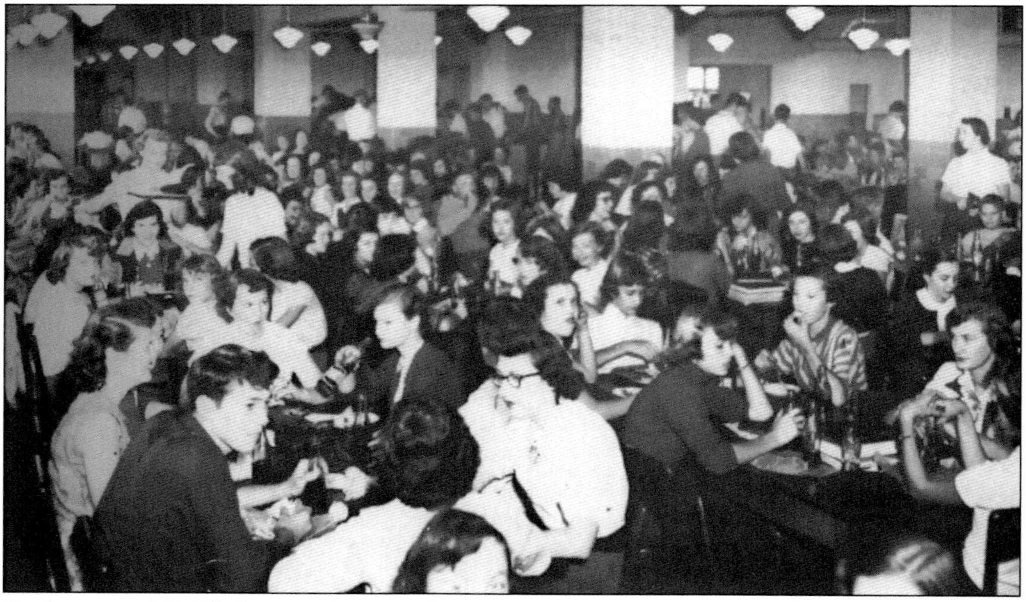

Students in 1952 fill the Dyersburg High School cafeteria at lunchtime. Many former students also recall being able to leave campus and eat lunch at home or at a restaurant that was located at the bottom of the hill.

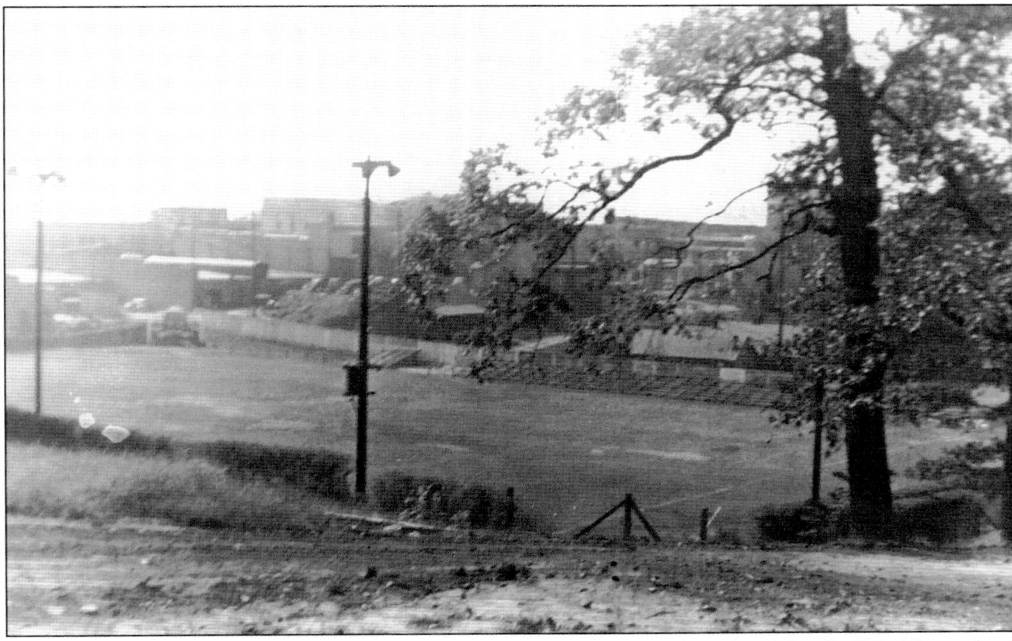

At the foot of what was called College Hill, the Dyersburg High School football field was built in 1936 to accompany the new high school. It was named Burks Stadium, after a student who died while training to become an aviator. Long ago, the site of the field was originally Dyersburg Commons, a grassy area where cattle grazed and military drills were held.

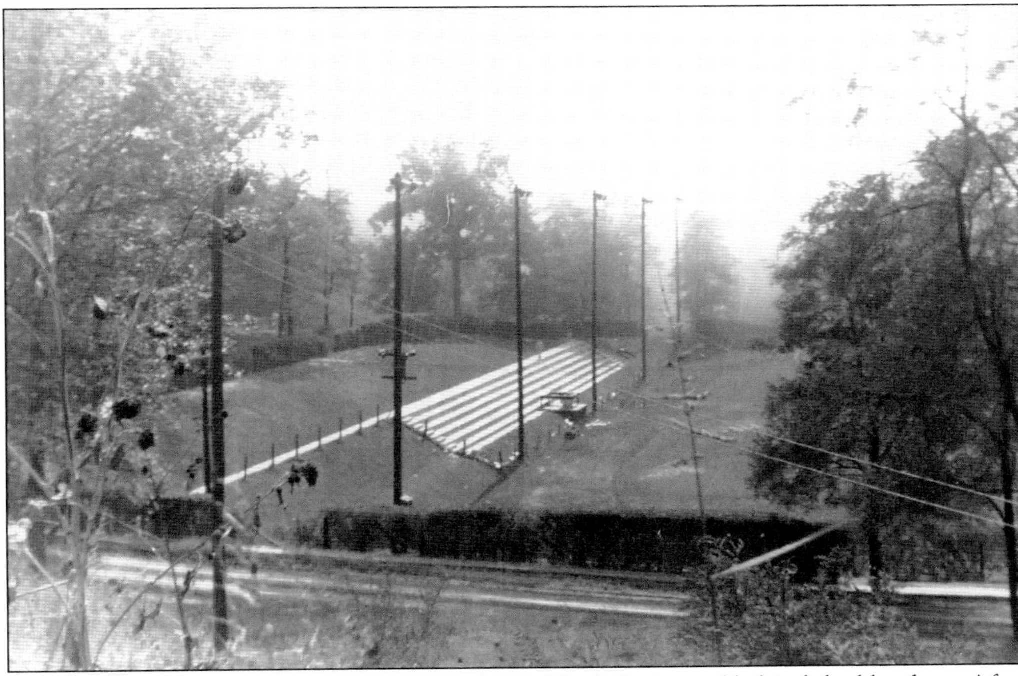

An upper deck and press box now stand in place of the hill pictured behind the bleachers. After the present-day Dyersburg High School was constructed in 1971, Burks Stadium was used by the local YMCA for soccer games.

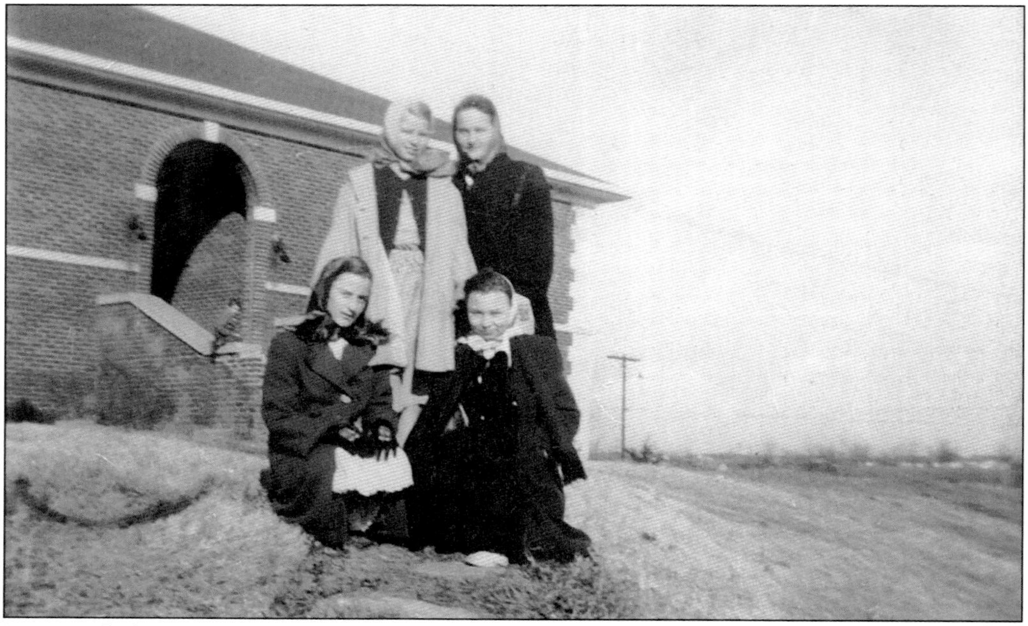

Jennie Bell Elementary School was attended by the children of Milltown for decades and was a popular spot for snapping photographs. In the image above, friends pose on a winter day in the early 1950s at the south entrance. Seated at front to the left is Joyce Flowers, and standing at the back to the right is her sister Nettie Jean Flowers. The others are unidentified. This area later became enclosed by a new wing, added to the school in 1957, so the steps in the background were eventually located inside the school rather than outside. In the image below, girls pose for the camera on a sunny afternoon in the mid-1950s. The hedges were part of the schoolyard at Jennie Bell for many years.

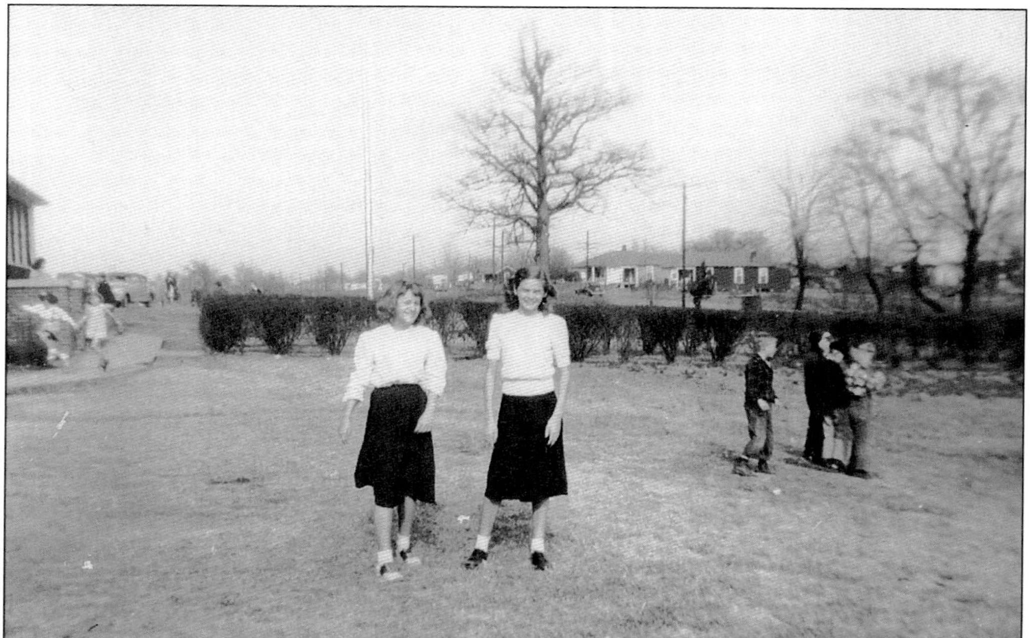

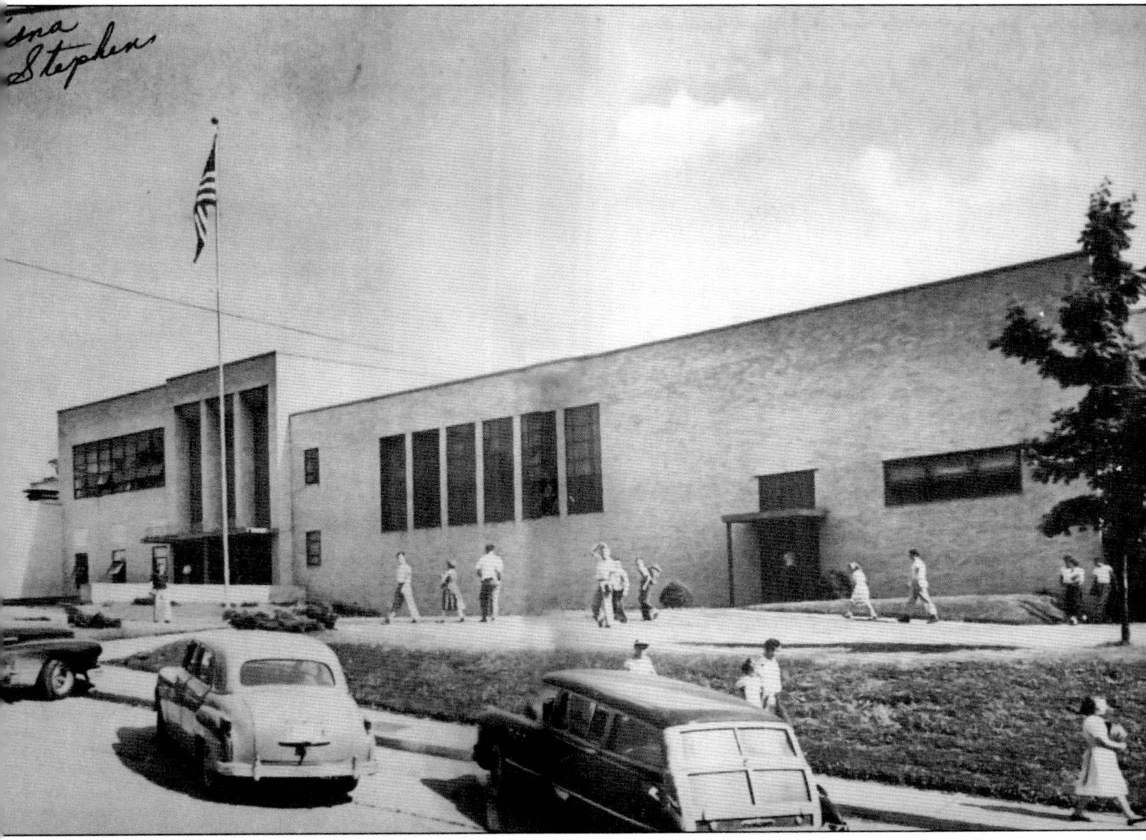

A panoramic photograph from the 1952 Dyersburg High School yearbook shows the school in its heyday. The children of millworkers and business owners filled the school each day. Trophy cases still hold numerous athletic trophies and awards from this time period, including Debate Champs 1931, 1934, 1936, 1938, 1939, 1941, and 1942; Track Champs 1910, 1911, and 1916; and Big Ten Football Champs 1947, 1948, and 1954.

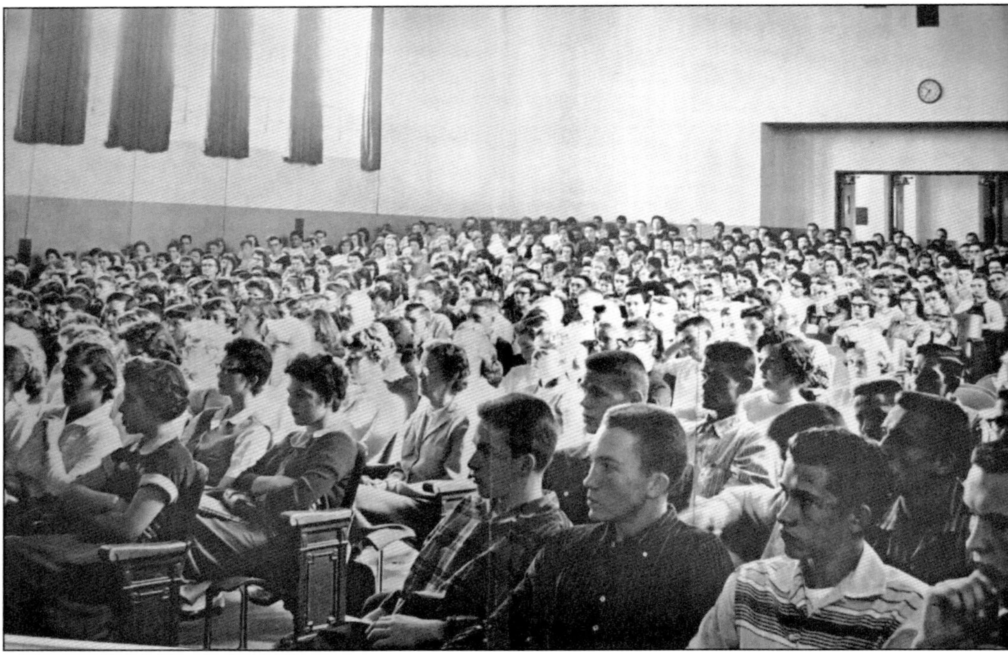

In the late 1950s, students fill the large auditorium at Dyersburg High School for an assembly. Girls had to sit on one side, and boys had to sit on the other. At that time, Future Farmers of America and Future Homemakers of America were very popular and boasted hundreds of student members. Schools were still completely segregated. African American students lived in the Bruce community of Dyersburg and attended Bruce High School.

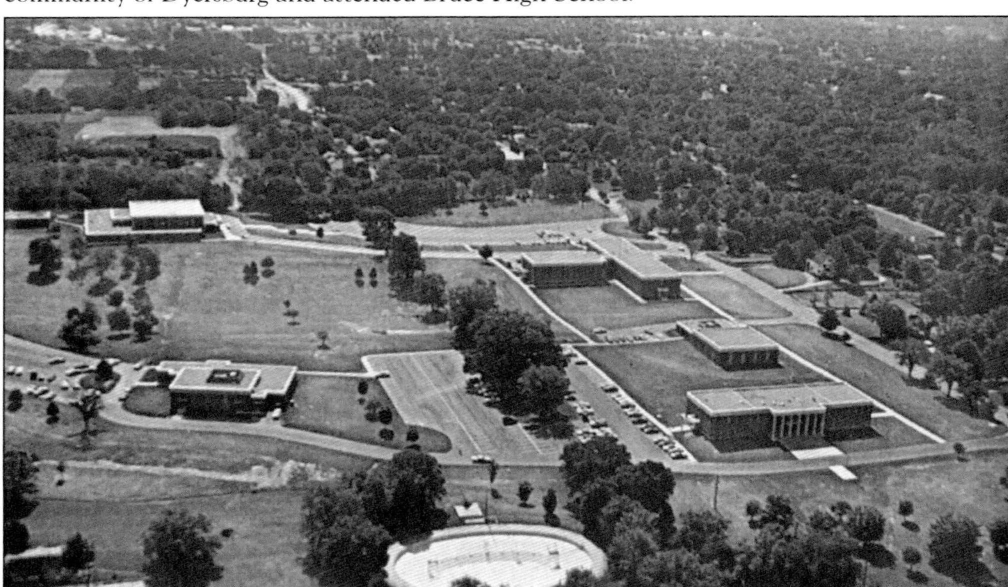

The biggest addition to Dyersburg's educational system in the 1960s was the construction of Dyersburg State Community College, a fully accredited two-year college. It was built on the old Okeena Golf Club course. At the bottom of this postcard, the Okeena municipal swimming pool, which was originally built in the 1920s, can be seen.

Six

Floods and Other Disasters

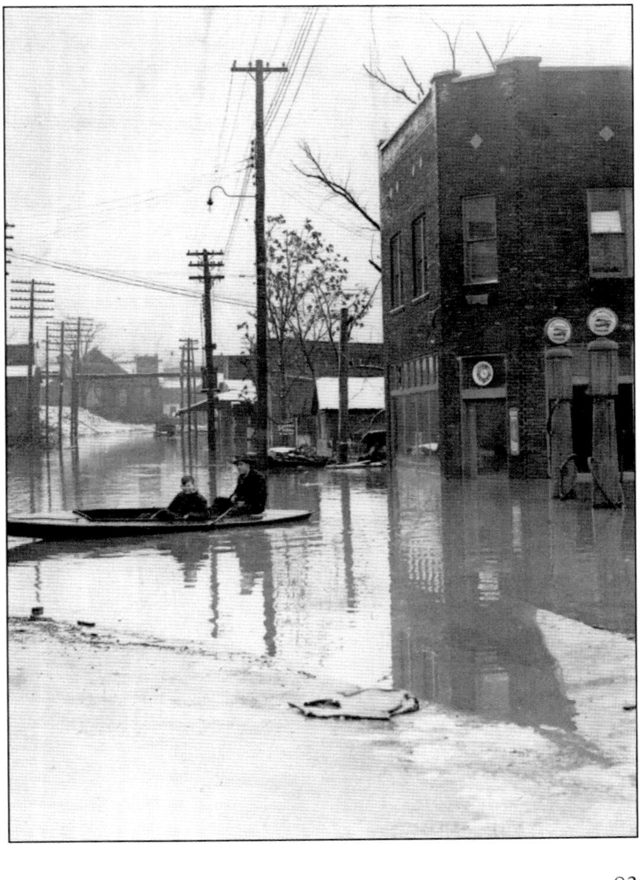

Residents use small boats to get around during the record-breaking flood in the winter of 1937. According to the National Weather Service, 21.24 inches of rain fell in January. January 24 was dubbed Black Sunday, as rivers overflowed in Tennessee and 11 other states, flooding over 12,000 square miles. Dyer County, with its rivers and tributaries, has always been susceptible to floods. (Courtesy Chris Gibbons collection.)

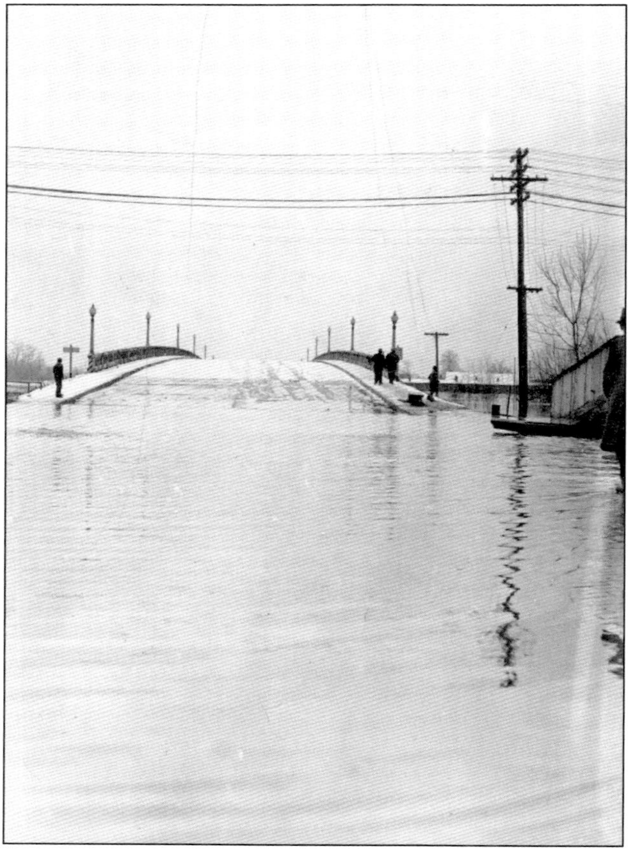

Floodwaters in 1937 encroach on the town, swamping the end of the long, high bridge into town over the Forked Deer River. The widespread southern floods of 1937 are believed to have caused at least 900 serious injuries and 250 deaths. (Courtesy Chris Gibbons collection.)

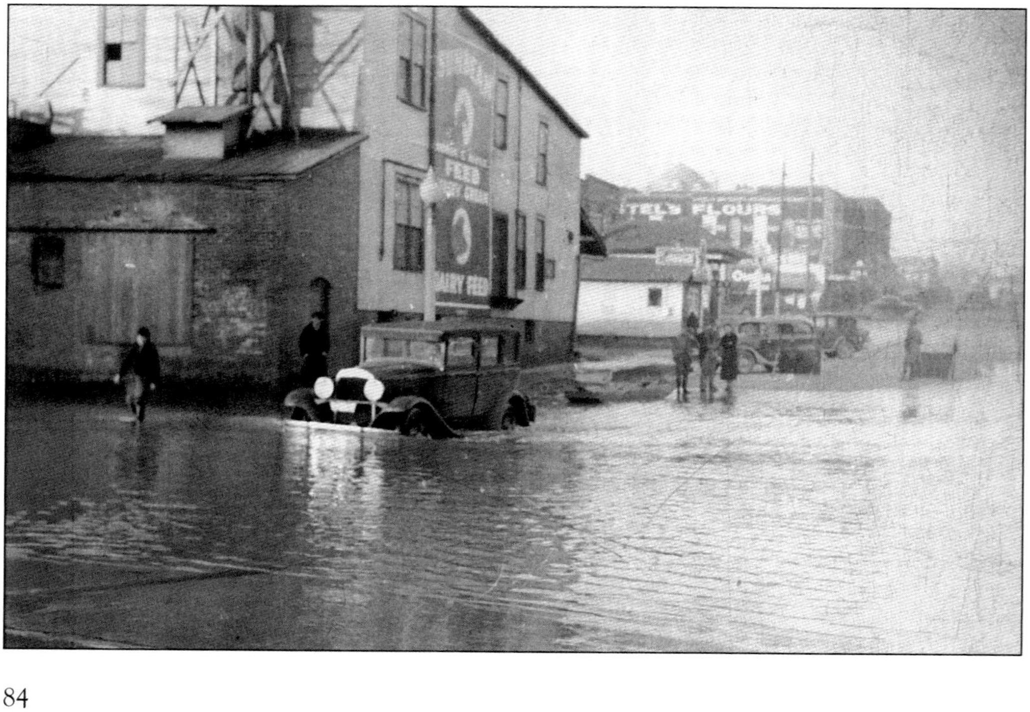

In 1937, a resident braves the high water on Main Street, hoping his car will make it through. The building to the left, with the feed sign, was later demolished to make way for Dyersburg's first water plant. The flour plant in the background was run by a Miss Monroe, one of Dyersburg's first female entrepreneurs. (Courtesy Chris Gibbons collection.)

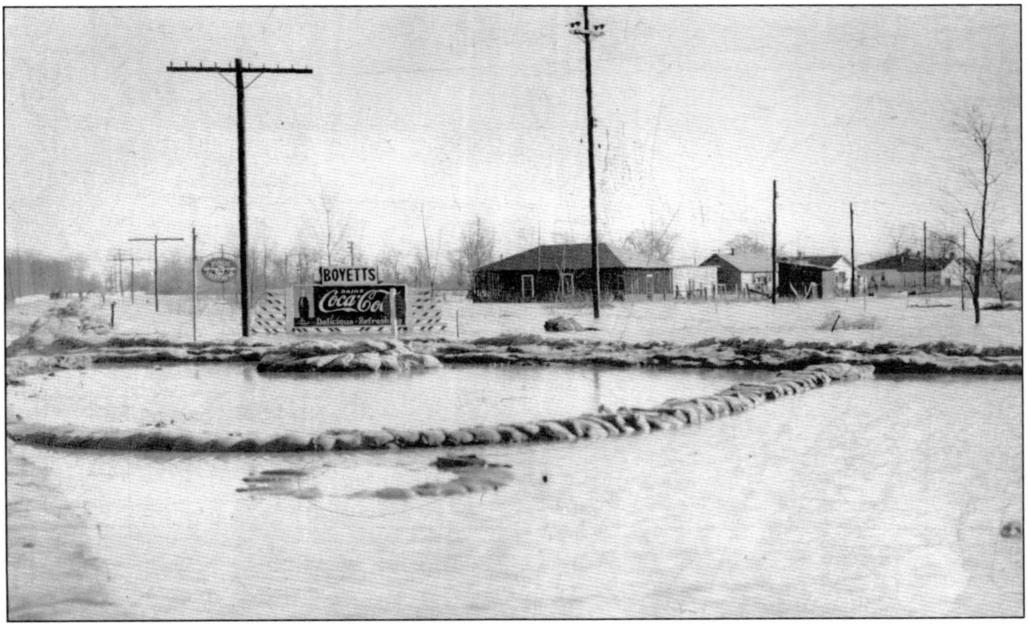

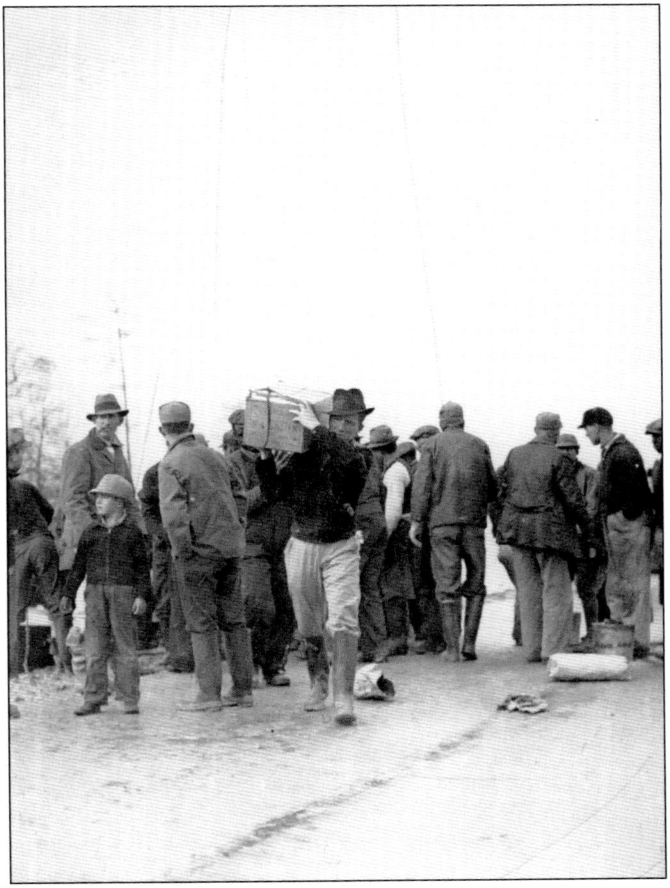

In the photograph above, a breach in the levee near Dyersburg can clearly be seen. In January 1937, Pres. Franklin D. Roosevelt issued a proclamation declaring "disastrous floods in the Ohio and Mississippi River Valleys already have driven 270,000 from their homes." In the image at right, refugees from flooded farmland in Dyer County troop into Dyersburg, carrying their belongings. Some 70 miles downriver from Dyersburg, the Memphis Fairgrounds was the site of a large refugee camp where some 60,000 people were fed, sheltered, and given medical attention. The fact that the flood happened during a bitterly cold winter led to many cases of pneumonia, influenza, and other diseases. (Both, courtesy Chris Gibbons collection.)

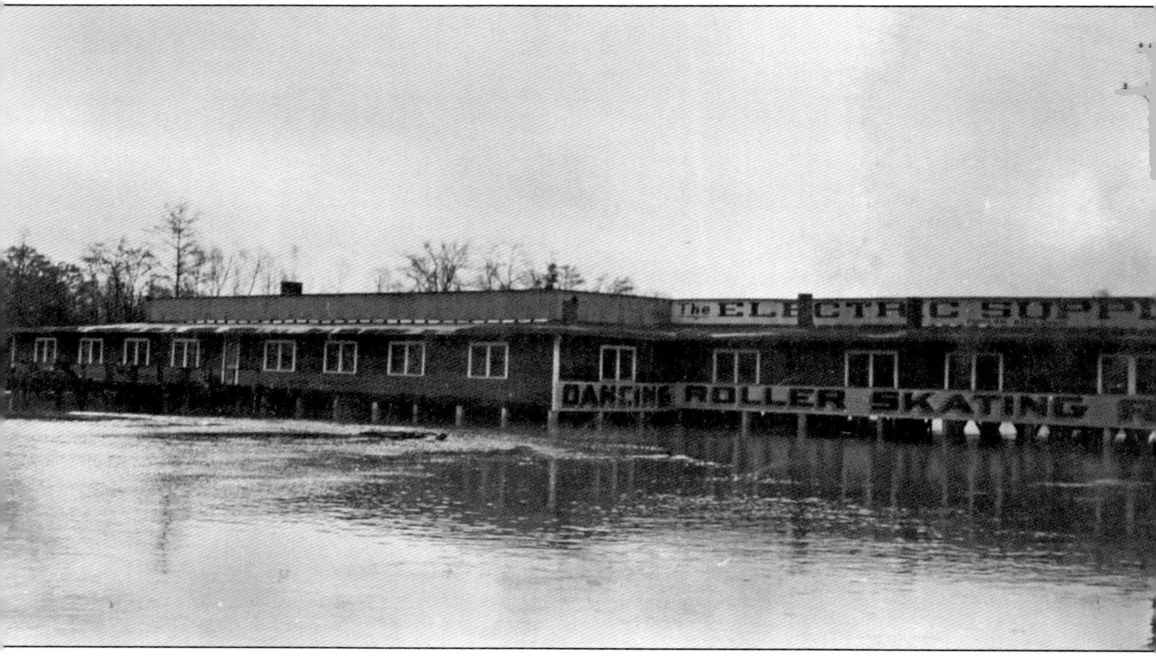

Dyersburg's local skating rink is seen during high water in the mid-1930s, probably during the flood of 1937. The old wooden structure stood on the right side of the levee as one entered town from the area called Southtown. Eventually, the old building flooded to such an extent that it collapsed and had to be demolished. (Courtesy Tennessee State Library and Archives.)

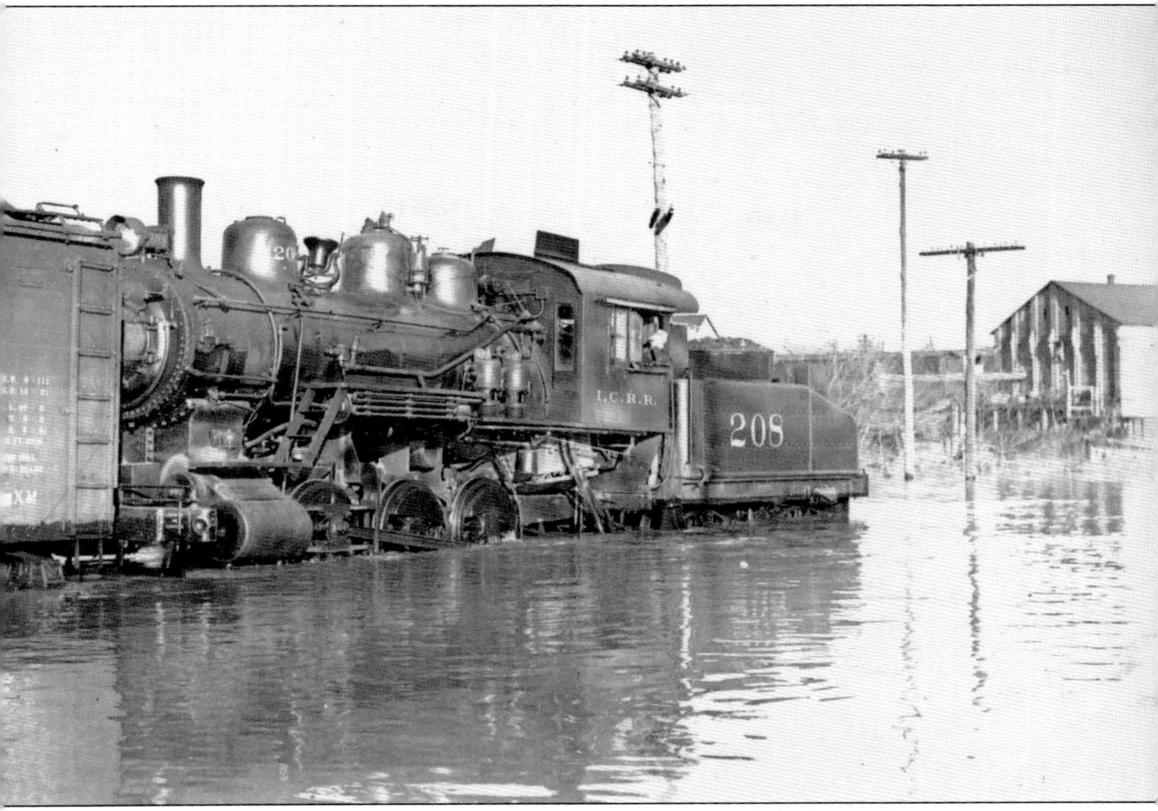

Floods have always been a part of life in Dyer County, occurring regularly despite the construction of levees. In this 1937 photograph, it would appear that the train engineer did not see the high water in time to stop. Most rail service along affected rivers, including the Mississippi, was suspended for months by the 1937 flood, which further added to the difficulty of evacuating refugees. (Courtesy Chris Gibbons collection.)

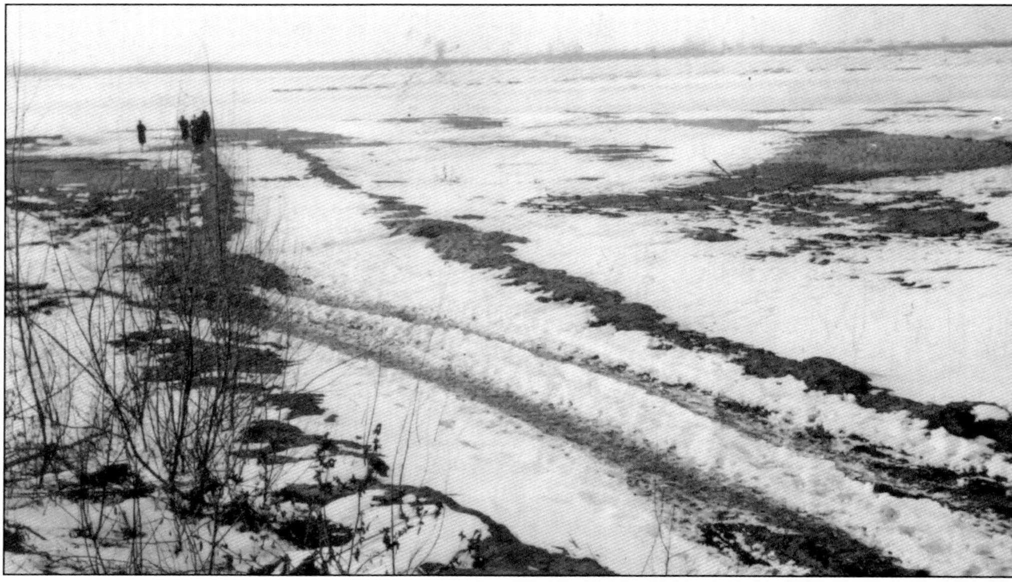

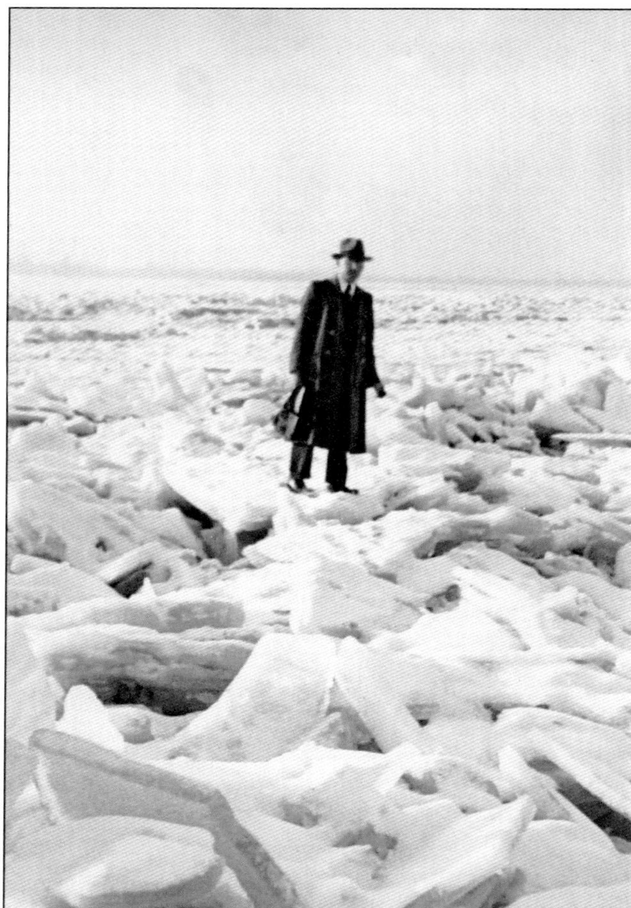

In these striking photographs, the Mississippi River is seen almost completely frozen over during the large flood in the winter of 1937. A few hardy Dyersburg residents venture down to the shore to see for themselves. Frozen ground contributed to the runoff that helped to make the 1937 flood so severe. Socially and economically, it was one of the worst disasters in American history up to that time. (Left, courtesy Chris Gibbons collection.)

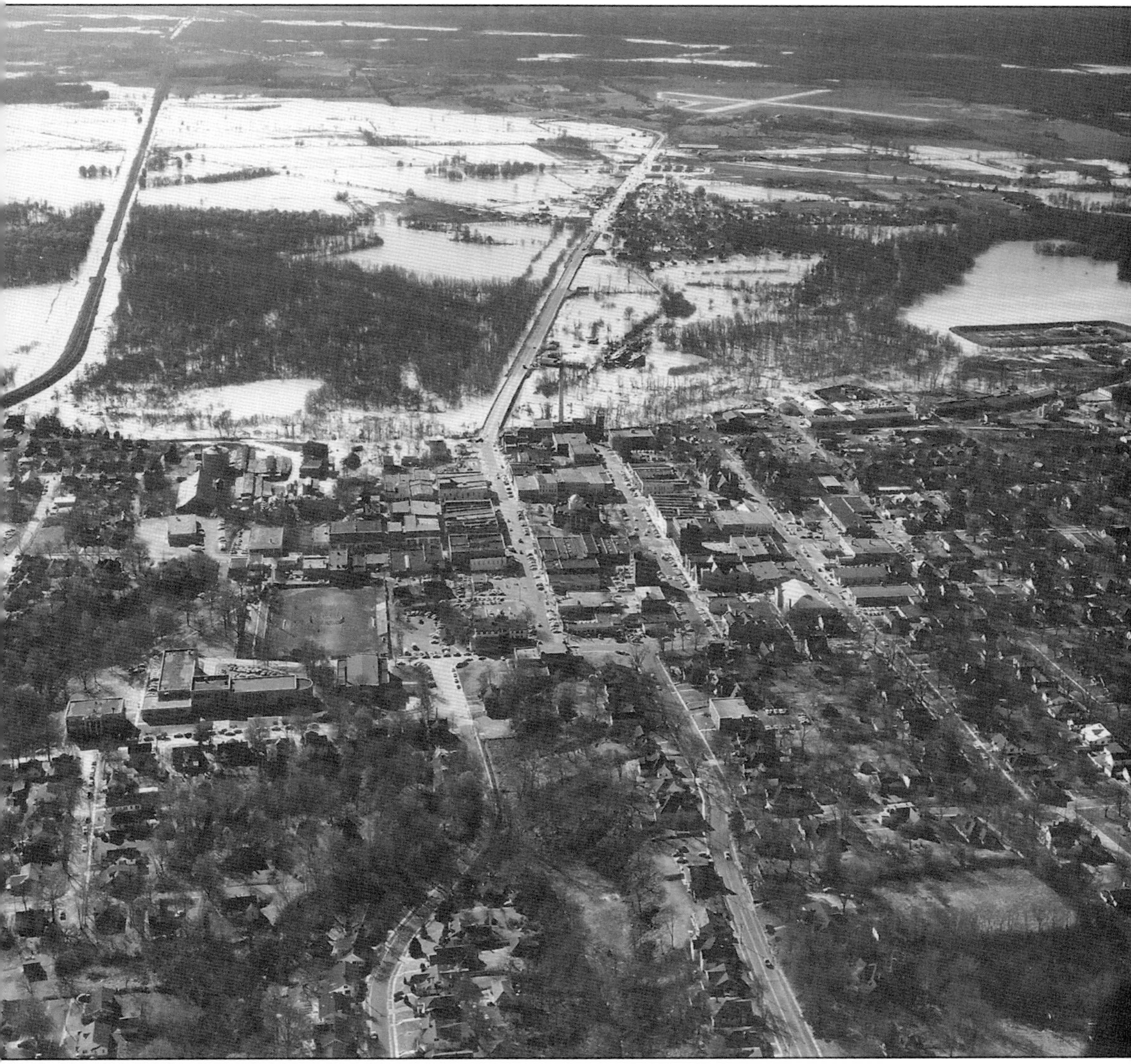

This c. 1955 aerial image clearly shows the parts of Dyersburg most often affected by floodwaters. The view is facing south. In the upper center of the photograph, Southtown is swamped, as is the Illinois Central Railroad line to the left. In town, the empty square of Burks Stadium is clearly visible at the lower left, and Dyersburg High School (the 1939 high school built by the WPA) is just below it. The dome of the courthouse rises at the center of the photograph. (Courtesy Paula Ledford.)

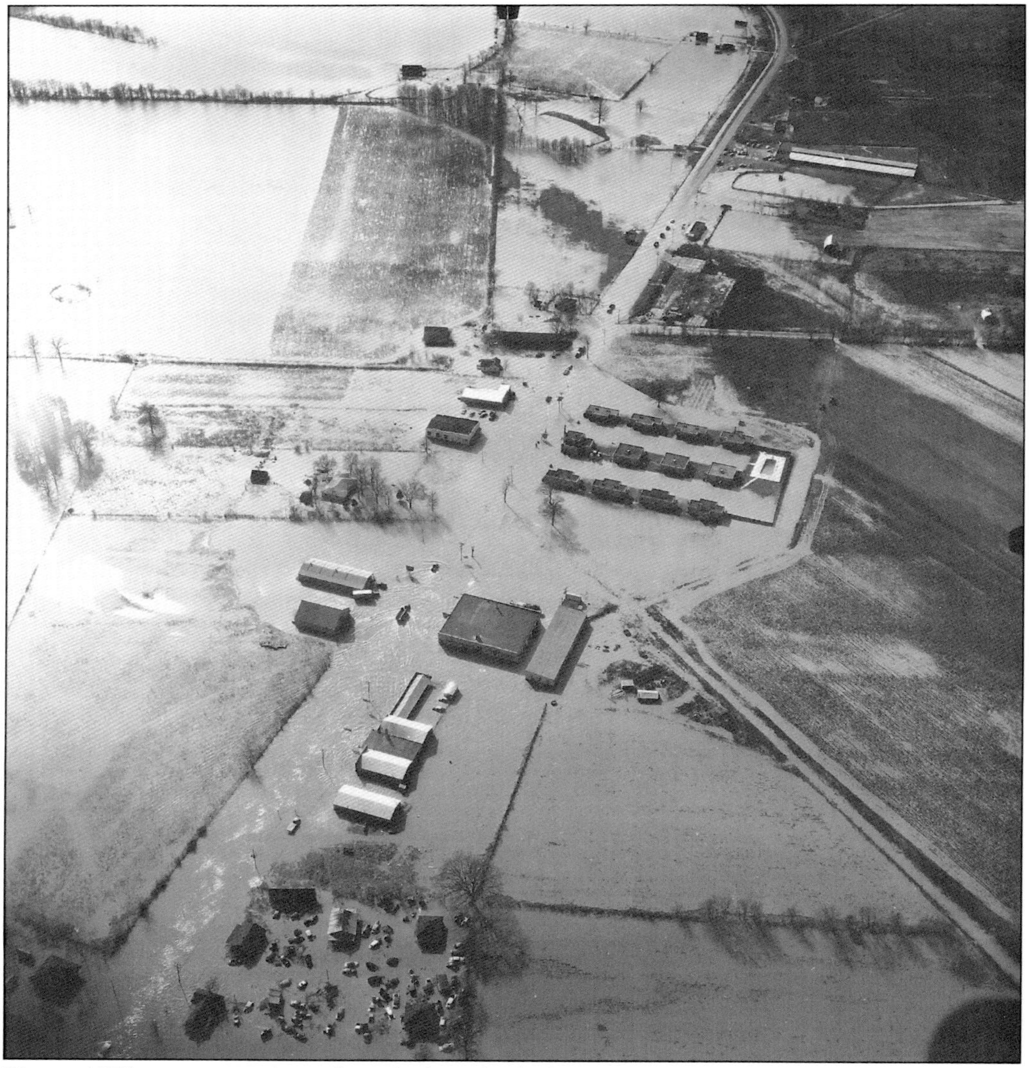

This c. 1955 image provides a closer look at the high water and includes the Plaza Court Motel, which is nearly submerged. Cars and trucks can be seen slowly making their way along the road that is the entrance to town, but their passage created waves of water that caused even more damage to the buildings. The square building at lower center, with the dark roof, at this time was the Plaza Coffee Shop and Food Center. It withstood this high water but was heavily damaged in 2010 and 2011. (Courtesy Paula Ledford.)

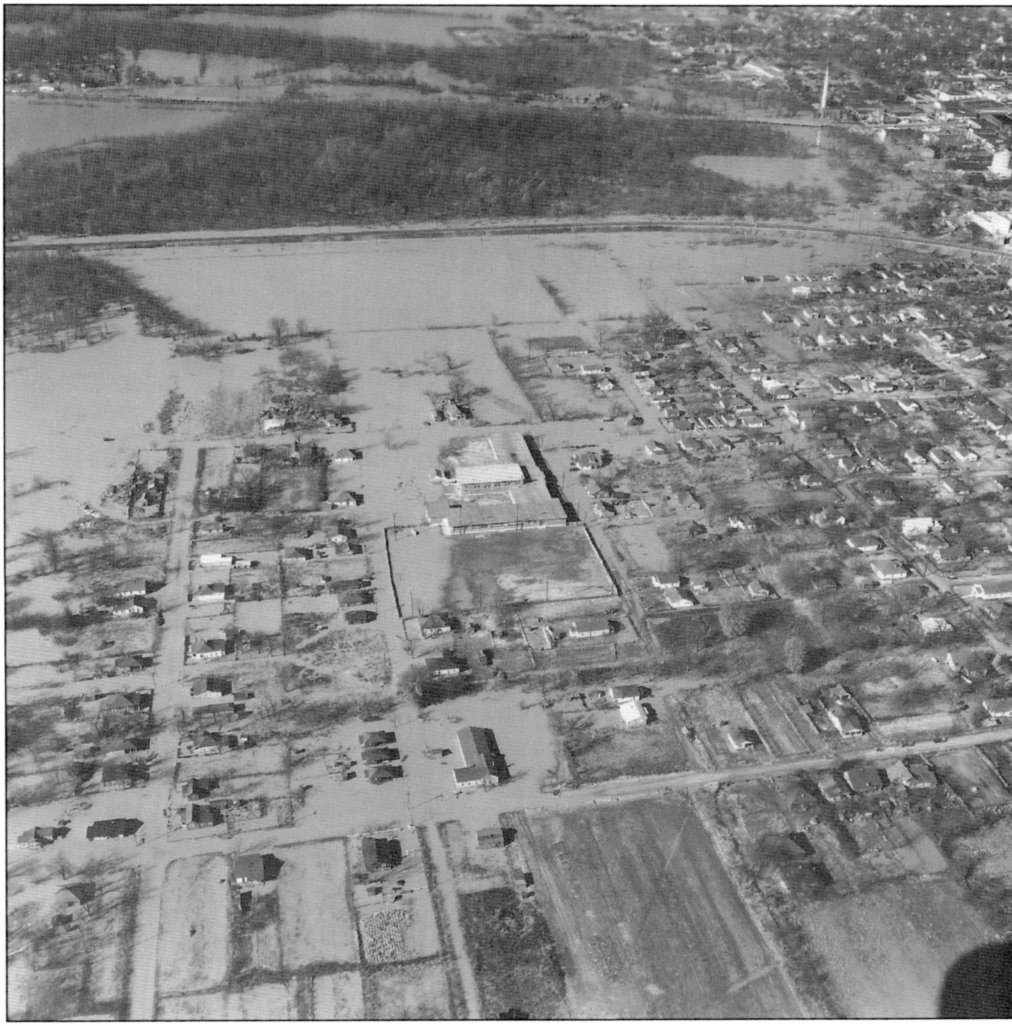

This c. 1955 aerial view of high water shows the Illinois Central Railroad running horizontally across the top of the photograph, with Highway 51 above. At the center of the photograph is Bruce School, which was established as an African American school serving the Bruce community, at right in this picture. (Courtesy Paula Ledford.)

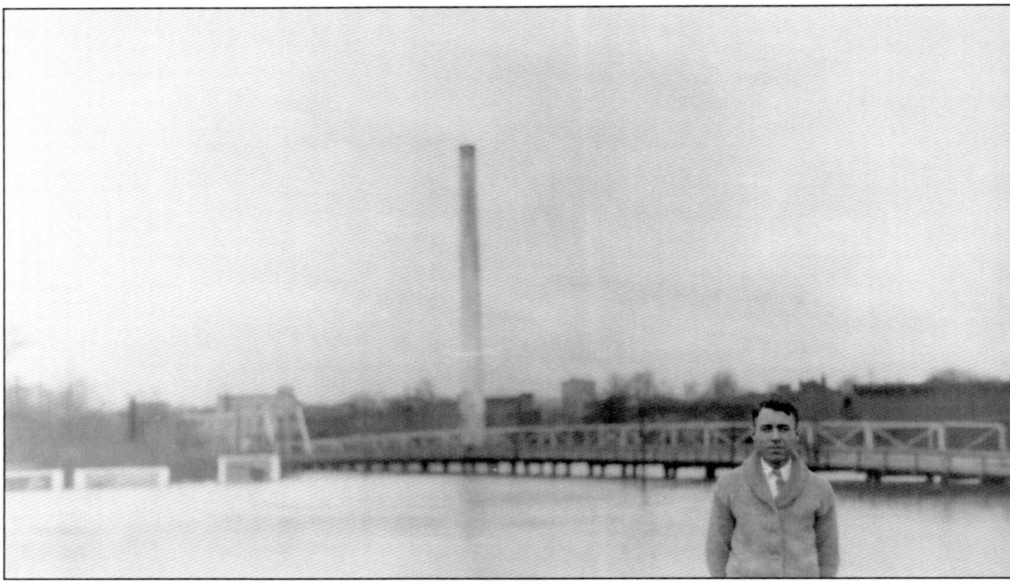

Jewell Reed, the son of town pharmacist Dr. John Reed, appears at the entrance to town in what is believed to be a snapshot of the 1927 flood that affected the entire Mississippi River, from Cairo to New Orleans. He is facing south, with the old Highway 51 bridge behind him. The 1927 Delta flood was one of the worst in recorded history, covering 27,000 square miles, causing $400 million in damages, and claiming at least 246 victims in seven states. (Courtesy John Reed.)

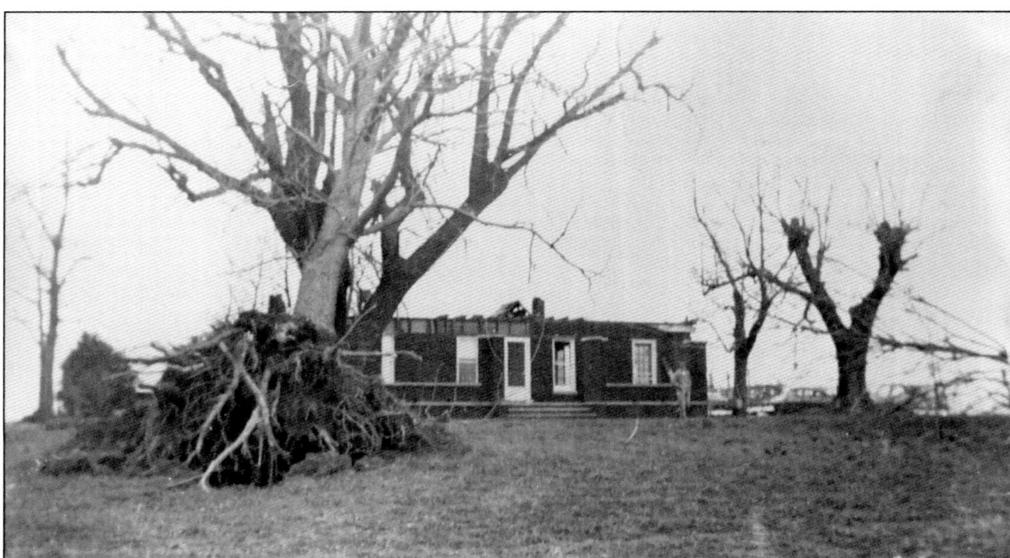

Dyersburg is located along what is commonly called Tornado Alley, where these storms tend to be most prevalent. In March 1952, houses, including this one at RoEllen, near Dyersburg, were damaged or destroyed by a F4 category tornado. The twister continued on a path through eastern Dyersburg, killing at least four people and causing as much as $500,000 in damages. It was one of the worst tornadoes ever recorded in Dyer County. (Courtesy Tennessee State Library and Archives.)

Seven

The Mill

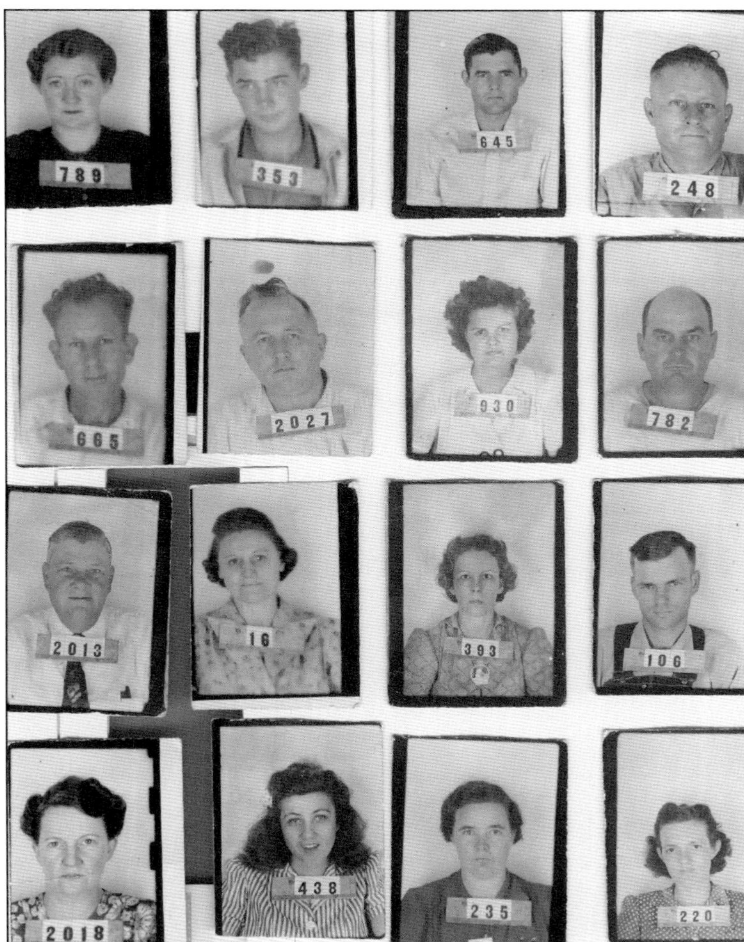

Some employees of Dyersburg Cotton Products in the 1940s are seen here in the photographs made for their identification badges. The company was born only seven months before the stock market crash of 1929. It struggled to survive before becoming a mainstay of Dyersburg that would employ as many as four generations of local families. In its early years, the mill produced cotton sweaters, long johns, and cotton gloves. In the late 1930s, it produced the first knitted fleece fabric, eventually becoming a leader in the fleece and pile industry. (Courtesy Billy Parmenter.)

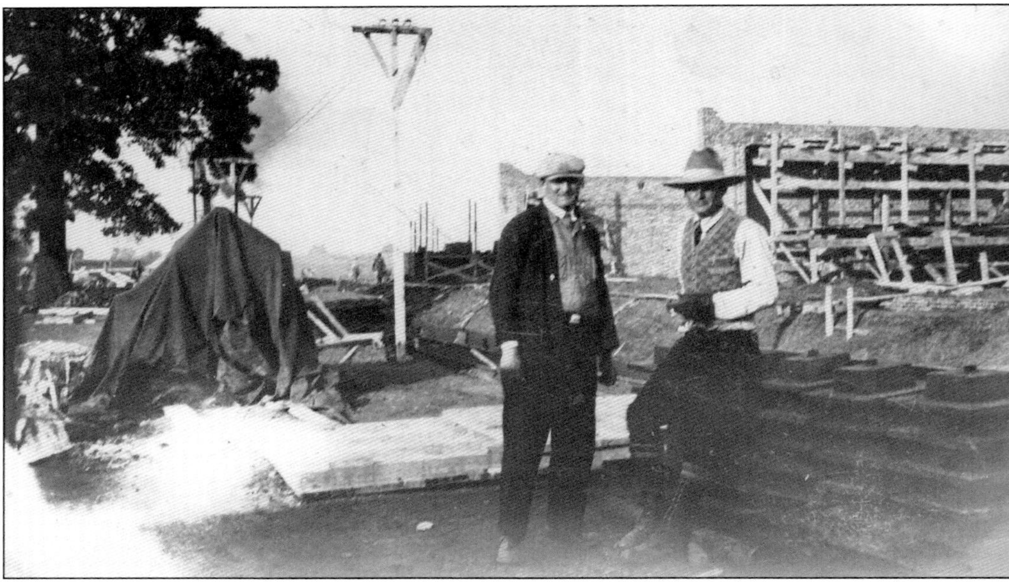

In 1928, R.H. Wheeler, representing Oswego Spinning Mill in New York, and Ladd J. Lewis, representing Adrian Spinning Mill in Michigan, took a train trip south looking for a site to locate a new plant. Dyersburg gave them a warm reception, and they lost no time in clearing cotton fields and constructing a 292,000-square-foot mill. (Courtesy Billy Parmenter.)

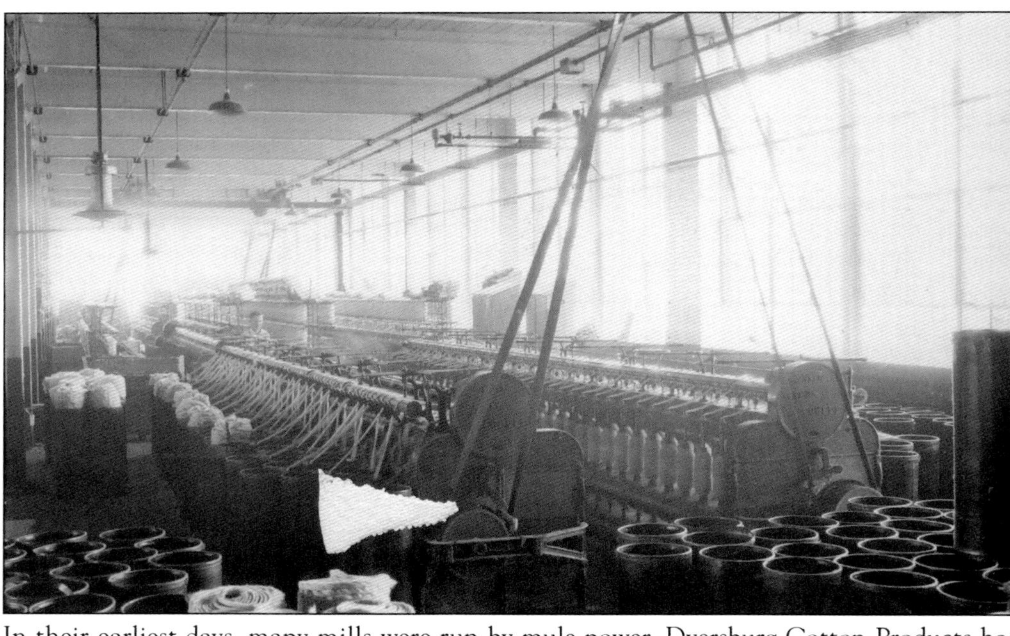

In their earliest days, many mills were run by mule power. Dyersburg Cotton Products had electricity from the beginning, but this room was still nicknamed the "mule room." Here, drawing machines slowly reduced the thickness of cotton strands as they wound through the machinery. (Courtesy Billy Parmenter.)

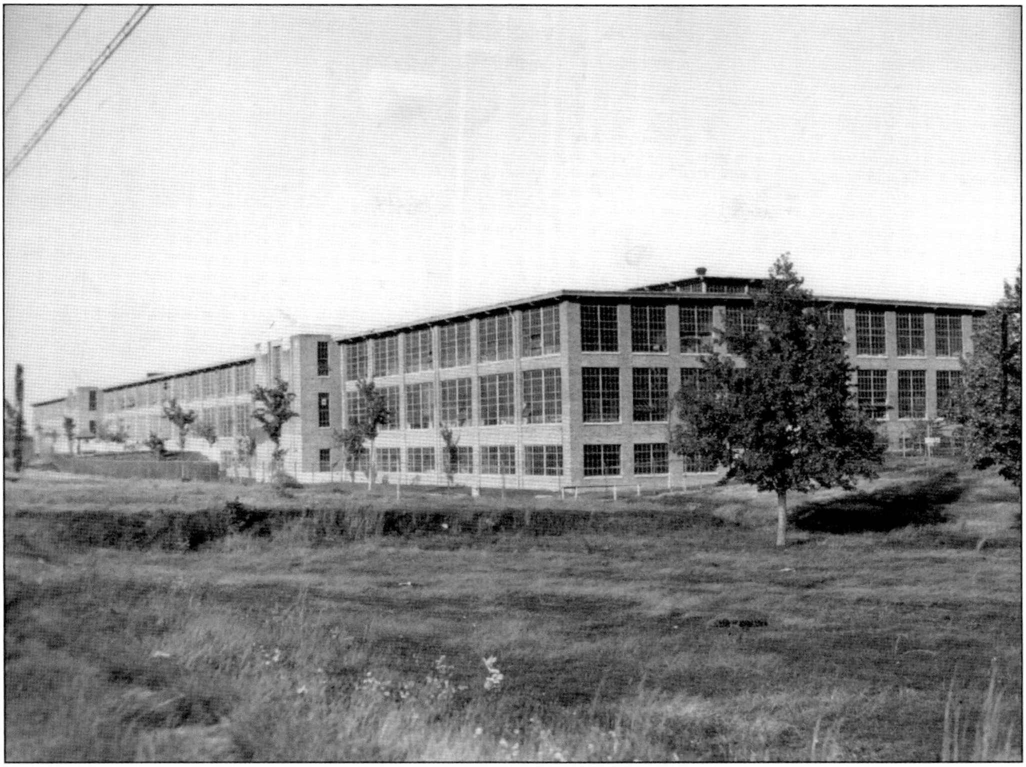

The plant was large from the very beginning, with around 1,500 employees. This was a time when producing cotton cloth was a labor-intensive process. Many women were required to cut and sew the fabric. The mill made "long-handled" underwear, knit material for gloves, cloth bags to hang meat for smoking and curing, cotton knit material for sweaters and other types of clothing, and later, cotton wadding for shells in World War II. (Courtesy University of Memphis Special Collections.)

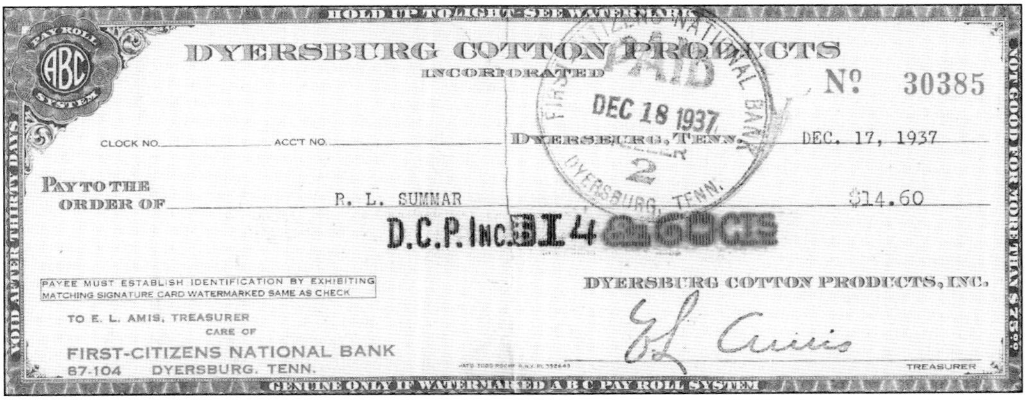

HOLD UP TO LIGHT—SEE WATERMARK

PAY ROLL ABC SYSTEM

DYERSBURG COTTON PRODUCTS
INCORPORATED

No 30385

CLOCK NO. ACCT NO. DYERSBURG, TENN. DEC. 17, 1937

PAY TO THE ORDER OF R. L. SUMMAR $14.60

D.C.P. INC.

PAID DEC 18 1937 FIRST CITIZENS NATIONAL BANK 2 DYERSBURG, TENN.

PAYEE MUST ESTABLISH IDENTIFICATION BY EXHIBITING MATCHING SIGNATURE CARD WATERMARKED SAME AS CHECK

TO E. L. AMIS, TREASURER
CARE OF
FIRST-CITIZENS NATIONAL BANK
87-104 DYERSBURG, TENN.

DYERSBURG COTTON PRODUCTS, INC.
E L Amis
TREASURER

VOID AFTER THIRTY DAYS

NOT GOOD FOR MORE THAN $75.00

GENUINE ONLY IF WATERMARKED A B C PAY ROLL SYSTEM

A pay stub from the early years of the cotton mill bears the stamp of E.L. Amis, an early officer of the mill. When the mill first opened in 1929, the average wage was about 18¢ an hour. Mill hands would work as much as 10.5 hours a day, five days a week, and sometimes a half day on Saturday, but the work was steady and it allowed the little town to grow. Even in the worst days of the Depression, the mill paid its workers with scrip that was redeemable at local stores. (Courtesy R.L. Summar family.)

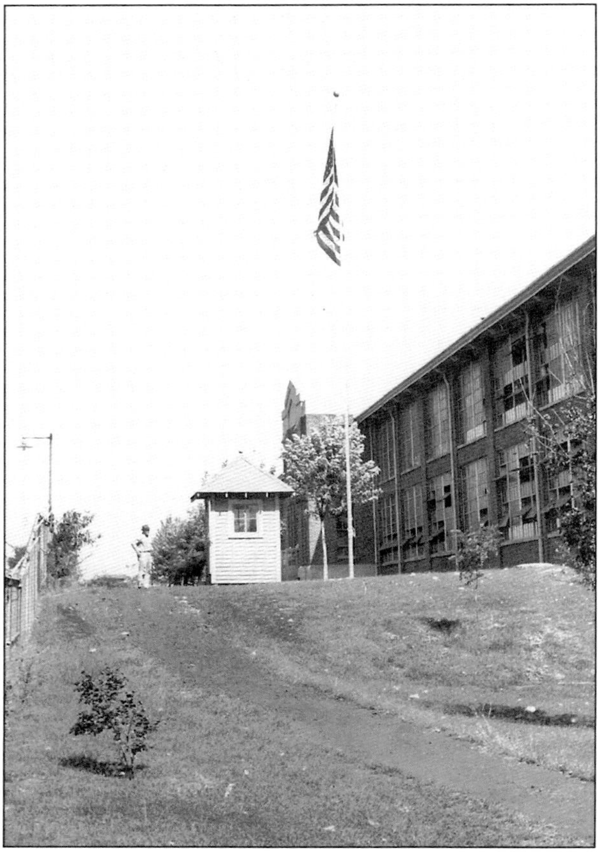

In the early 1930s, R.H. Wheeler took over as president of the mill, and it truly flourished. Accountant E.L. Amis was given the assignment of employee relations, and he took steps to deeply attach the company to the Dyersburg community. In this photograph can be seen the flagpole and guard shack put up at the outbreak of World War II. (Courtesy R.L. Summar family.)

By 1940, the payroll had settled to about 650 people. This reflected the arrival of better equipment, which resulted in fewer women being needed to cut and sew the fabrics by hand. Also, many Dyersburg men had left the mill to serve in World War II. (Courtesy R.L. Summar family.)

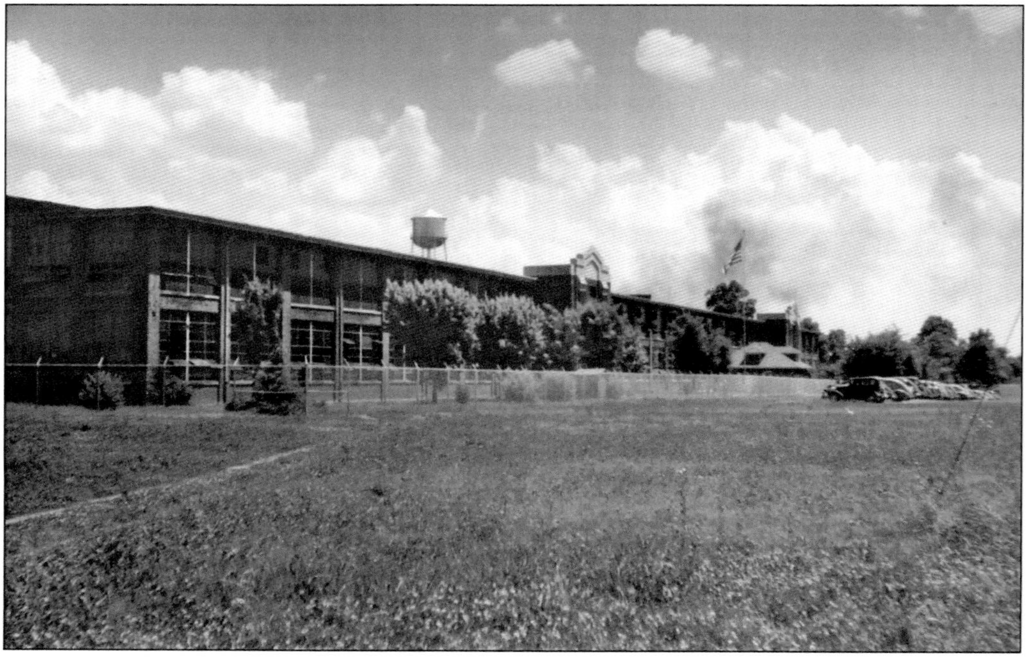

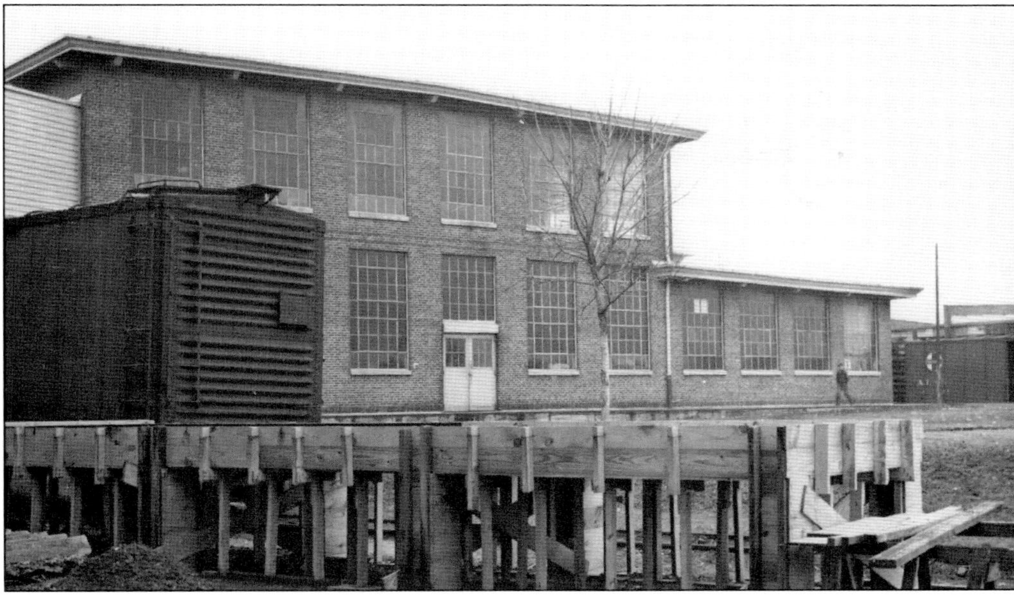

The wooden structure behind the mill is the shuttle track that was used to unload coal from boxcars; a small pile of coal can be seen to the left. The coal was used to provide steam in the boiler room of the mill. (Courtesy Billy Parmenter.)

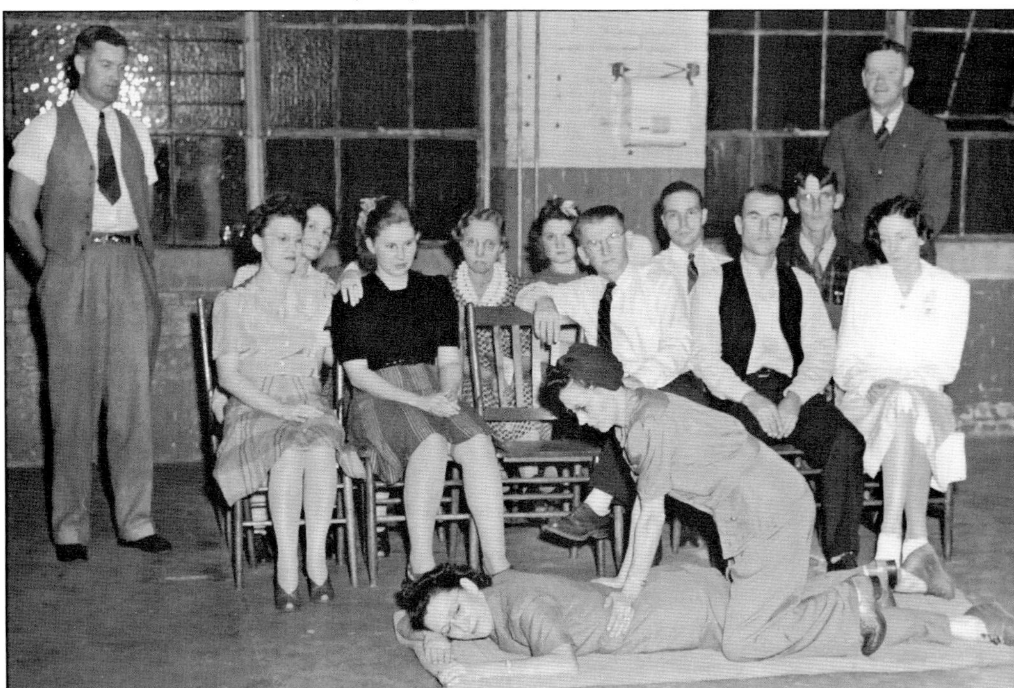

In the early 1940s, company employees attend a CPR training class. As World War II approached, the mill geared up to prepare its employees for any necessity or emergency that might arise. The mill launched a war bond drive with 100-percent participation, which earned it the Treasury Department's Minute Man Award. (Courtesy R.L. Summar family.)

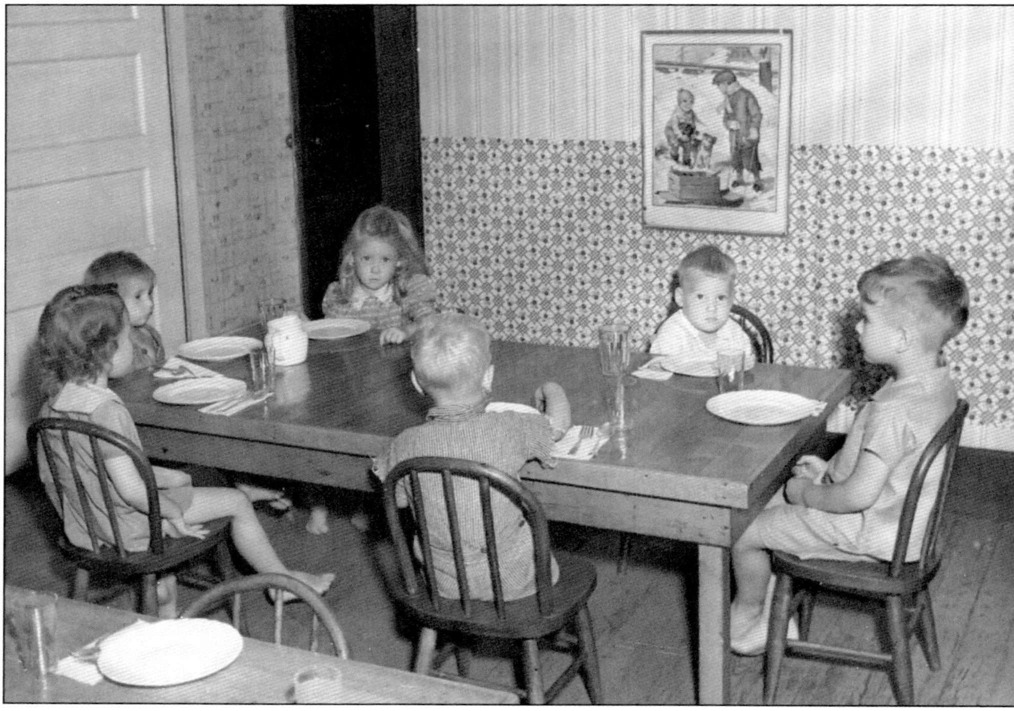

During World War II, as men left to serve in the war, many women came to work at the mill, creating a need for child care. The company solved this problem by renting a home in nearby Milltown and creating a nursery school. Complete with lessons and meals, it provided care for Milltown children as their parents spent long hours at work. (Both, courtesy Billy Parmenter.)

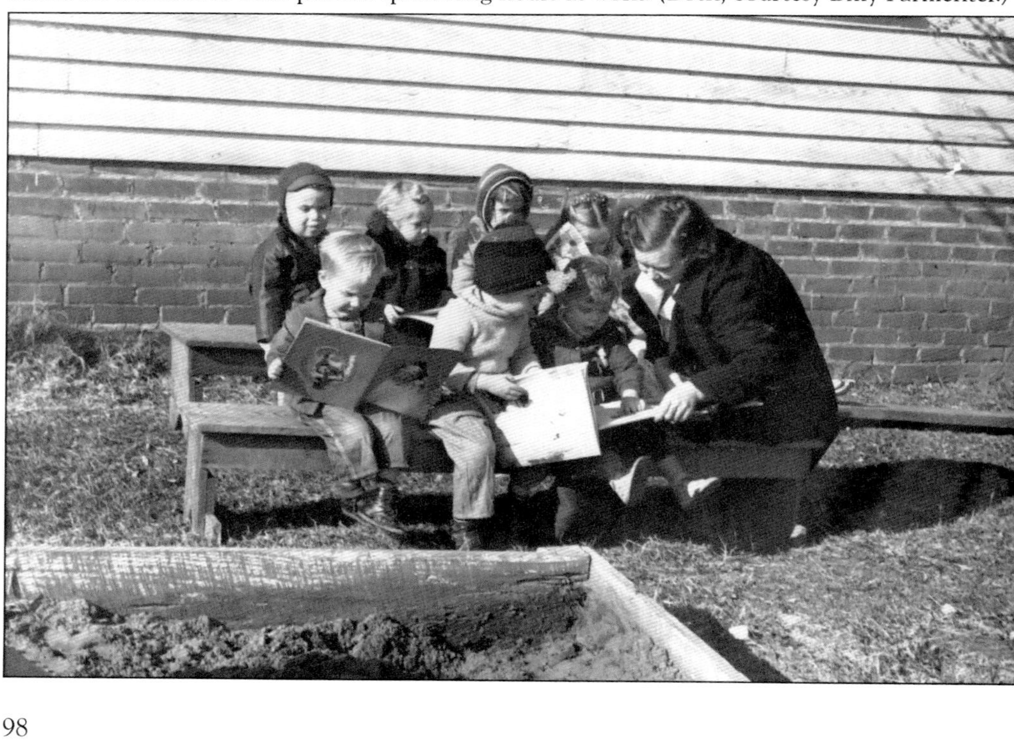

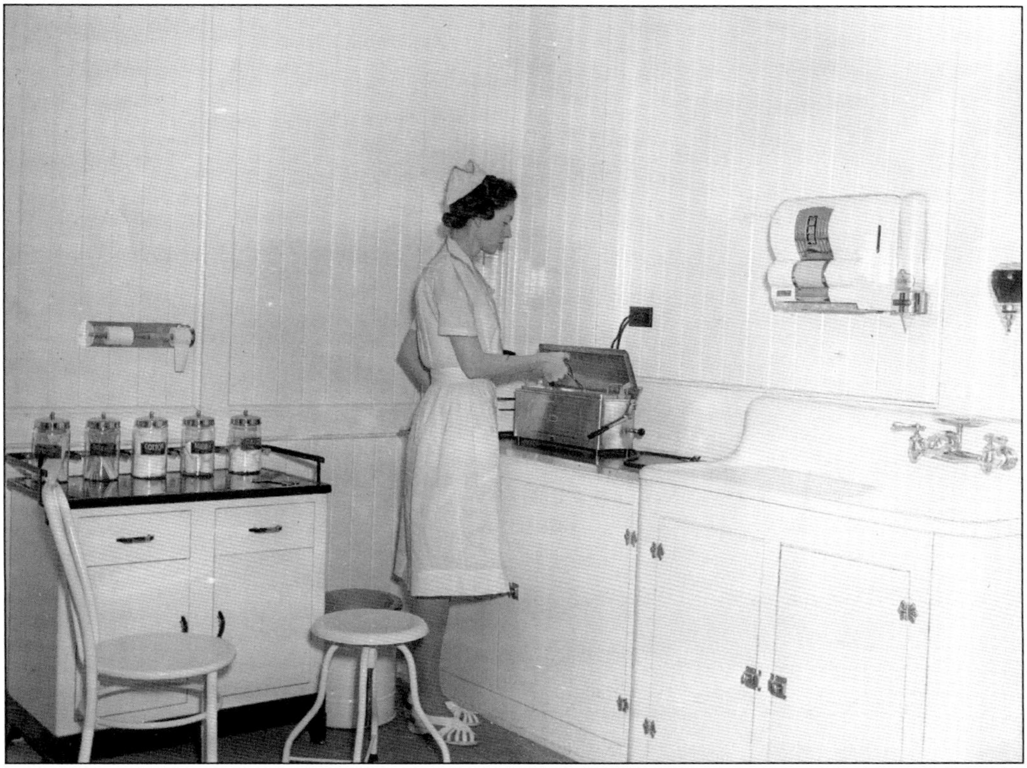

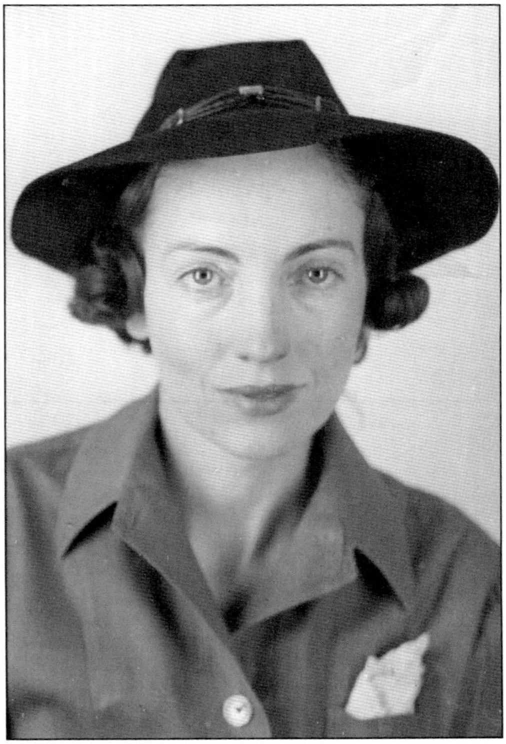

Oma Caldwell was head of the Dyersburg Cotton Products' first aid department, and she ran the infirmary for many years. There was a fully equipped nursing station in the mill for employees' needs. During World War II, Caldwell organized female employees to help fold bandages for the armed forces. (Both, courtesy Billy Parmenter.)

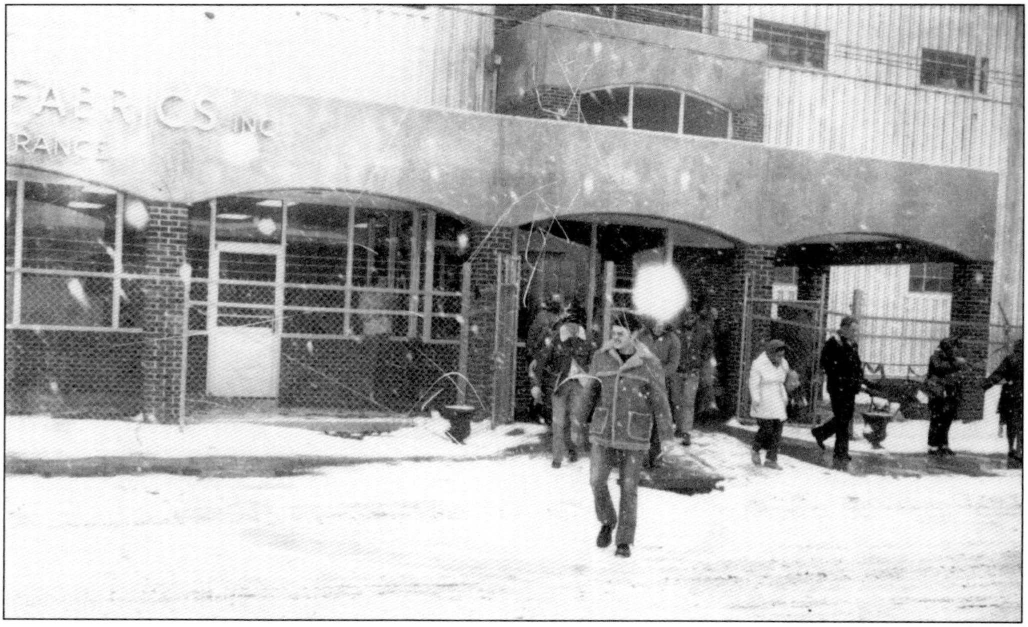

Unlike the children at nearby Jennie Bell Elementary School, millworkers did not get "snow days" off. Cold weather often inspired humorous tall tales in the mill's newspaper, the *Spinnit*, such as stories of how icicles grew so long around someone's roof that they finally lifted the house off the foundation, so that the homeowner needed a ladder just to climb in and out of his house. (Both, courtesy Billy Parmenter.)

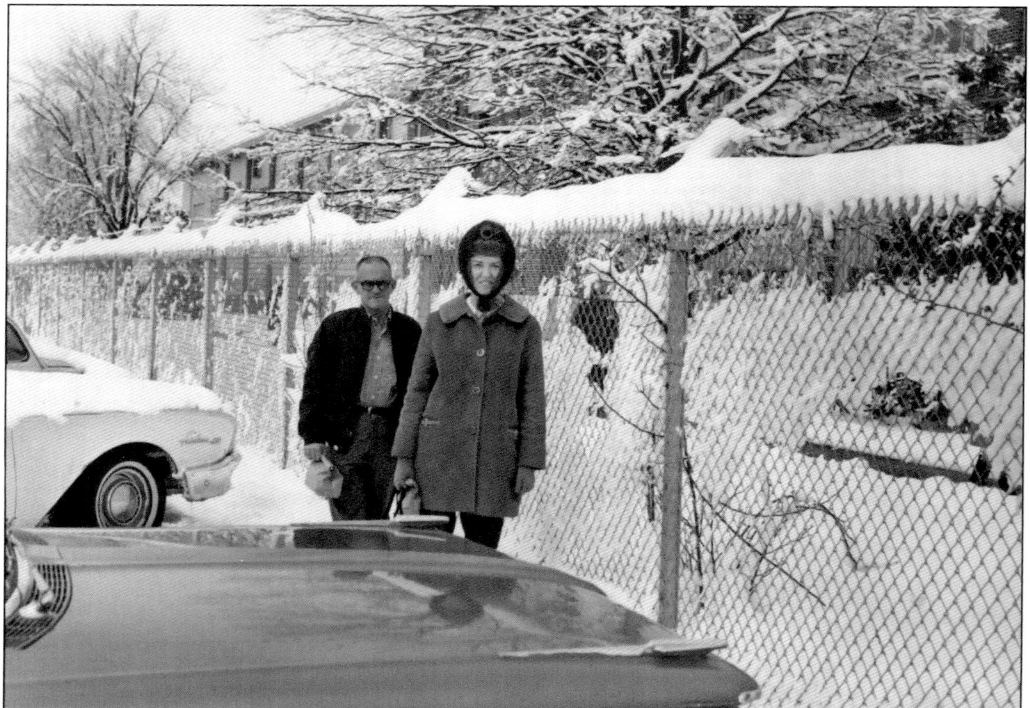

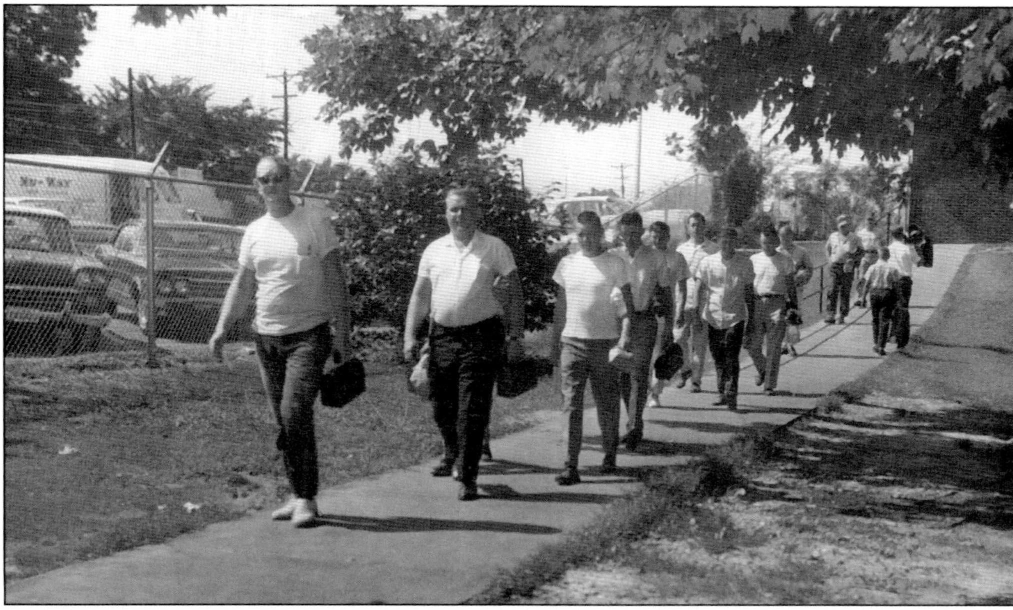

Dye House employees file toward the south entrance of the mill at shift change time, carrying their lunch boxes. For many years, Dye House workers had to bring their own lunches rather than use the mill cafeteria because they could not leave the fabric once the dye process started. Millworkers remember days when the work was so busy, no one had time to eat at all, and they had to take lunch back home at the end of the day. (Courtesy Billy Parmenter.)

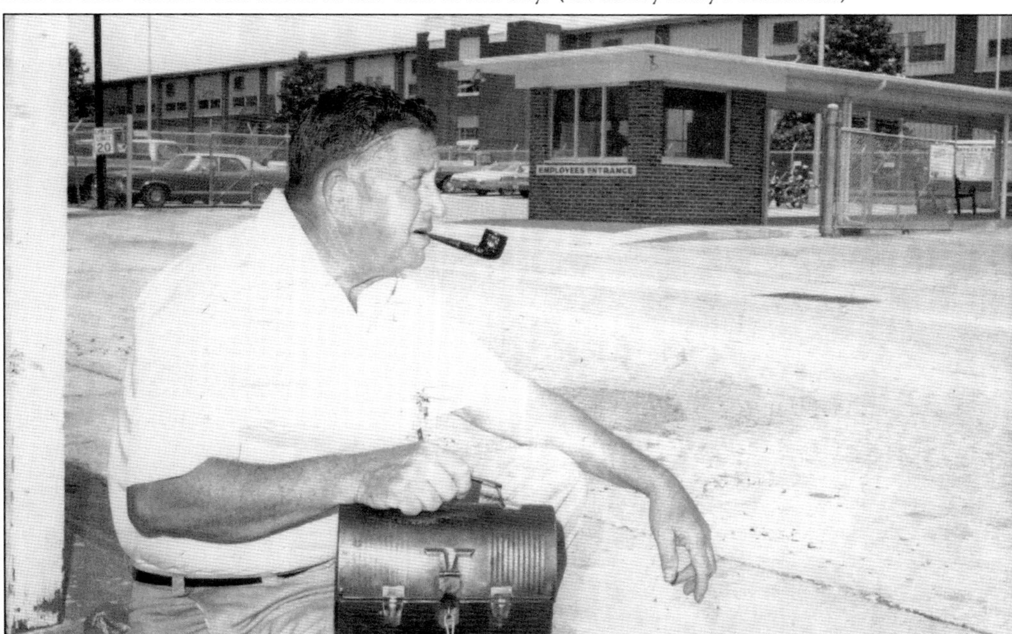

Willie Wheeler (no relation to R.H. Wheeler), a longtime employee of the mill, waits to report to work on the second shift. Coworkers remember that he was so superstitious, if there were 13 rolls of cloth in a batch, he would separate a roll in order to keep them from totaling 13. (Courtesy Billy Parmenter.)

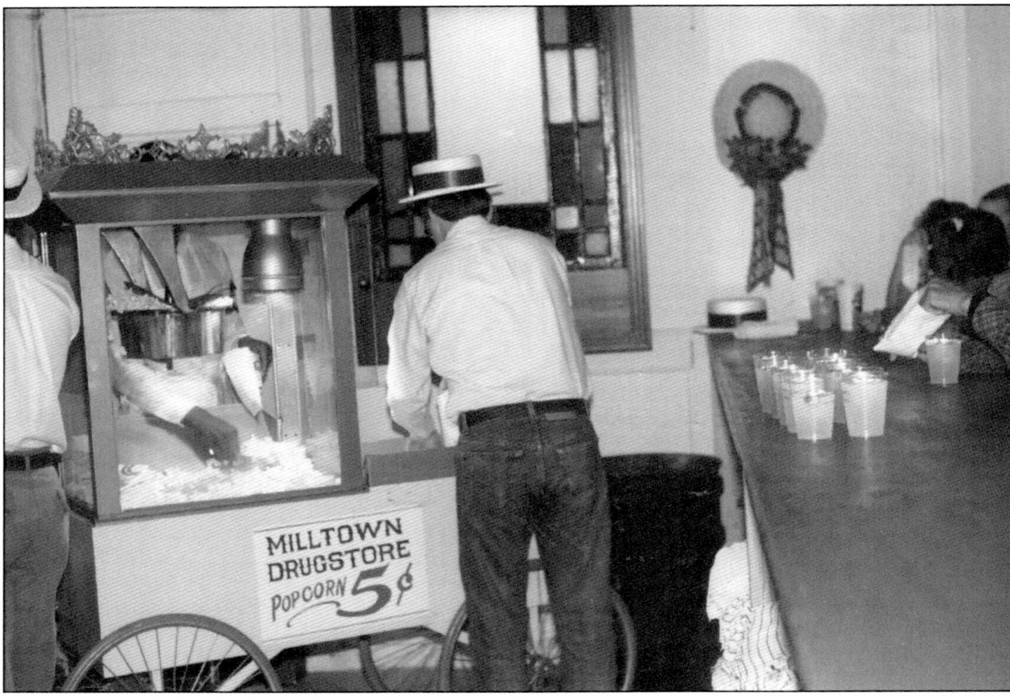

A popcorn machine highlights one of the many fun events that the mill management provided for employees. There were parties and celebrations, and the mill had its own bowling league that played on Tuesday nights. Each December, on a designated Saturday morning, there was a pancake breakfast that was well attended, and each November, beginning in 1959, there was an annual employee recognition dinner honoring longtime employees. (Courtesy Billy Parmenter.)

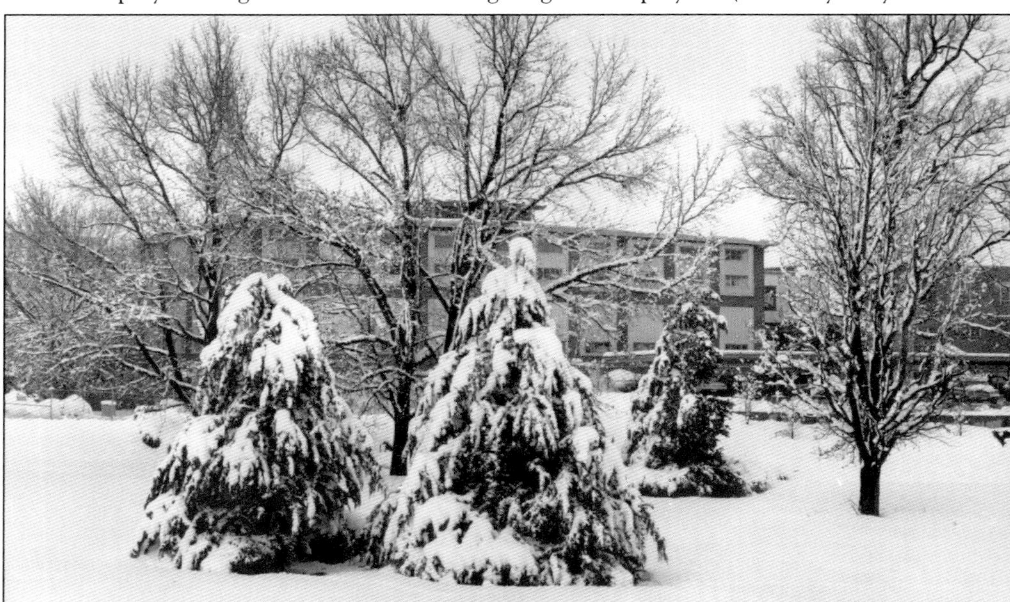

A rare Southern snow decorates the trees around the mill. During the Christmas season, the small evergreen trees in the center of the photograph were strung with lights. (Courtesy Billy Parmenter.)

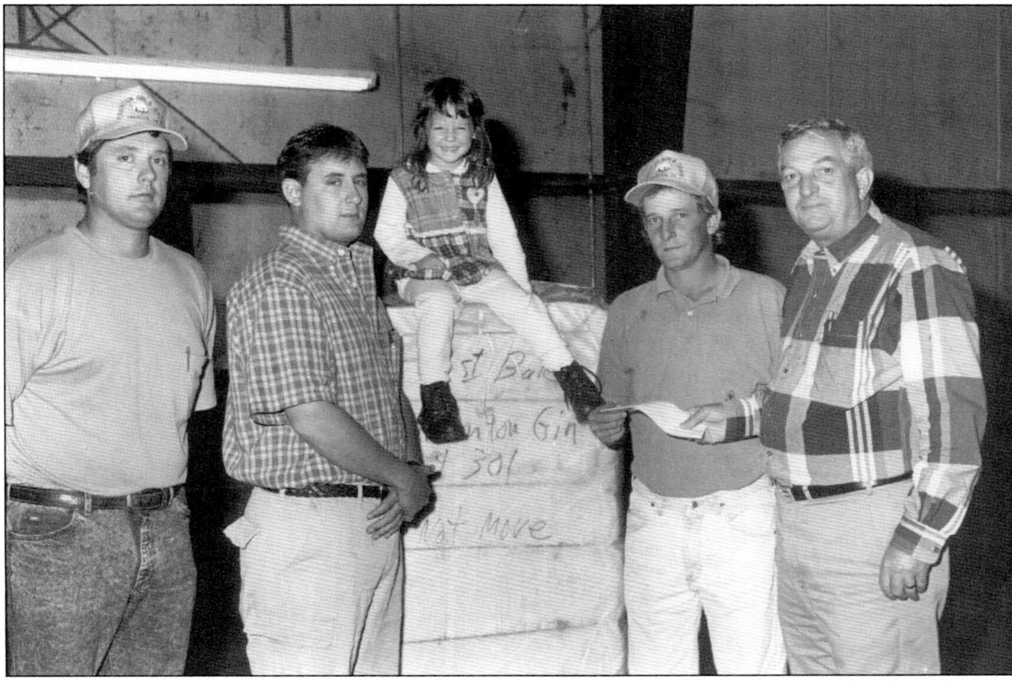

Each year, the first bale of cotton ginned in Dyer County was proudly put on display. This one is from the early 1980s. Each year, the mill would purchase the first ginned bale for a premium price and put it on display in the lobby of First Citizens National Bank. This was no small feat as a single cotton bale can weigh as much as 600 pounds. (Courtesy Billy Parmenter.)

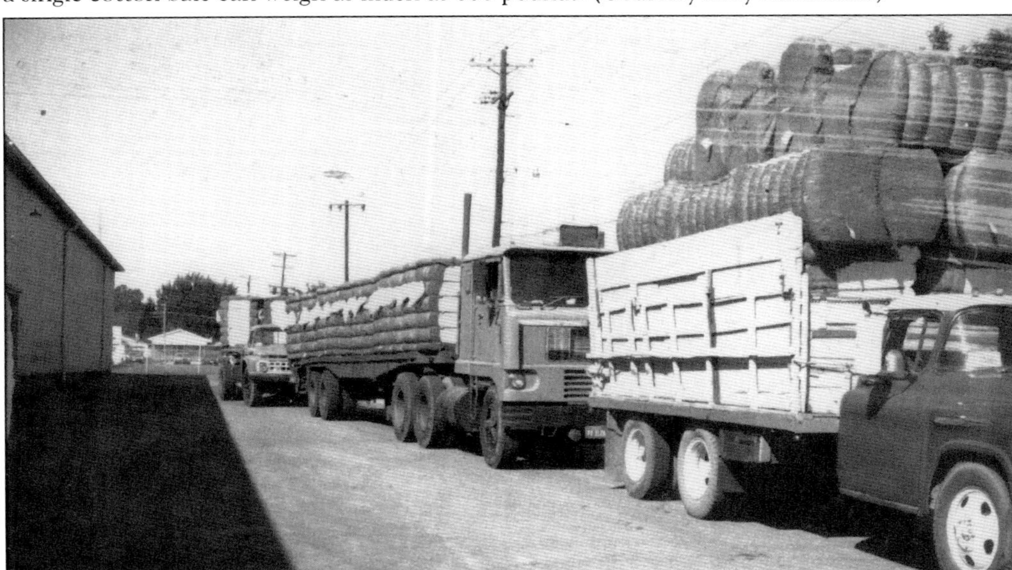

Trucks line up at the mill, bringing their loads of cotton bales purchased from local gins. The bales would be taken inside and processed into cloth. For decades, there were more than two dozen cotton gins in Dyer County, and cotton was the mainstay of the town. (Courtesy Billy Parmenter.)

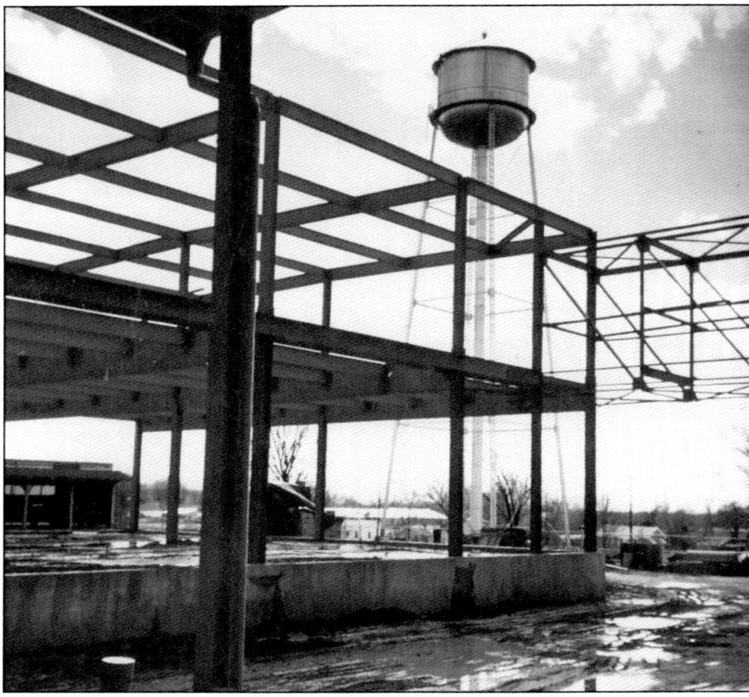

The cotton mill's original water tower was made of wood. Eventually, a more modern tower made of metal replaced it. The metal tower is seen here through scaffolding as a new part of the mill—an expansion of the Dye House—was constructed in the mid-1980s. In the photograph below, also taken in the mid-1980s, the Goodyear Blimp hovers over the tower on a trip downriver to Memphis, 70 miles away. (Both, courtesy Billy Parmenter.)

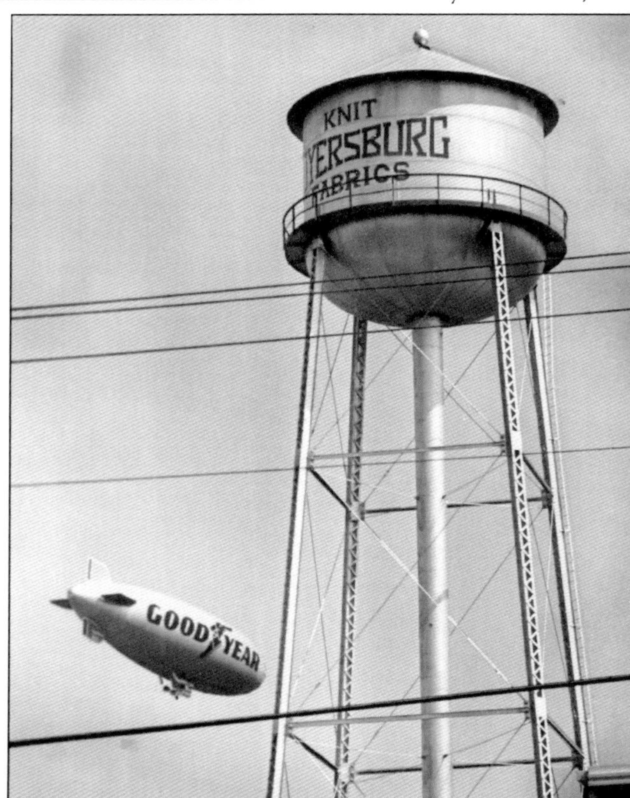

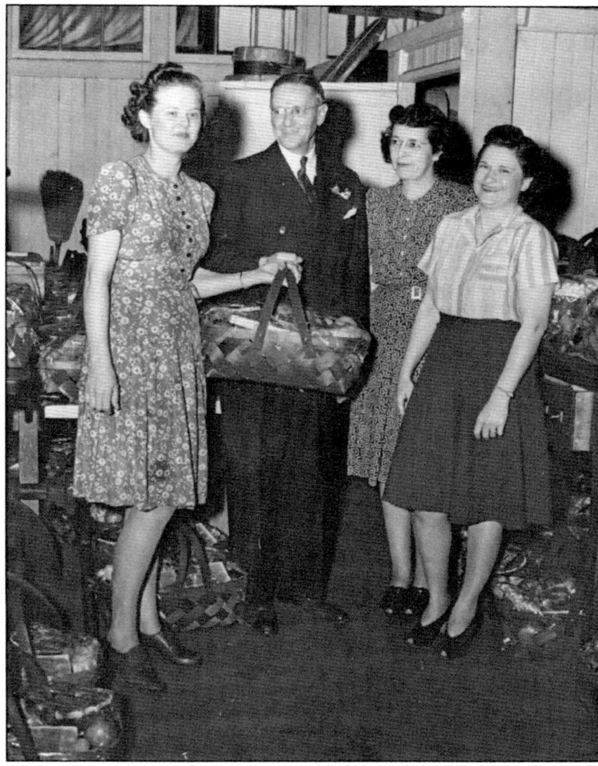

In a photograph from the 1940s (right), employees receive Christmas baskets from R.H. Wheeler, company president. The mill provided fare for Christmas dinner to the families of Milltown for decades. In the image below, employees file out at the end of the day carrying the split oak baskets home to their families. The *Spinnit* often carried accounts of employees' holiday plans and the large family dinners they hosted. (Both, courtesy Billy Parmenter.)

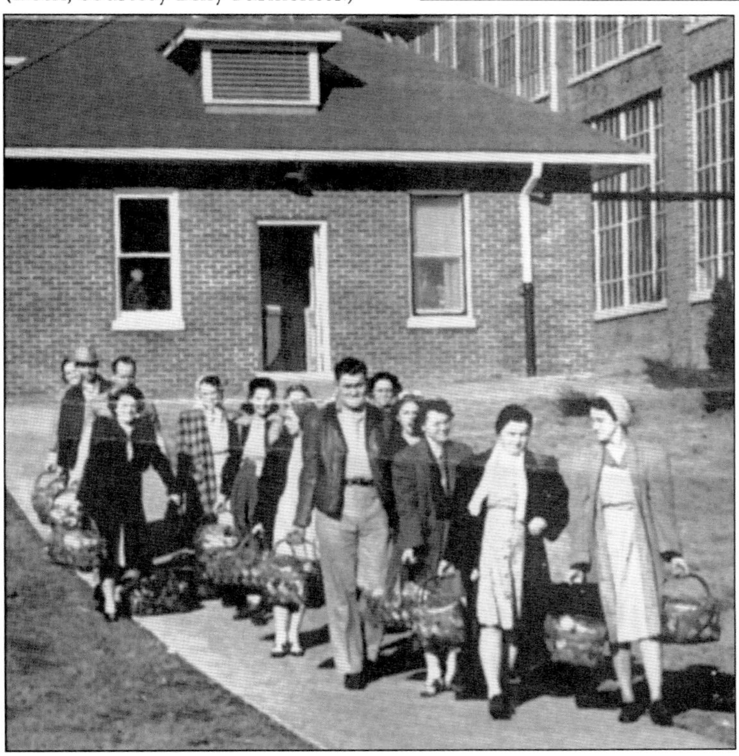

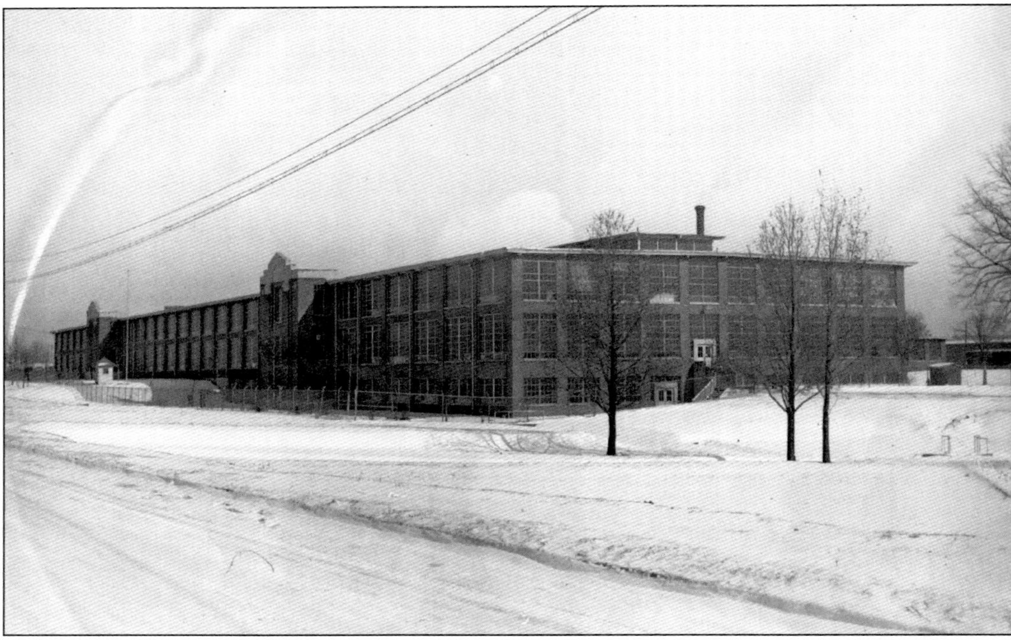

In the photograph above, snow blankets the cotton mill on a quiet day in the 1930s. The southwest corner is facing outward. The facility was still new, and most of the landscaping was yet to be done. The image below, taken on another snowy day about 20 years later, reveals a view from one of those corner windows. A sidewalk now leads from the mill to the corner of Harrell Avenue and Phillips Street, and juniper trees have been planted along it. During the holiday season, the evergreens were decorated with strings of lights. (Above, courtesy Chris Gibbons collection; below, courtesy R.L. Summar family.)

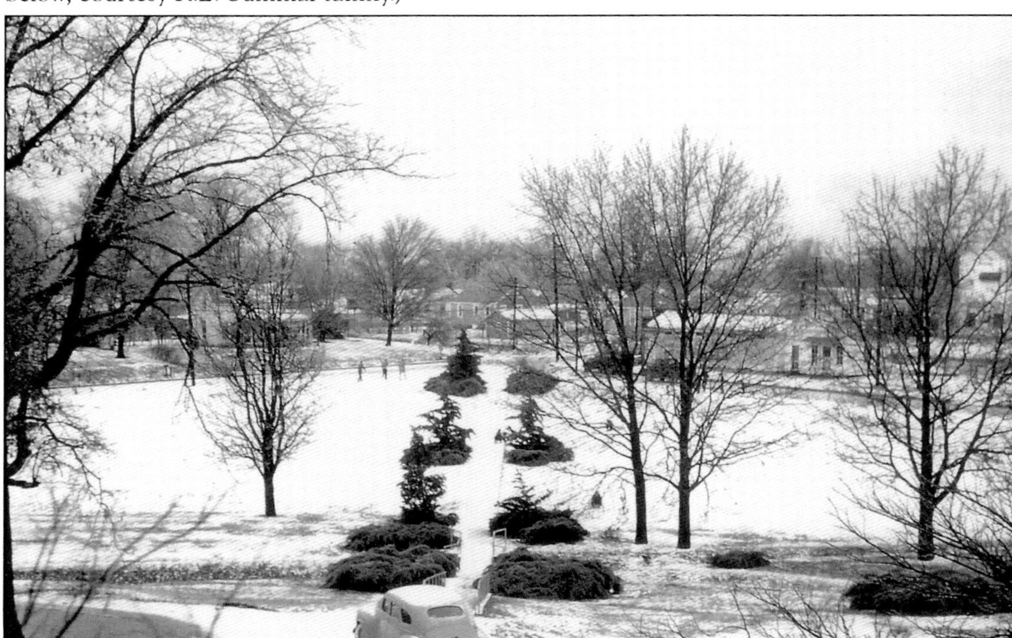

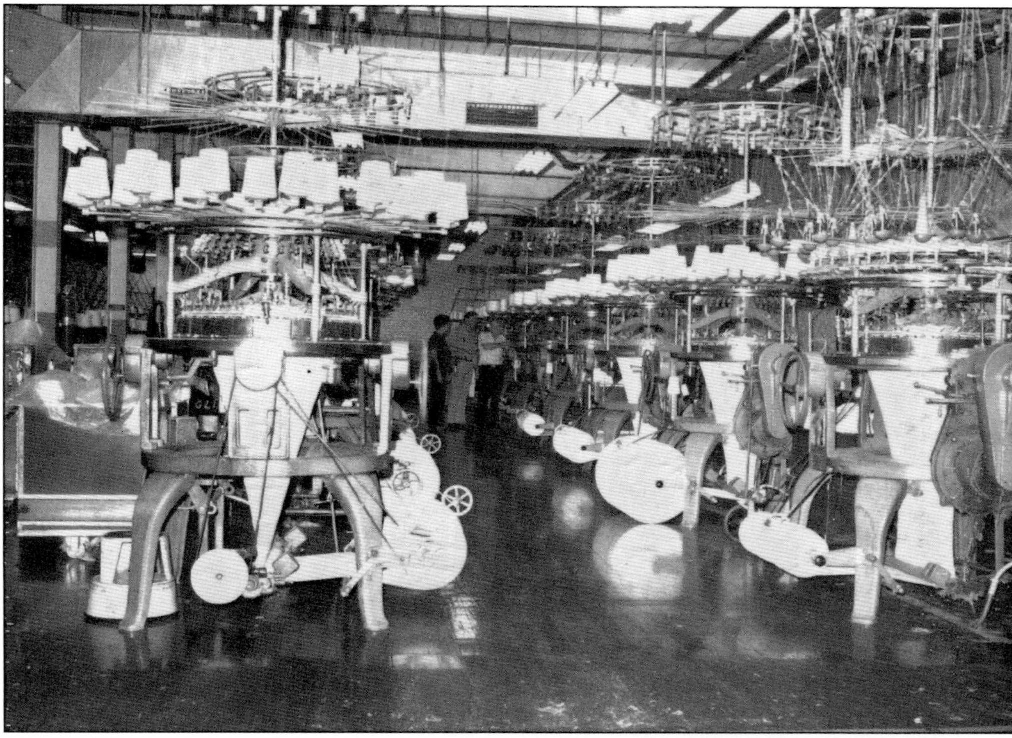

Pictured above is one of the mill's knitting rooms, where thread was knit into rolls of cloth. The latch-needle machinery in this photograph is one of two types of knitting machines; the other type was spring-needle. In the image at right, a mill employee is making cones of thread like those seen at the upper left in the photograph above. (Both, courtesy Billy Parmenter.)

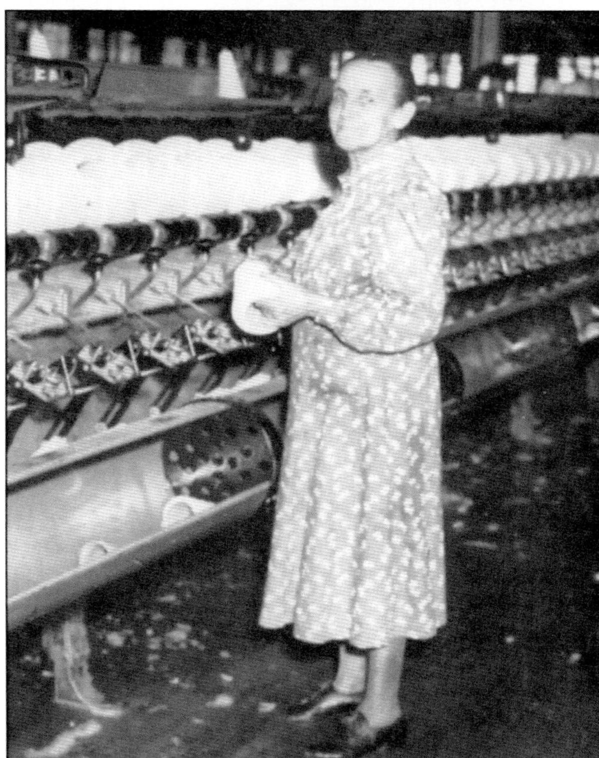

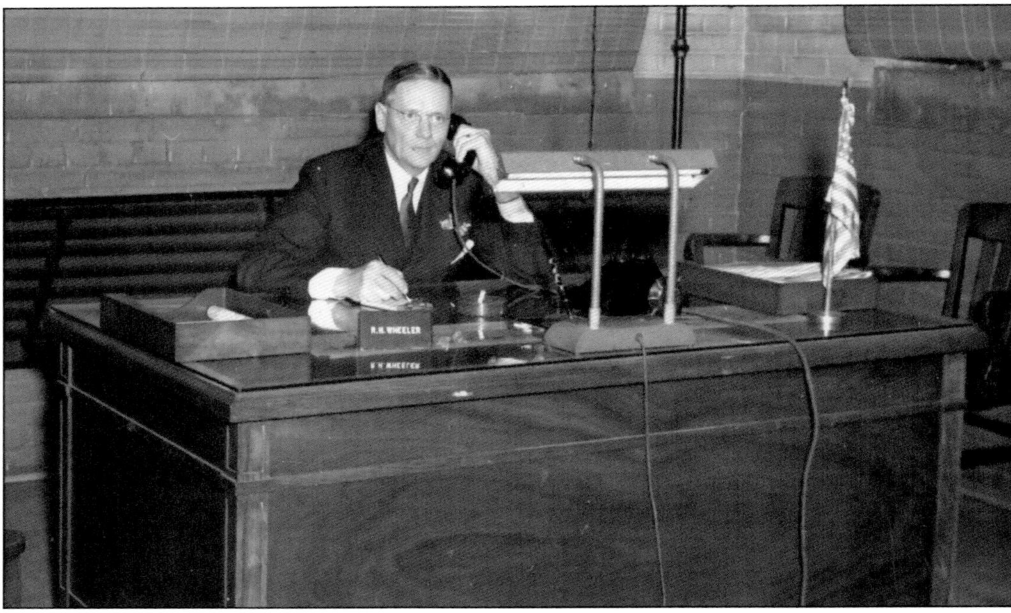

R.H. Wheeler, mill president, is pictured at his desk in the late 1940s. After more than 40 years of manufacturing all-wool, wool-blend, and cotton fabrics, the mill expanded into synthetics in the 1960s, becoming a leader in the fleece and pile industry. In 1969, the company changed its name to Dyersburg Fabrics to more accurately reflect its products. (Courtesy Billy Parmenter.)

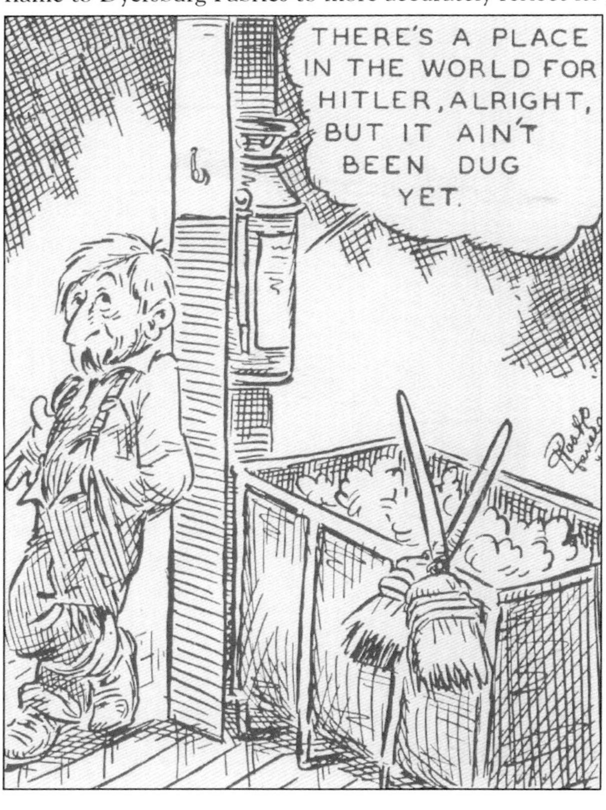

In 1940, the *Spinnit* published its first issue. E.L. Amis edited it and took the photographs. The first editions were only four pages long, but by the 1970s, the paper ran 12 to 14 pages. Amis drew his own original cartoons for the paper, including this one about Hitler. He would often be caught in meetings quietly sketching ideas for the next issue.

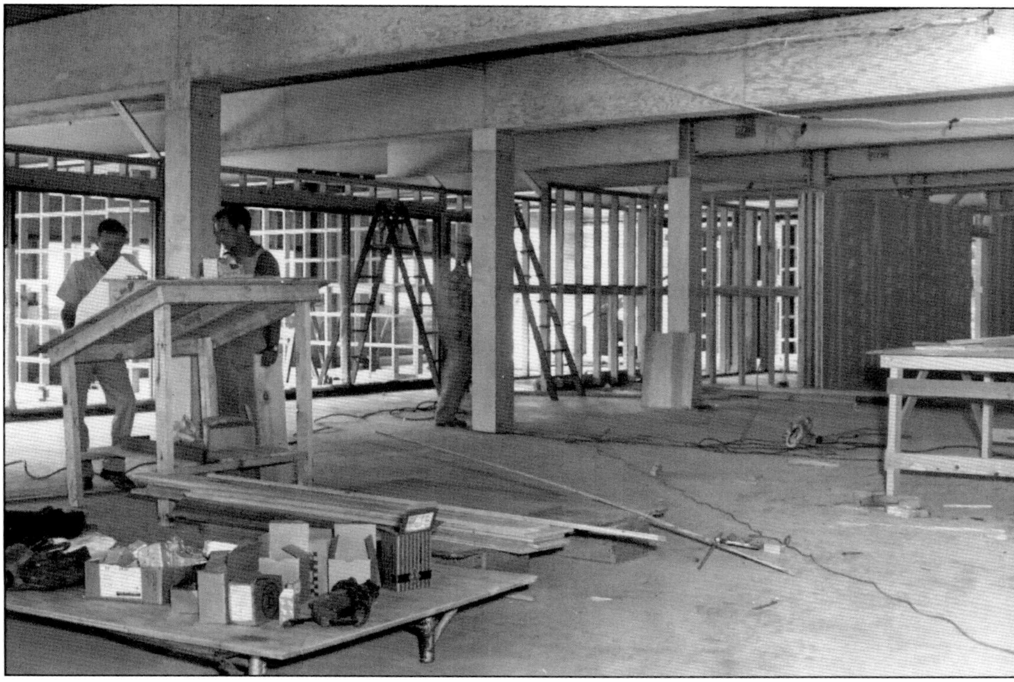

The mill grew steadily through the years. In the photograph above, new construction is underway in the 1980s, and below, knitting machines are loaded onto a crane to be moved to the new Knitting Building complex. During the 1960s, Congress called for regulations that would make children's clothing, especially nightwear, more flame resistant. Dyersburg was the first facility to produce material that met the government's new standards, and the mill expanded. By 1976, it had become the country's top acrylic fleece producer. (Both, courtesy Billy Parmenter.)

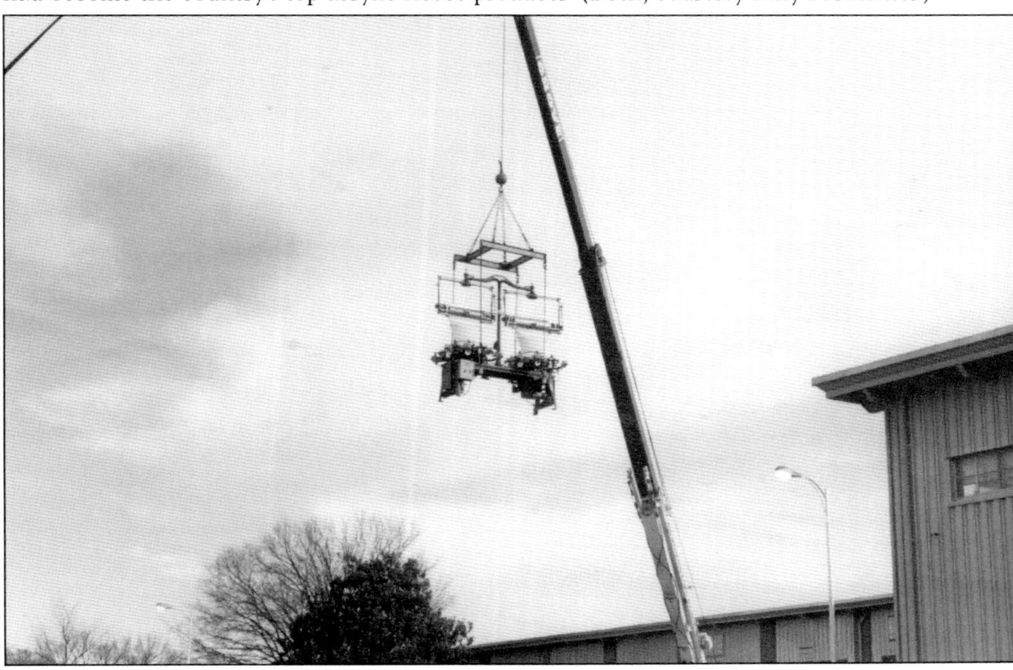

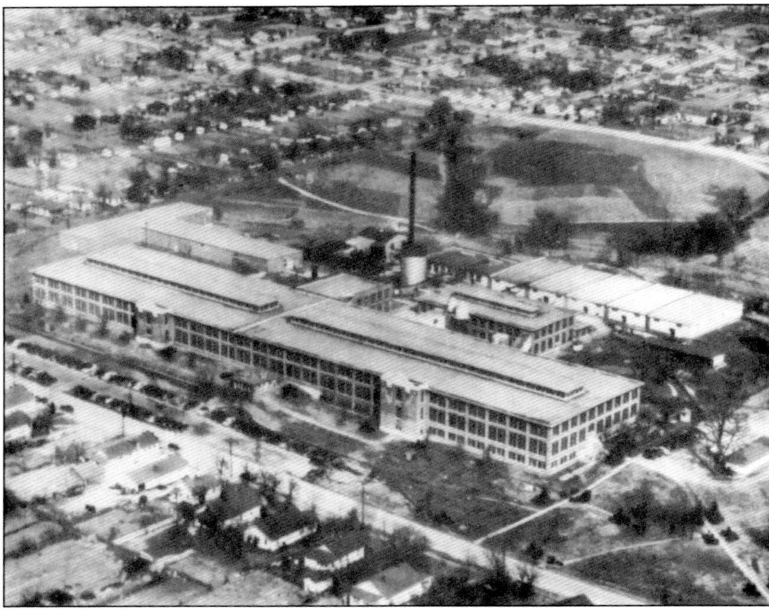

Aerial views of the cotton mill through the years show how the mill grew to become the centerpiece of the town. In its early days, employees worked from 6:00 a.m. to 6:00 p.m. At the height of production, there were four shifts, including weekends. In later years, the work was divided between two shifts.

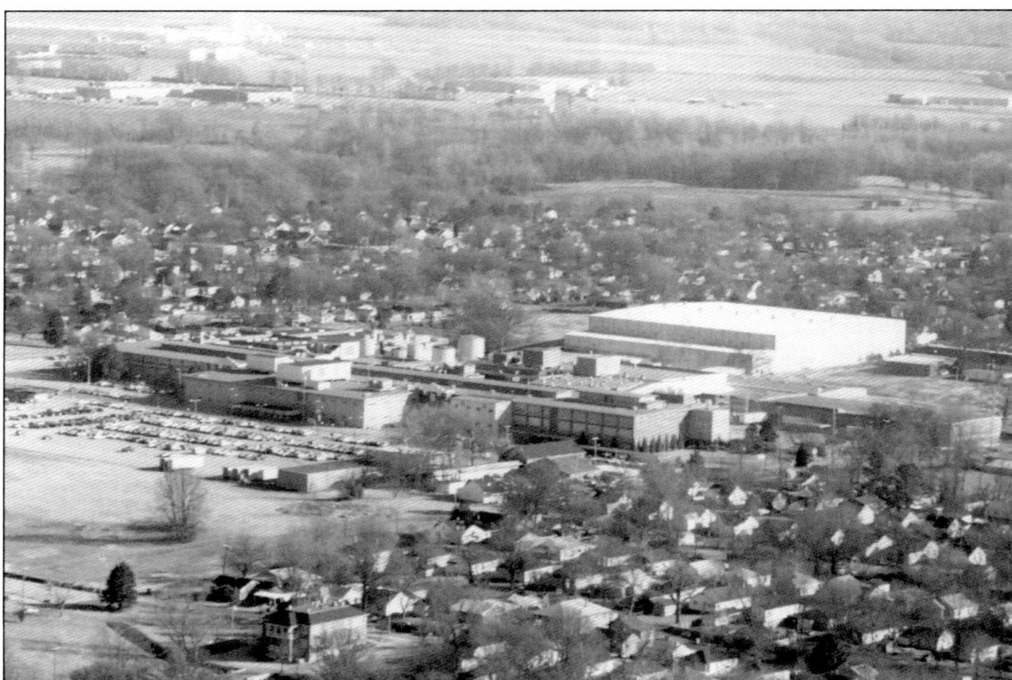

In the early 1990s, the company did well with its own branded outerwear fleece products. Its fleece fabric was the first to be made from recycled plastic soda bottles. In December 1993, the company opened its new knitting facility. It had 155,000 square feet and was located at the Dyersburg Industrial Park, which covered 30 acres, including the original facility. At times, three generations of the same family were working at the mill at the same time. In the photograph above, some of the nearly identical houses of Milltown can be seen. There were 99 houses in all. (Courtesy Billy Parmenter.)

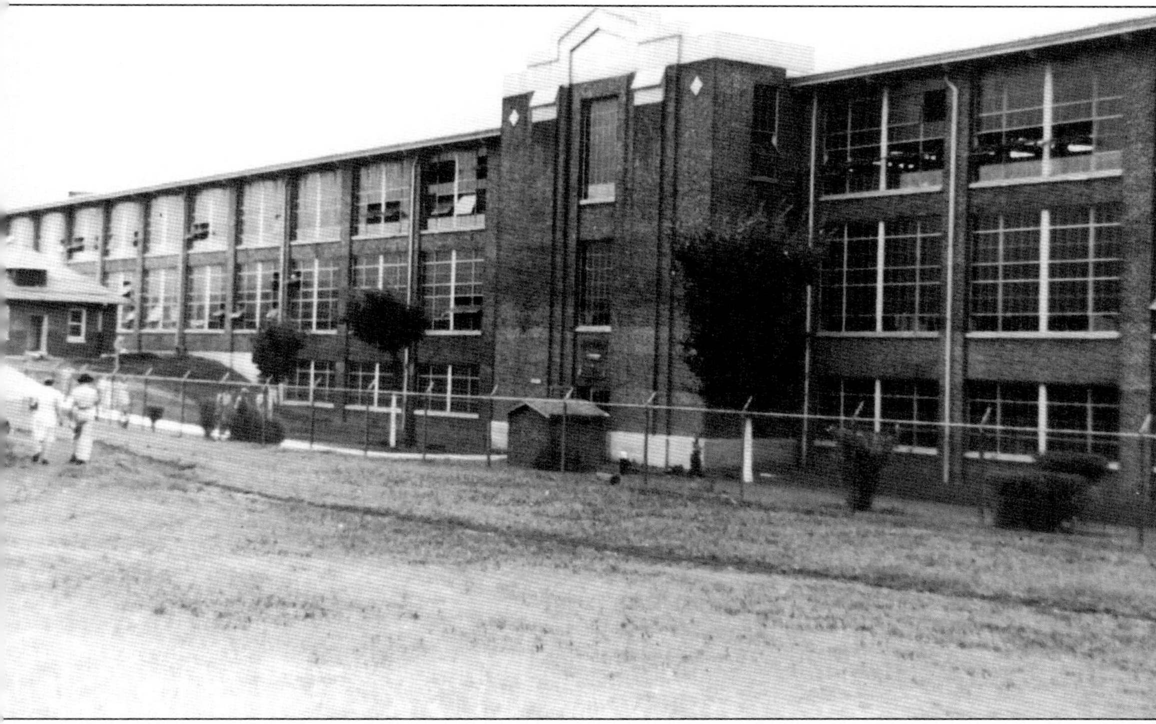

The small structure at the center of this photograph is the original firehouse. Especially after it was expanded, the firehouse was the spot where smokers gathered. They called themselves "the Hunkerin' and Hankerin' Club" because they were hunkering down in the firehouse and hankering for a cigarette. The louvered windows seen in this photograph were later removed when central air-conditioning came to most of the mill.

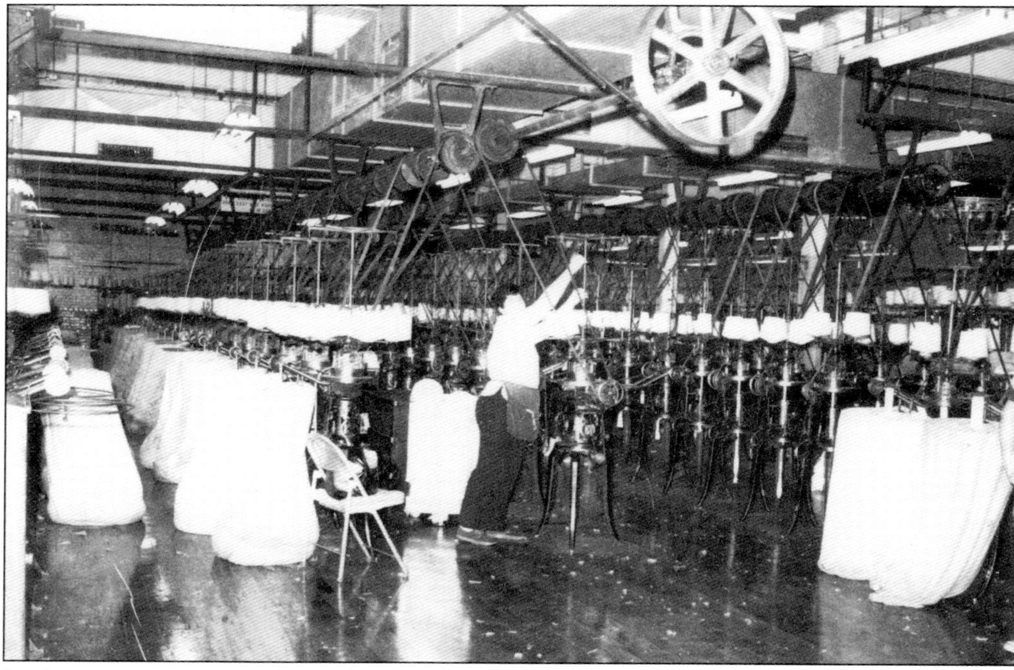

In the equipment room, these white bags would catch yarn as it unspooled. It was said that the mill was constantly in a state of new construction for most of its existence, as demand for its products grew. (Courtesy Billy Parmenter.)

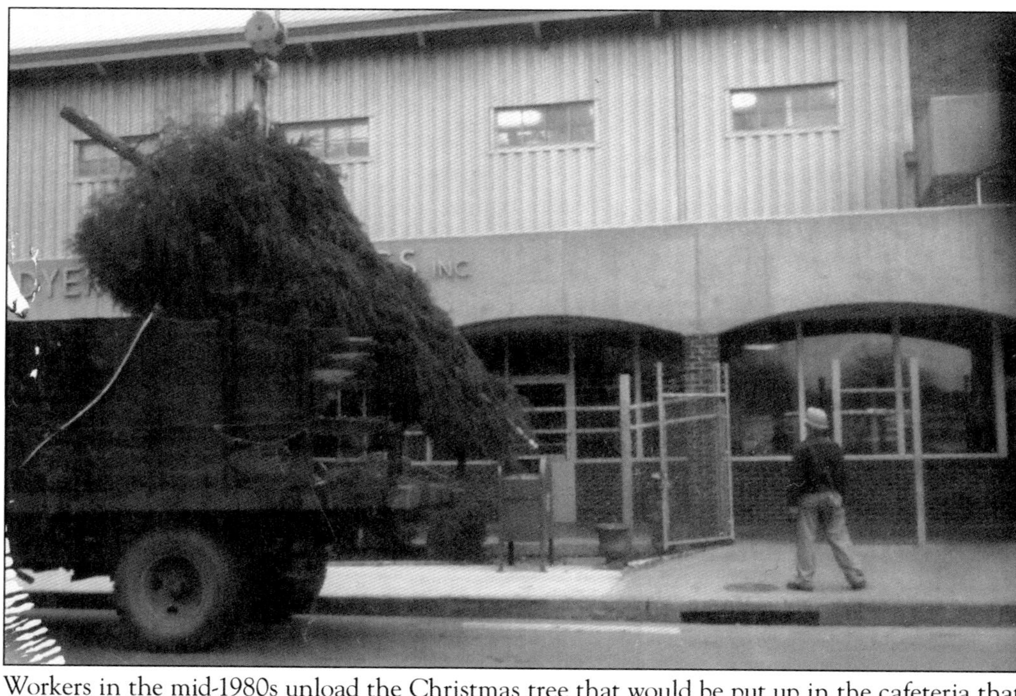

Workers in the mid-1980s unload the Christmas tree that would be put up in the cafeteria that year. This photograph provides a good view of the new construction completed at that time, in which a new guardhouse and a wing with a cafeteria were built. (Courtesy Billy Parmenter.)

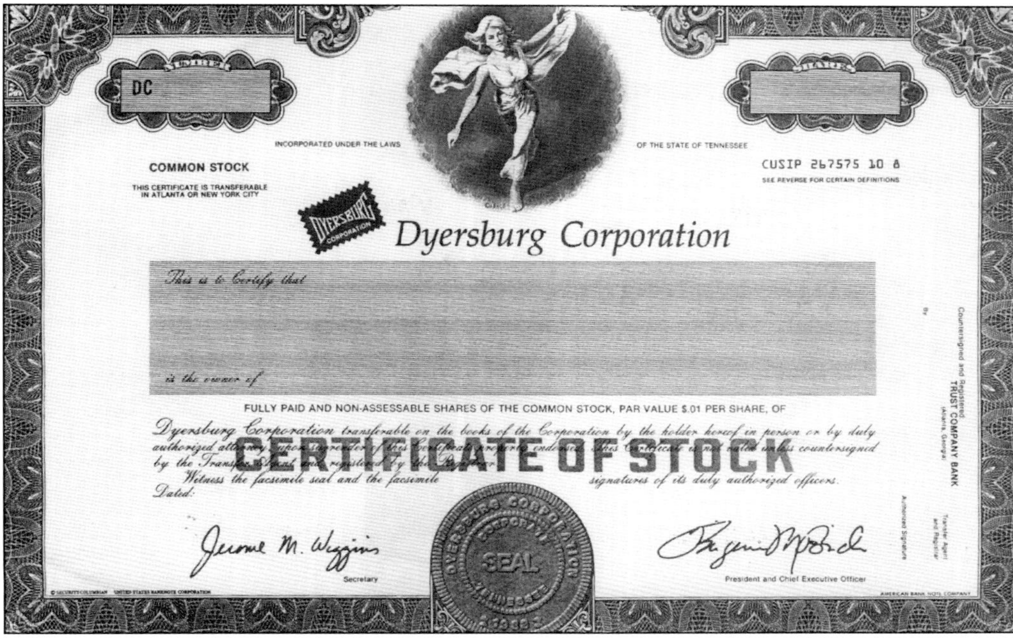

Dyersburg joined the trend of management-led leveraged buyouts in 1986, when it was purchased by a group of investors. In 1988, the name was changed to Dyersburg Corporation. The structure was also changed, allowing shareholders of Dyersburg Fabrics to exchange their shares for stock in the new corporation. In 1992, the company went public, trading on the New York Stock Exchange, but the stock eventually became worthless. (Courtesy Billy Parmenter.)

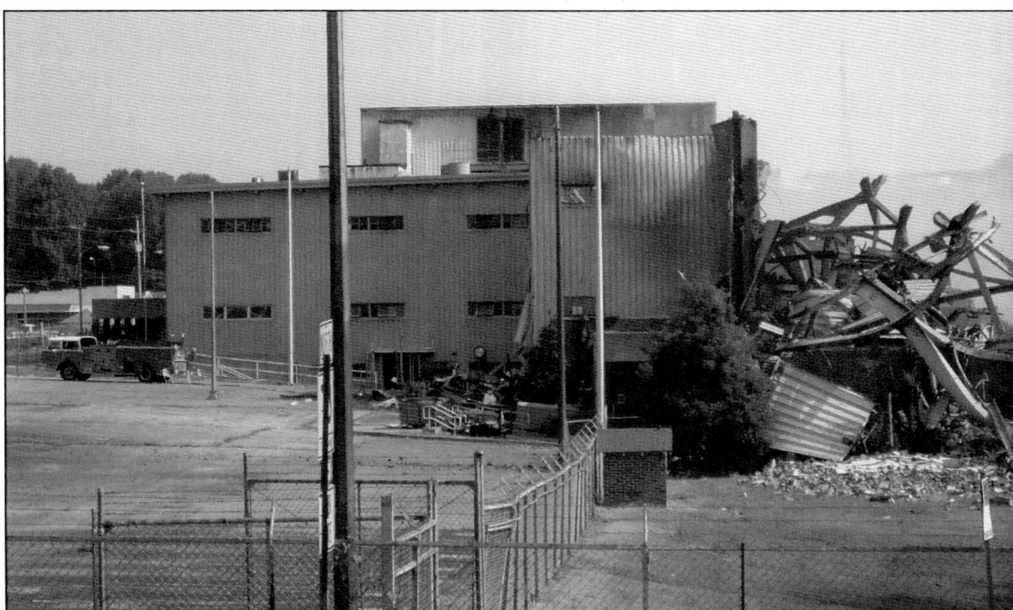

The cotton mill lies in ruins on July 23, 2007, after a huge fire broke out in the middle of the night. The fire smoldered for six days before it was fully extinguished. The facility was unoccupied at the time, and no one was injured. As of 2011, no official cause for the fire had been established.

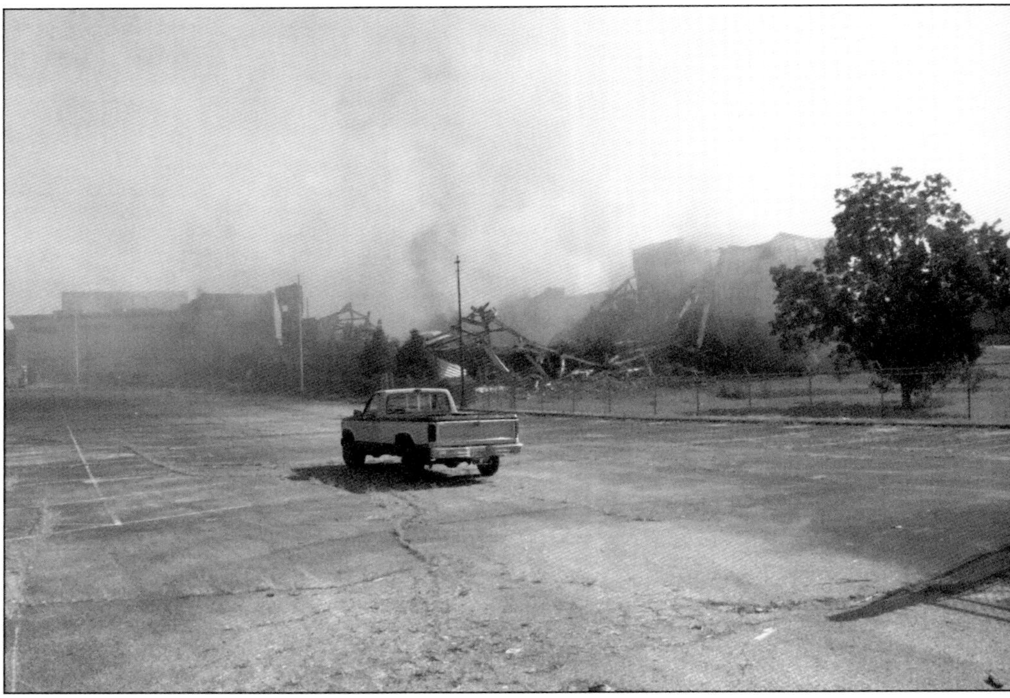

The facility closed for the last time in April 2006, as much of the US textile industry declined. The building was empty when it caught fire in July 2007 and burned to the ground. Eventually, the rubble was cleared away, leaving the site empty. Now, the corner of Harrell Avenue and Phillips Street is occupied by warehouses and parking lots. The mill safe—still containing original documents from 1929—survived the fire. It was recovered and donated to the Dyer County Historical Society for display in its museum.

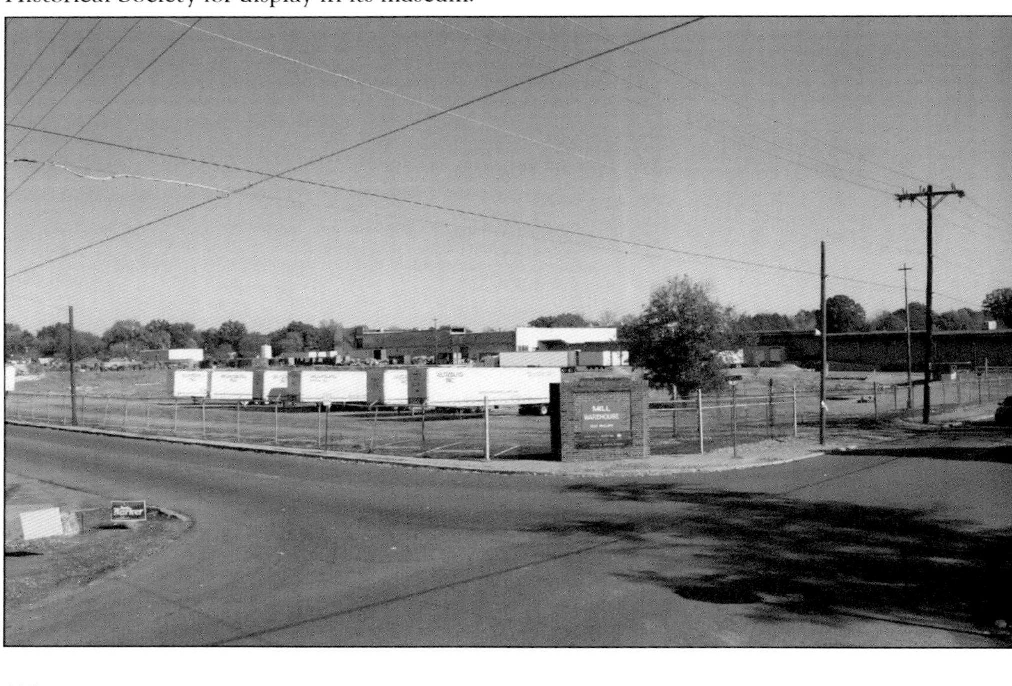

Eight

PEOPLE

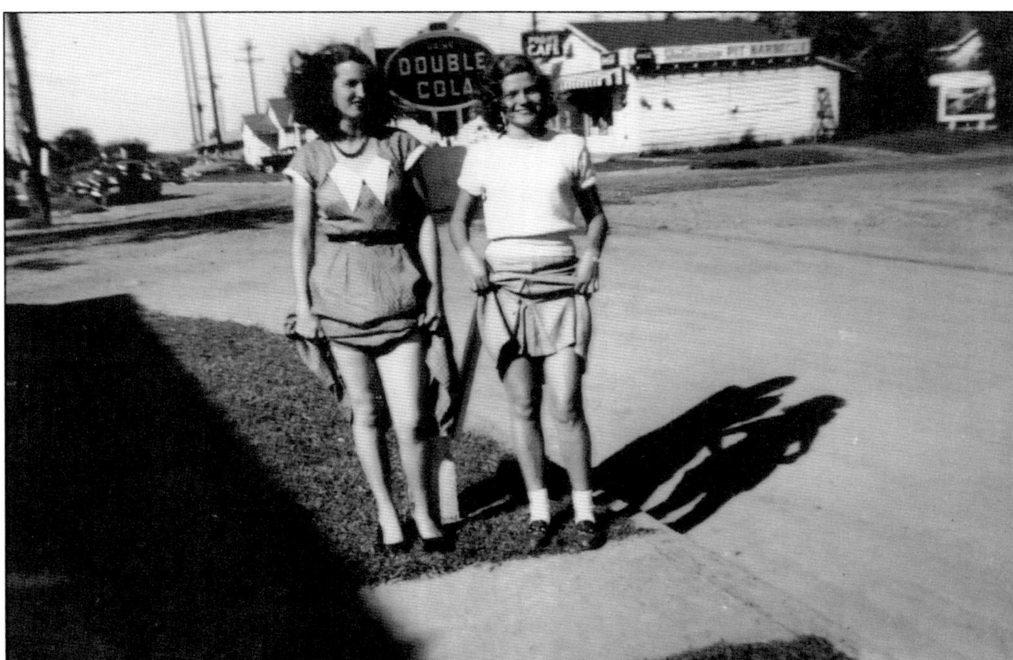

Two comely residents of Milltown surely disrupted traffic with this lighthearted display on a pleasant afternoon in the mid-1950s. In the background is the intersection of Shelby Drive and Harrell Avenue, always a busy spot for stores and other establishments. The white building, which was at this point a barbecue café, later became the popular Chuckwagon Restaurant. In the background, the tall lights of Burnham Field are visible.

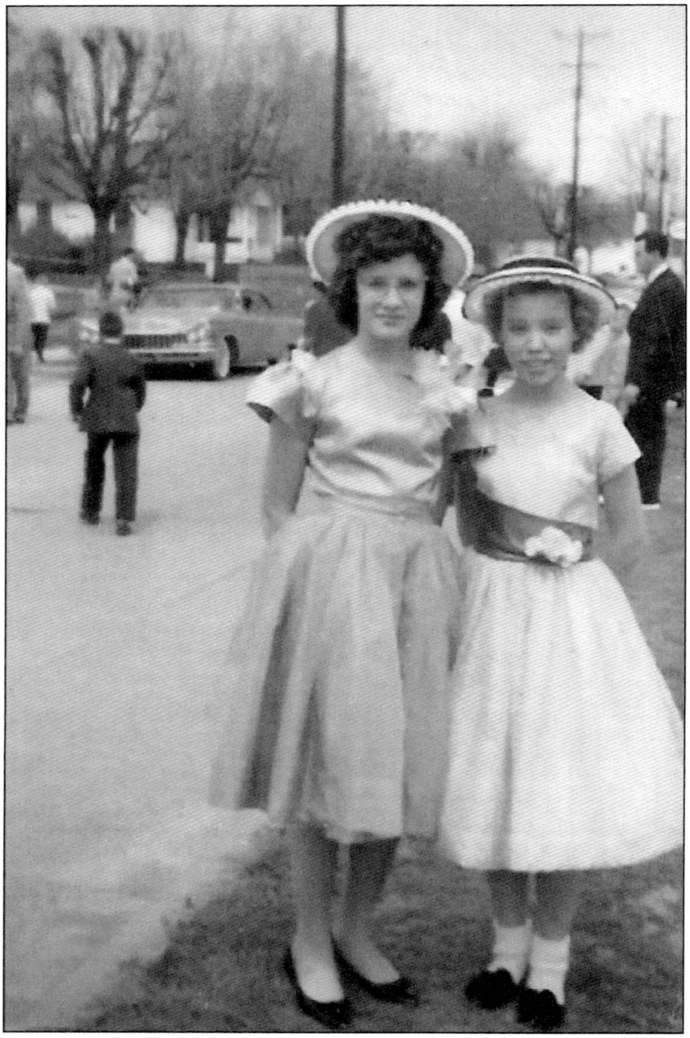

In the photograph at left, Sandra Gibson Phillips (left) and Joan Johnson Clark pose in front of the Church of God on Harrell Avenue on Easter Sunday, 1960. Joan played piano for the church at that time and later became a music teacher. They are standing at the edge of the cotton mill's front yard. In the background, the sign is visible at the Esso gas station owned by Ted "Buck" Dycus. In the image below, snapped from a window in the mill a few years earlier, the church is seen on a snowy day. The church had their Easter egg hunt in the front yard of the mill for many years, until a metal fence was erected around it. The low building to the left was Pritchard's Grocery Store. (Left, courtesy Sandra Gibson Phillips; below, courtesy R.L. Summar family.)

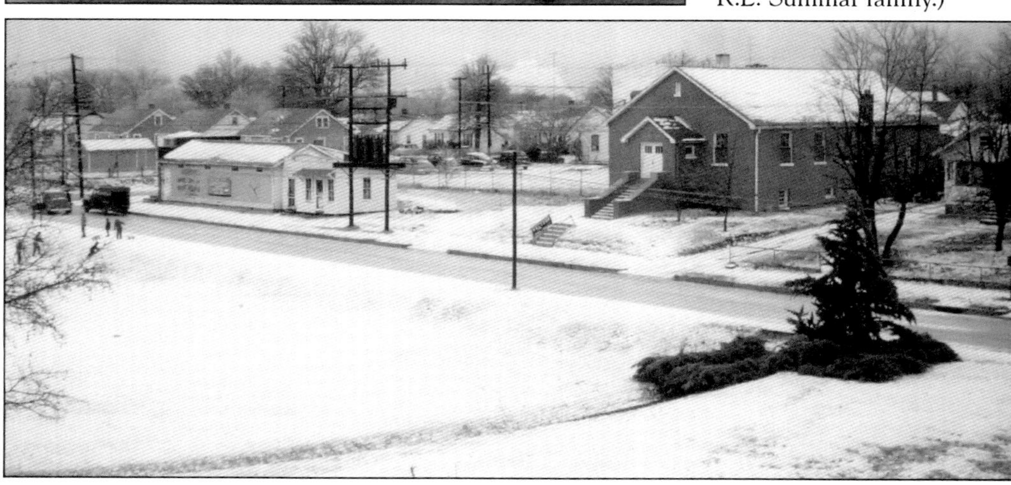

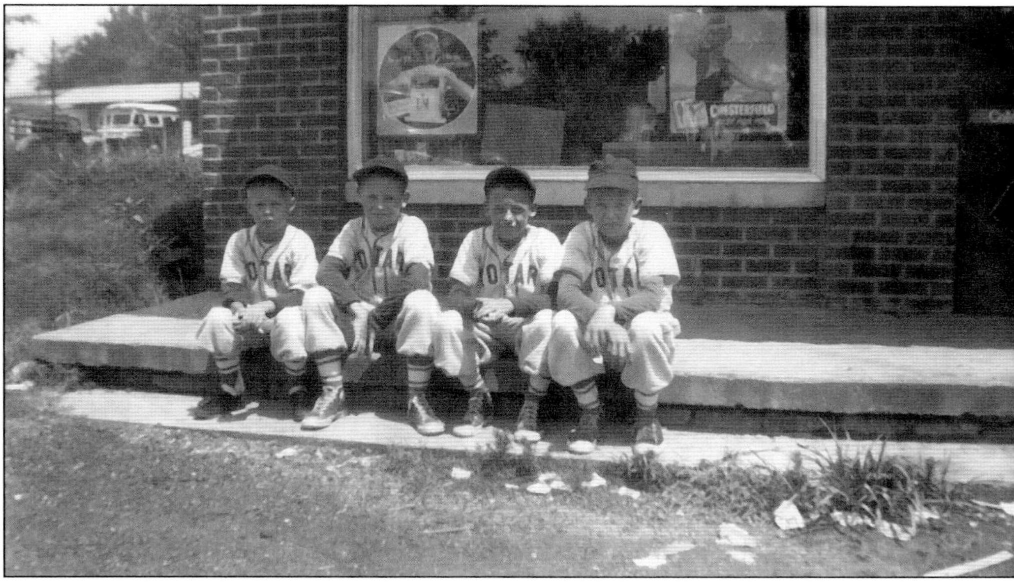

Four young baseball players, sponsored by the Rotary Club, take a break on the front porch of Pritchard's Grocery Store in the late 1950s. The store was located across the street from the front yard of Dyersburg Cotton Products. The building no longer exists. (Courtesy Gaylon Reasons.)

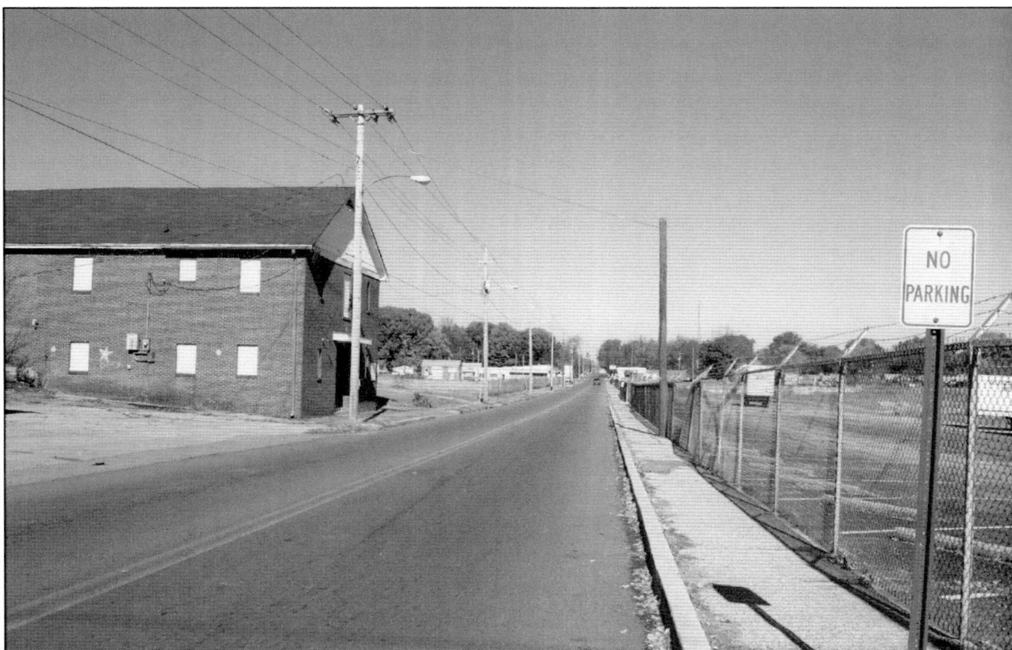

The Church of God (left) on Harrell Avenue was expanded in the 1960s, enclosing the long flight of front steps. It remained in use until a new building was constructed around the corner on Phillips Street. Since then, the old building (pictured in 2010) has stood abandoned. A metal fence now surrounds the parking lot that was once the large front yard of the cotton mill (where the girls are standing on the previous page). Dycus's Esso station, which was down the street, and Pritchard's Grocery, which would be on the left edge of this photograph, are both gone.

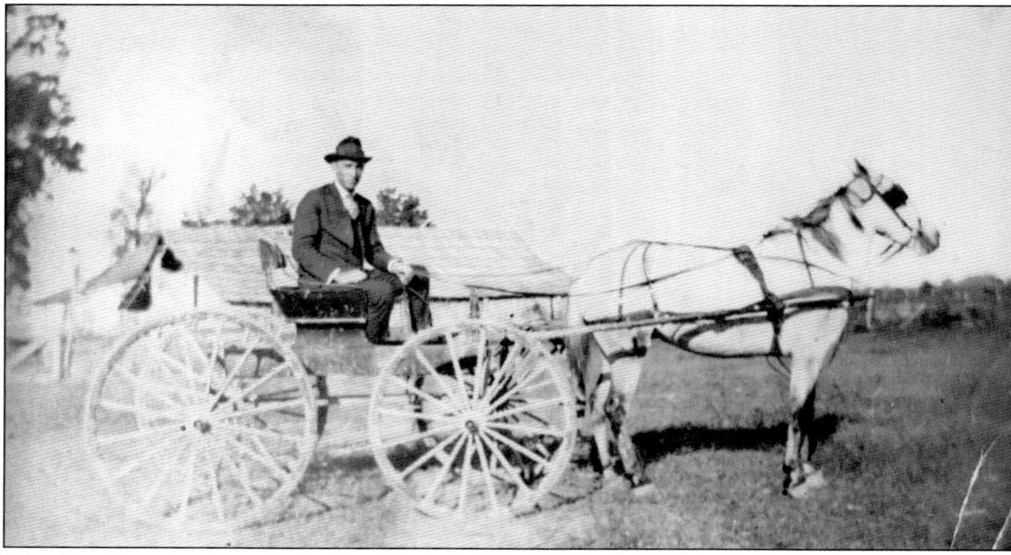

This Dyersburg man is dressed up, and his horse and wagon are clean and tidy, as he sets out to go courting sometime around 1900. The photograph was taken on what was then called Hogwaller Road, which became Phillips Street, south of where the cotton mill would eventually be constructed. The road was originally named Hogwaller because a large hog farm was located in the area. (Courtesy Tennessee State Library and Archives.)

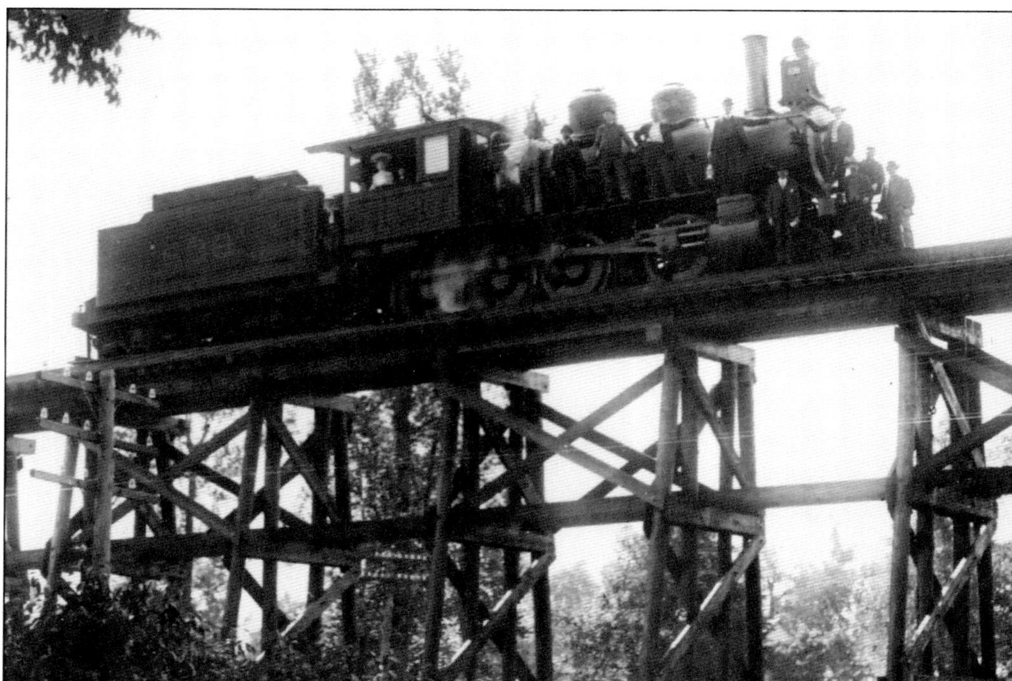

In a photograph taken April 30, 1900, men pose with a locomotive that was a twin to the doomed train that carried engineer Casey Jones to his death. Trains similar to this one were used to haul logs to Menglewood, a nearby box company in rural Dyer County. The musical history of that community inspired that name of Minglewood Hall, a concert venue in Memphis.

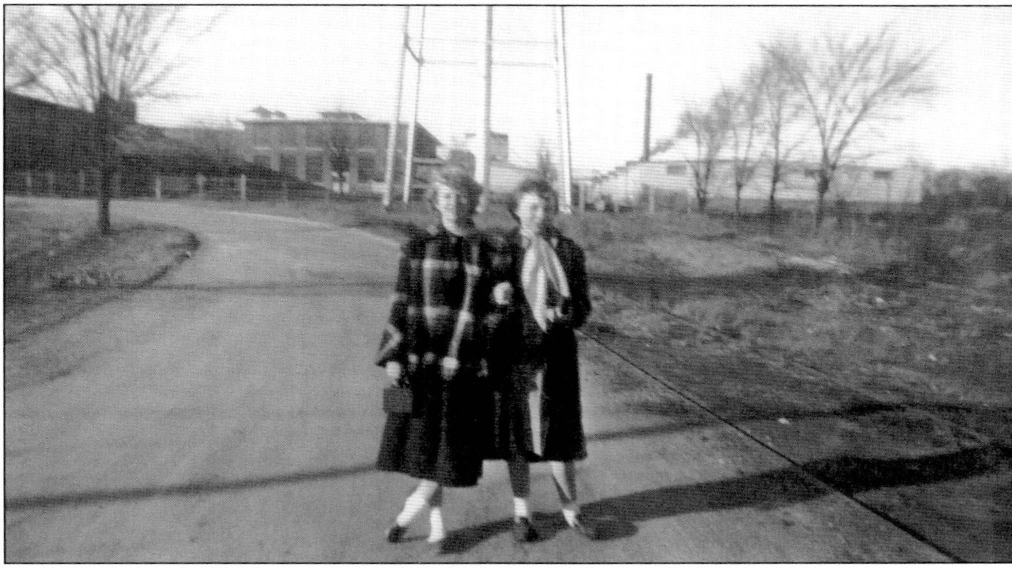

In the c. 1953 photograph above, Milltown friends pose in front of Dyersburg Cotton Products on a winter afternoon. Behind them can be seen the metal legs of the water tower. In the image below, a young girl plays in the front yard of a Milltown house with its dark tar siding. In the early days of the textile industry, workers had to walk or ride great distances to work, since farmland populations tend to be spread out. Ladd Lewis, first president of Dyersburg Cotton Products, quickly realized this was counterproductive, so he planned the construction of small, identical homes close by the business. The "mill town" approach was already well established and successful in the Northeast. They intended to build 100 homes, but when three good contractor bids were received, the decision was made to give each 33 homes to build. So 99 homes were eventually constructed, and workers paid a small amount of rent each month. Coal to heat the houses was supplied by the mill.

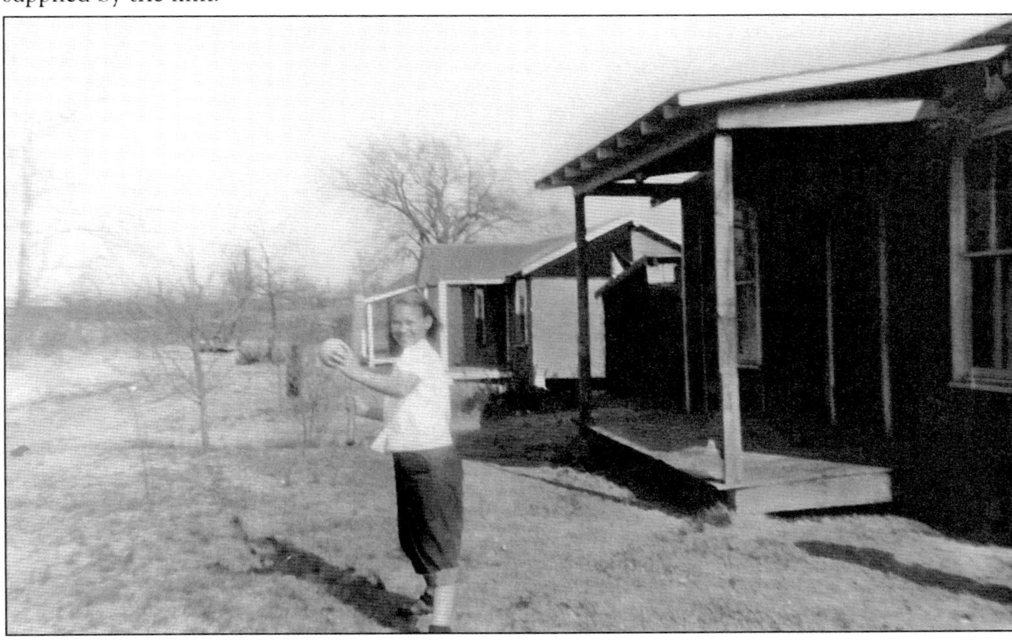

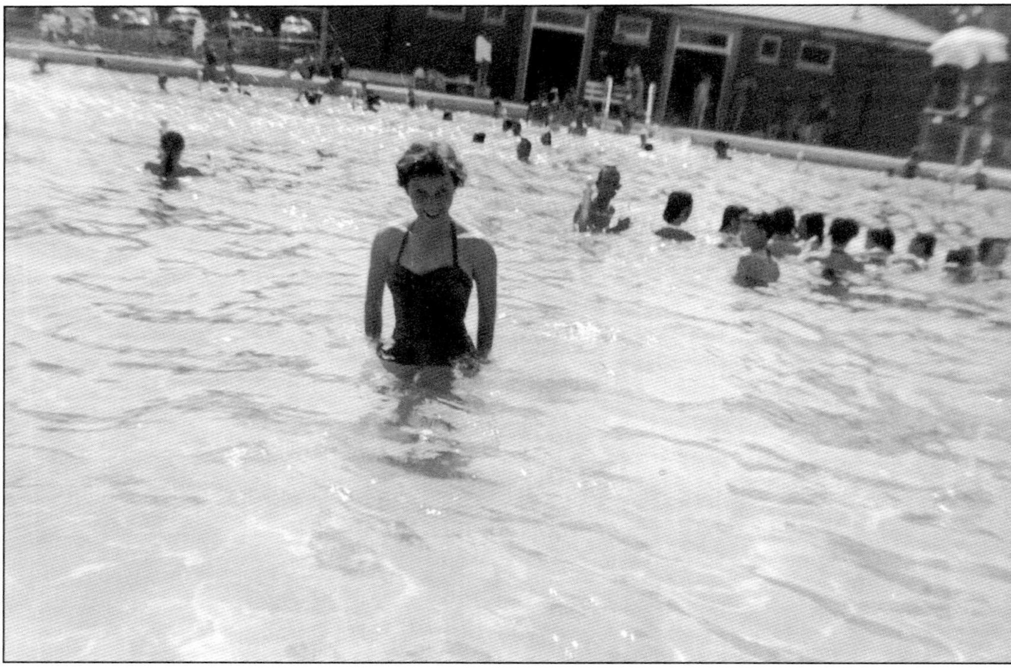

Nancy Trout was one of many Dyersburg residents cooling off in Okeena Pool on a hot day in the mid-1950s. In the background, small children form a line as they hang on to the chain separating the shallow and deep ends of the pool. The Okeena Bathhouse, in the background, was built in the 1930s and remains in use today. The pool, once at the edge of a park and golf course, is now next to Dyersburg State Community College.

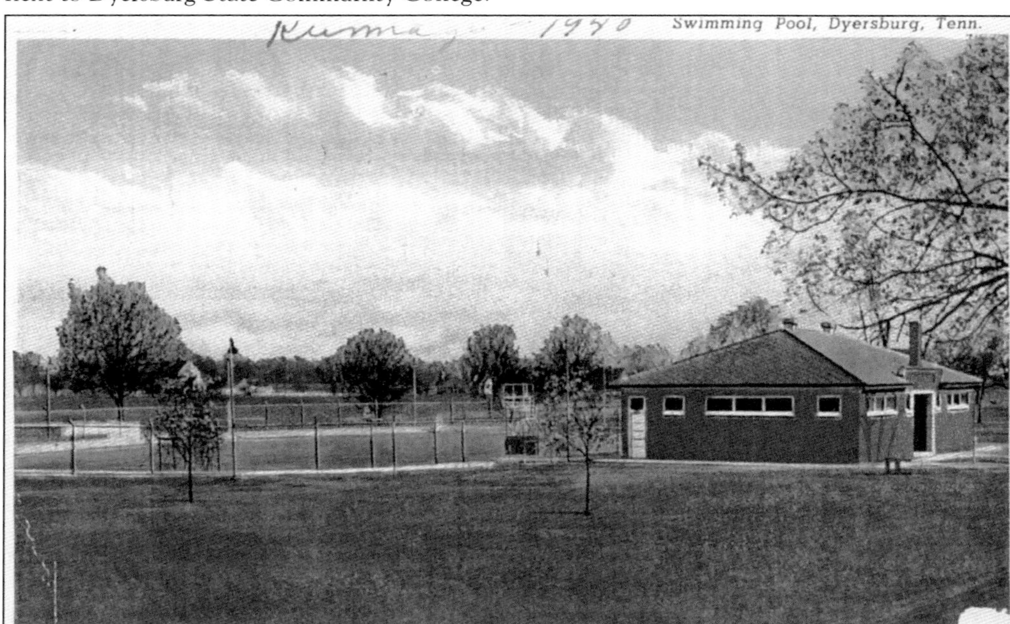

This 1940s postcard shows Okeena's pool and bathhouse on a summer day. The pool held 55,000 gallons of water. A wading pool for small children was added later.

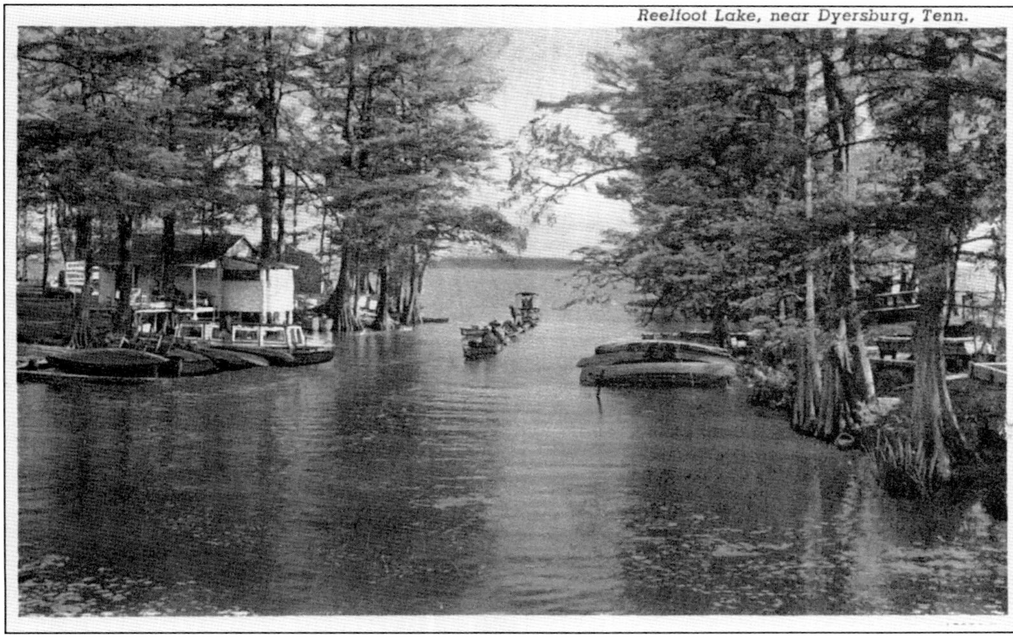

Reelfoot Lake, just a few miles from Dyersburg, was created by the most violent earthquakes in recorded history: the ones that occurred in 1811 along the New Madrid Fault. The few residents in the area at that time reported a sound like distant cannon fire, followed by sudden heavy darkness, the cries of panicked animals, and then the roar of entire forests falling to the ground. The course of the Mississippi River was altered, and the river actually flowed backwards briefly from the violence of the quake. When the disaster was over, a large lake was left behind, some 100 miles long and from one-half mile to eight miles wide. It was named Reelfoot Lake. Legend holds that because it was formed by an earthquake, there are places in the lake where the bottom has never been found.

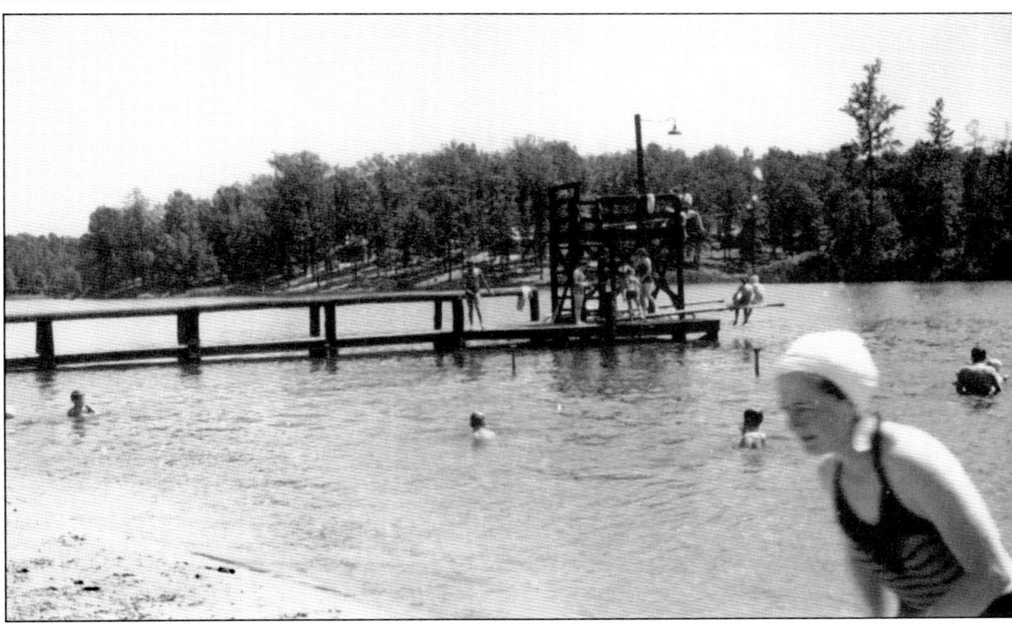

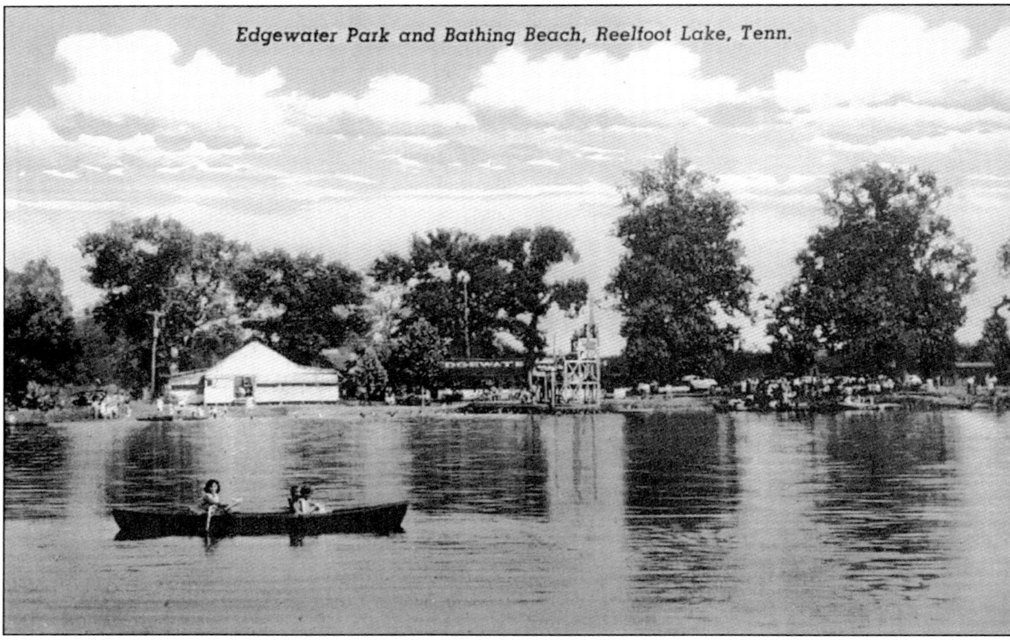

Reelfoot Lake once had three sandy public beaches: Edgewater (above), Sunkist (below), and Magnolia. In the 1960s, sand was trucked in to make the beaches larger. Although the beaches are now privately held by homeowners, Reelfoot remains a popular hunting and fishing spot in West Tennessee. American bald eagles are often spotted in the winter months making their nests, and Boy Scout troops and bird enthusiasts from all over the Southeast make pilgrimages to see them in their natural habitat.

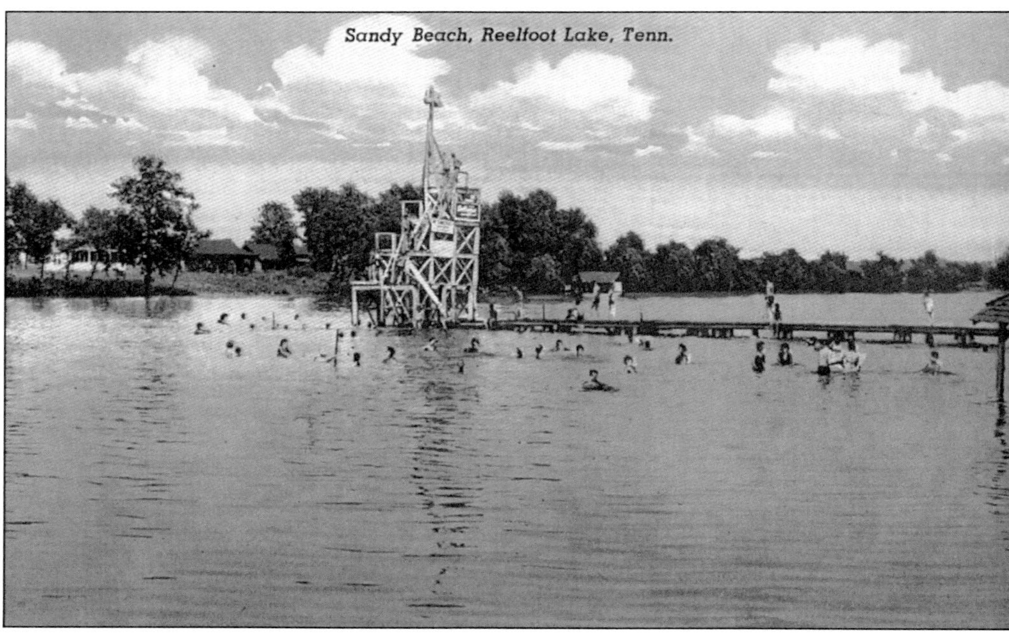

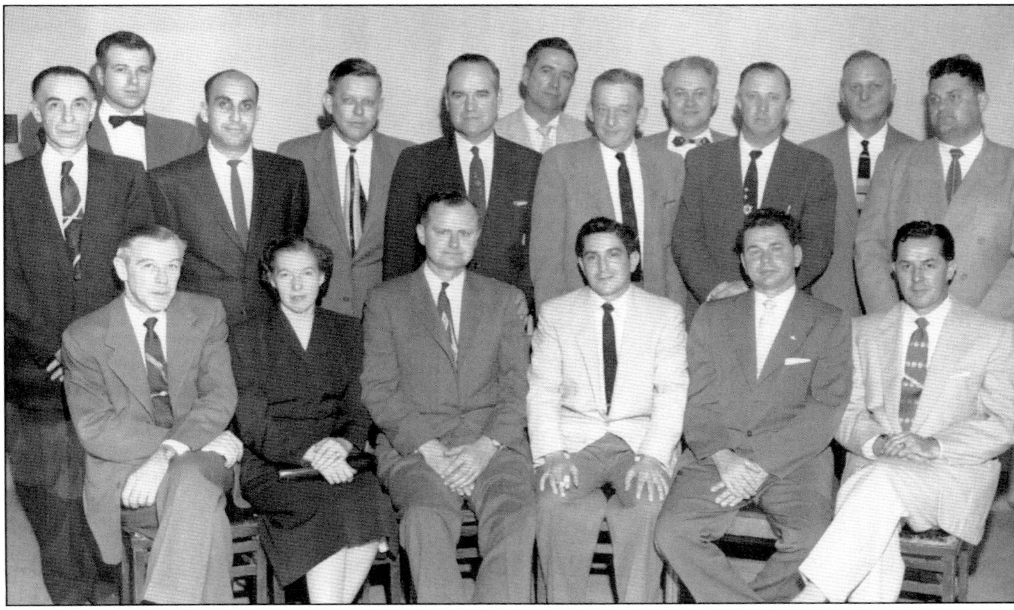

The West Tennessee Medical Association held periodic meetings in the Dyersburg area. Pictured in this undated photograph are, from left to right, (first row) Dr. Paul Baird, Dr. Lydia Watson (daughter of Dr. William Watson, who established Dyersburg's first hospital), Dr. Robert Kerr, Dr. Joe Criapie, unidentified, and Dr. Tom Baird; (second row) Dr. Orren B. Landrum, Dr. W.I. Thornton, two unidentified, Dr. J. Chalmers Moore, unidentified, Dr. W.E. Anderson, and four unidentified. (Courtesy Flowers Studio.)

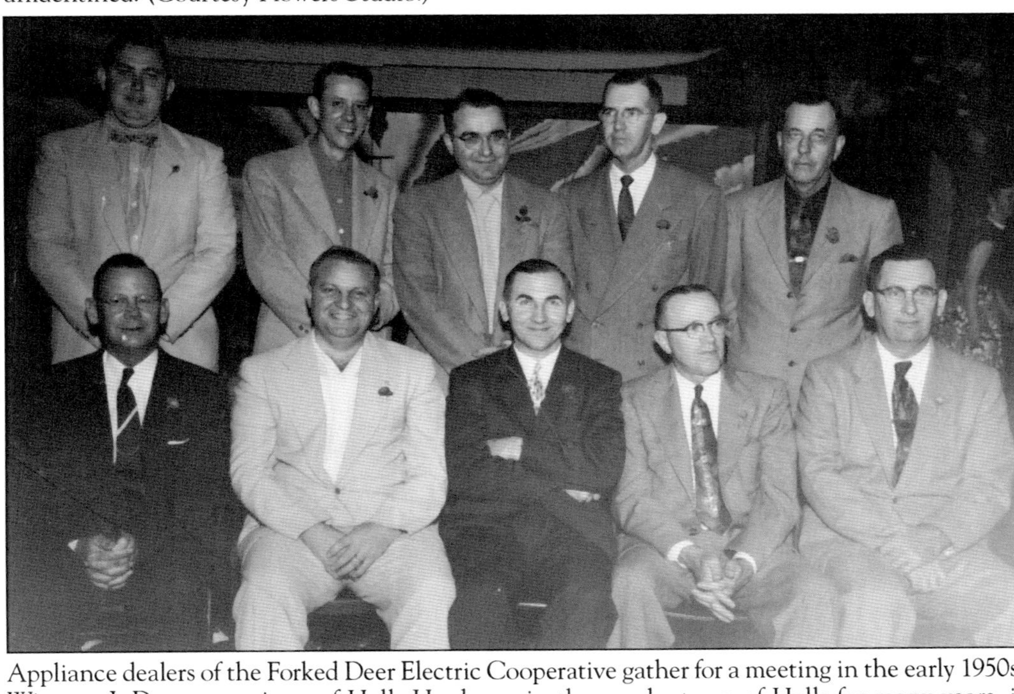

Appliance dealers of the Forked Deer Electric Cooperative gather for a meeting in the early 1950s. Winston J. Daws, proprietor of Halls Hardware in the nearby town of Halls for many years, is pictured at the front in the center.

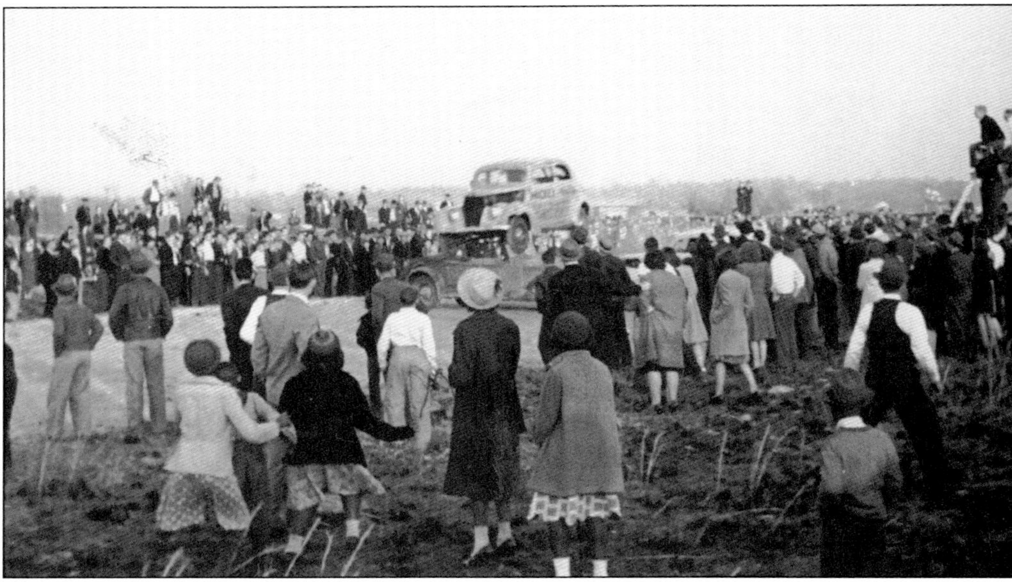

A snapshot from the 1930s shows a typical amusement of the period—watching a staged event in which one car is driven up a ramp and over another. Children crowd forward to witness the excitement. Events such as this were often staged in the open farmland around Dyersburg, and the whole town would turn out to see them. Traveling circuses, rodeos, and stunt performers would travel up and down the Mississippi River, stopping to entertain along the way. (Courtesy Chris Gibbons collection.)

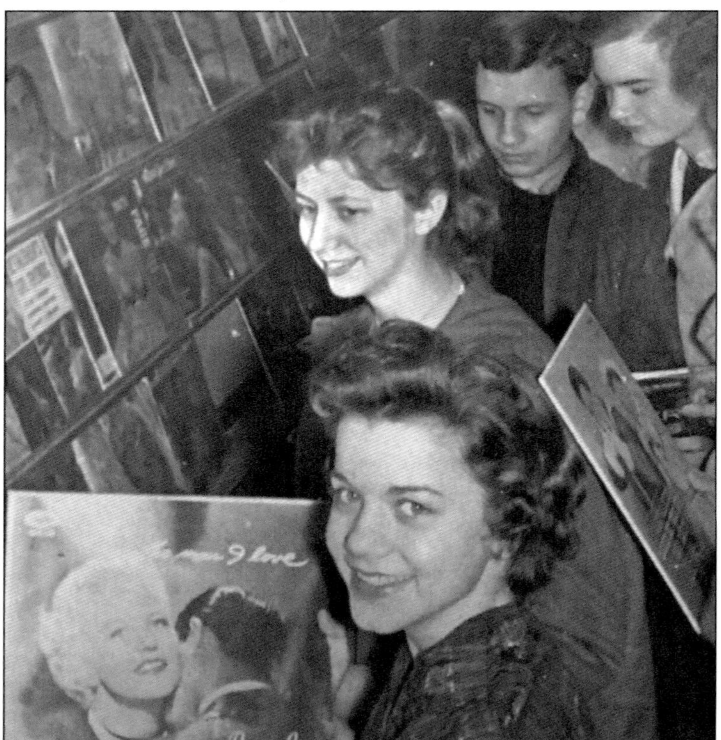

In a snapshot from a Dyersburg High School yearbook, bright-eyed teenagers hurry to the record shop after school to snap up their favorite albums. The girl in the foreground is clutching a copy of *The Man I Love*, a popular 1957 album. It was recorded by vocalist Peggy Lee, accompanied by the Nelson Riddle Orchestra conducted by Frank Sinatra. Lee's career would eventually span nearly seven decades.

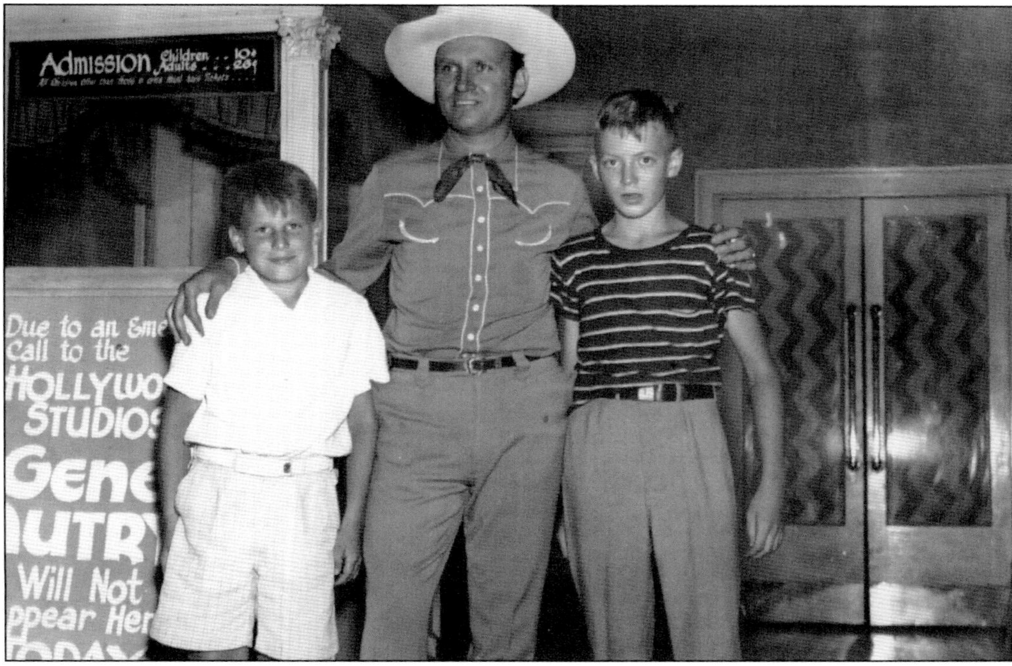

Despite what the sign says, cowboy singing star Gene Autry did appear at one of the Dyersburg movie theaters on July 9, 1939. Fans originally gathered on Thursday, when he was slated to appear, but he was delayed a few days. Autry's career was in full swing at that point. It was the year he recorded what would become his biggest hit, "Back in the Saddle Again." (Courtesy Chris Gibbons collection.)

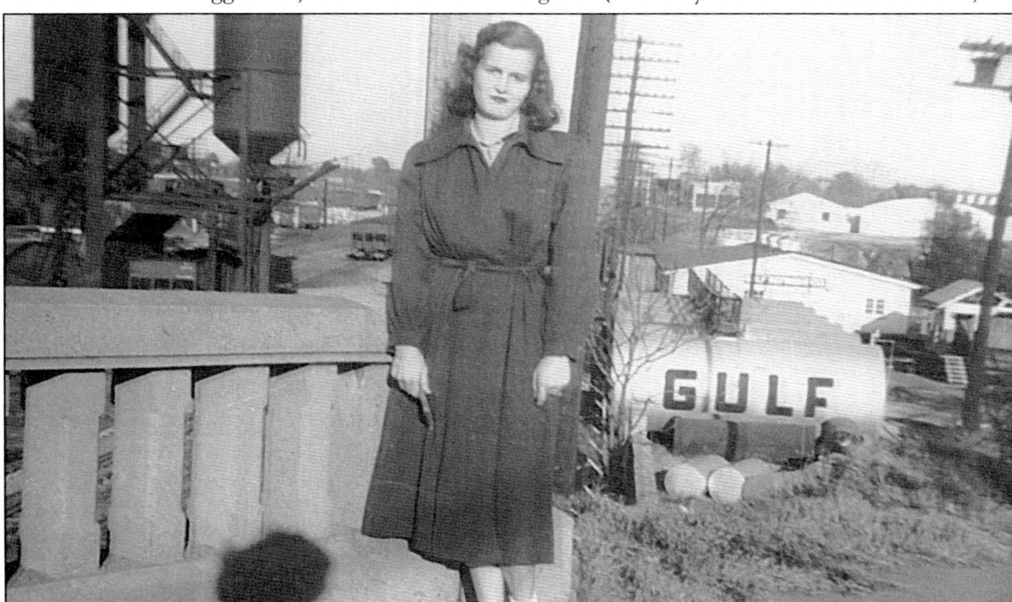

Dyersburg teenager Joann Campbell is pictured in the 1950s on the East Court overpass of the railroad on the north end of Dyersburg. The Gulf Oil distributorship is visible in the background. On the left, the coal chute that dispensed coal for steam locomotives can be seen. Telegraph poles, strung heavily with wires, are visible behind her; they followed the path of the railroad.

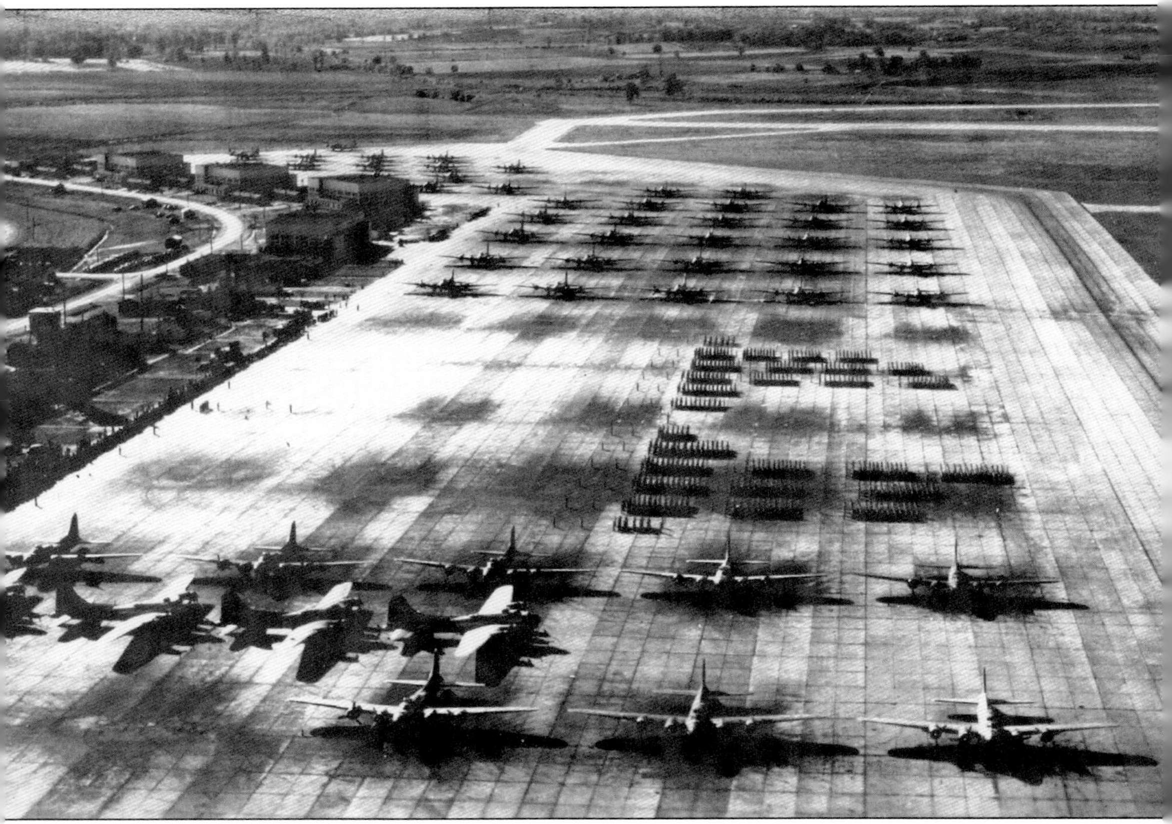

In 1942, the Army Air Force built the largest World War II training base in the southern United States—the Dyersburg Army Air Base. It was located on farmland at the border of Dyer and Lauderdale Counties, only a few miles from Dyersburg. It was here that 7,700 servicemen received their stateside training before shipping out. Training missions were flown daily, with B-17s filling the skies over the towns of Halls, Ripley, Gates, and Dyersburg. The base was closed after the war and remained empty for decades until a small airport was established. A growing Veterans Museum now occupies the site. (Courtesy Pat Higdon.)

About the Organization

The Dyer County Historical Society's mission is to preserve and promote the history of Dyer County. Since its inception in 2004, this organization has nurtured a higher level of interest in local history. The board of directors is made up of 15 dedicated volunteers who meet monthly to conduct the business of the society. The membership has grown to nearly 100 people, and the Dyer County Museum has opened in the old Dyersburg High School in downtown Dyersburg. Interviews of local citizens have been recorded and archived, field trips to areas of local historical importance have been scheduled, and a Web page has been established.

Historical exhibits are on display in various locations, including the communities of Bogota, Trimble, Newbern, and Finley. The Bruce community is currently planning a museum to be housed in the old Bruce High School. Stories about Dyer County's past are being collected, verified, and stored in the Dyer County Museum, along with artifacts from the past. Improvements to the museum include exhibit panels and display cases, a video surveillance system, and the purchase of a database software program.

The society has partnered with other area museums and civic clubs to create fundraising opportunities that support its mission. The public is invited to attend any of the regular monthly meetings of the board of directors. The board meets on the second Tuesday of each month in the Professional Development Center at 305 College Street.

Anyone with an interest in Dyersburg, Newbern, Trimble, or any part of Dyer County is encouraged to contact the Dyer County Historical Society. The society stands ready, willing, and able to assist with questions, artifacts, photographs, or stories that will help those who share our passion for our part of this wonderful world.

Please visit www.dyerhistory.com for more information.